Off The

Portugal

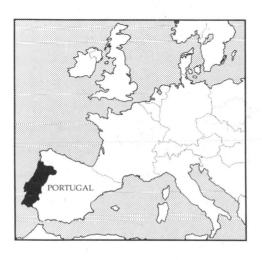

Off the Beaten Track
PORTUGAL

Nick Timmons

MOORLAND PUBLISHING

Published by:
Moorland Publishing Co Ltd,
Moor Farm Road West, Ashbourne,
Derbyshire, DE6 1HD England

ISBN 0 86190 501 6 (UK)

The Globe Pequot Press,
6 Business Park Road,
PO Box 833, Old Saybrook,
Connecticut 06475-0833

ISBN 1-56440-297-5 (USA)

First published 1992
Revised 2nd edition 1994
© Moorland Publishing Co Ltd 1994

Front Cover: fishing boats on the
Algarve (*International Photobank*).

The illustrations on pp56, 73, 74, 89 and
107 have been supplied by P. Gray. All
the remaining black and white
illustrations and all the colour illustrations have been supplied by Nick
Timmons and Tanya Draude.

Printed in Hong Kong by:
Wing King Tong Co Ltd

British Library Cataloguing in Publication Data:
A catalogue record for this book is available from the British Library.

Library of Congress Cataloging-in-Publication Data
Timmons, Nick
  Off the beaten track. Portugal/Nick Timmons. — Rev. 2nd ed.
    p. cm.
  Includes Index.
  ISBN 1-56440-297-5 (USA)
  1. Portugal — Guidebooks. I. Title. II. Title: Portugal.
DP516.T56 1994
914.6904'44 — dc20   93-1450
                                                          CIP

Contents

Key to Maps

● Town /City

—— Main Road

=== Motorway

River

Lake/Reservoir

·············· Boundary

Note on Maps
The maps for each chapter, while comprehensive, are not designed to be used as route maps, but rather to locate the main towns, villages and places of interest.

Museums and Other Places of Interest
Wherever possible opening times have been checked and are as accurate as possible. In general many museums are closed on Mondays and national holidays. Some churches are not open to visitors during services. Those in the country are frequently kept locked and it is neccessary to find the caretaker for the key. Remember that churches are places of worship as well as historical monuments, so dress and conduct should be appropriate.

A Note to the Reader
We hope you have found this book informative, helpful and enjoyable. It is always our aim to make our publications as accurate and up to date as possible. With this in mind, we would appreciate any comments that you might have. If you come across any information to update this book or discover something new about the area we have covered, please let us know so that your notes may be incorporated in future editions.

As it is the publisher's principal aim to produce books that are lively and responsive to change, any information that readers provide will be a valuable asset in maintaining the highest possible standards.

The Author

Nick Timmons was born in Dublin in 1962 and educated in Liverpool. He studied English Literature at Wadham College, Oxford, and after a range of employment from nursing auxiliary at a psychiatric hospital to motorcycle courier, he qualified as a teacher of English and Media Studies at the Institute of Education, University of London. Since then he has taught in schools in Essex, Cheshire and Liverpool, and is currently a lecturer in Media Studies at Accrington and Rossendale College.

He has travelled extensively in the Iberian Peninsula over the last ten years, and in particular has developed a keen interest in Portugal after becoming aware of its rich culture and great beauty, especially in the north of the country.

Acknowledgements

The author would like to thank Ros Ballaster at UEA and Sue at Blacon High School for the Portuguese lessons. Also thanks to Mr and Mrs Clark Hutchison for their hospitality and to Pete for his expert guidance, not forgetting the warm welcome received in Porto and Gêres from João, Claudia, Cristina, Monica and David. Thanks are also due to my parents and sister Margaret for their support and and determination to get this project off the ground. Above all thanks to Tanya, no better companion on a long journey.

This book is dedicated to my father.

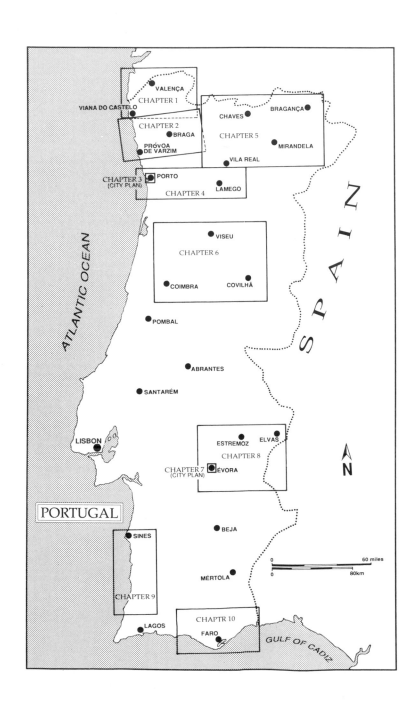

Introduction

Western Europe is a continent of great diversity, well visited not just by travellers from other parts of the globe but by the inhabitants of its own member countries. Within the year-round processes of trade and commerce, but more particularly during the holiday season, there is a great surging interchange of nationalities as one country's familiar attractions are left behind for those of another.

It is true that frontiers are blurred by ever quicker travel and communications, and that the sharing of cultures, made possible by an increasingly sophisticated media network, brings us closer in all senses to our neighbours. Yet essential differences do exist, differences which lure us abroad on our annual migrations in search of new horizons, fresh sights, sounds and smells, discovery of unknown landscapes and people.

Countless resorts have evolved for those among us who simply crave sun, sea and the reassuring press of humanity. There are, too, established tourist 'sights' with which a country or region has become associated and to which clings, all too often, a suffocating shroud — the manifestations of mass tourism in the form of crowds and entrance charges, the destruction of authentic atmosphere, cynical exploitation. While this is by no means typical of all well known tourist attractions, it is familiar enough to act as a disincentive for those of more independent spirit who value personal discovery above prescribed experience and who would rather avoid the human conveyor belt of queues, traffic jams and packed accommodation.

It is for such travellers that this guidebook has been written. In its pages, no more than passing mention is made of the famous, the well documented, the already glowingly described — other guidebooks will satisfy the appetite for such orthodox tourist information. Instead, the reader is taken if not to unknown then to relatively unvisited places — literally 'off-the-beaten-track'. Through the specialist knowledge of the author, visitors using this guidebook are assured of gaining insights into the country's heartland whose heritage lies largely untouched by the tourist industry. Occasionally the reader is urged simply to take a sideways step from a site of renowned tourist interest to discover a place perhaps less sensational, certainly less frequented but often of equivalent fascination.

Portugal is the ideal country for those wishing to get off-the-beaten-track. Once one of the world's richest nations the magnificence of its palaces, castles, cathedrals and churches awaits the enterprising traveller. From the mountains of the Peneda-Gerês National Park to the beaches of the South-West Alentejo — the most beautiful and unspoilt in the Iberian Peninsula — this book will help you discover the essence and true flavour of Portugal, a country which time seems to have passed by. It guides you to the valley of the Douro — one of the most spectacular, yet least known of all European rivers — to beautiful ancient towns such as Évora, Bragança and Coimbra, and to fascinating out of the way villages where you are still more likely to see oxen and donkeys used for transport than motor cars.

1 • The Alto Minho

The Alto Minho is the northernmost region of Portugal and is named after the River Mihno that is the historical and the current political frontier between Portugal and the northern Spanish province of Galicia. It is an area of outstanding natural beauty enclosing to the east two mountain ranges, the Serra de Soajo and the Serra de Peneda, and the northern section of the Peneda-Gerês National Park.

It was in many ways this hilly and mountainous region of the country that established an identity and culture different from that of the rest of the Iberian Peninsula. For it was this type of terrain that suited the hill dwelling, agricultural Suevi people that migrated into the area from Swabia in Germany after the collapse of the Roman Empire during the fifth century after Christ. The rest of the peninsula was settled by the Visigoths during the same period, whose nomadic, herding lifestyle suited the hot expanses of the plains of the South and West. Very little evidence remains today of the Suevi except the heavy type of ploughshare that is still used in the area. Nonetheless, it was their independence and distinct culture that formed the bedrock of the eventual nation state.

The natural place from which to begin an exploration of the region is **Viana do Castelo** — its largest town and home of the most important festival of folklore in Portugal. Viana lies 59km (36 miles) north of Porto on the fairly recently modernised main route, the N13, and has good bus and train connections to the cities of Porto, Braga and Lisbon.

Set on the north bank of the wide estuary of the River Lima, the skyline of the city is dominated by the neo-Byzantine basilica of the church of Santa Luzia. Designed by Ventura Terra and rather obviously modelled on Sacre Coeur in Paris, it was completed at the beginning of the twentieth century. It can be reached by road or by funicular. The interior, though, with its rather crude painted ceiling

11

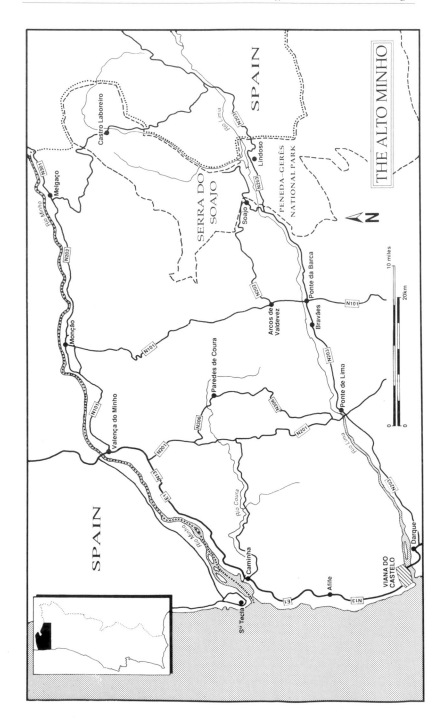

is very disappointing. The view across the estuary to the long, sandy, delightful beach at Amorosa is quite spectacular in compensation. Next to the church is a large luxury hotel named after it. Just below the hotel, set amongst very attractive woods, and which can be reached by a pleasant walk, is the first of the town's many sites of historical interest.

This is the ruined remains of the original Celtic settlement in the area, known as a *citania*. The most remarkable of these, the *Citania de Briteiros*, is situated near Braga, but this one, too, has its points of interest. Scattered around are roofless, circular granite walled huts that once were homes, some sections of a defensive wall, and the roughly paved remains of streets. They were probably occupied from around 500BC up until the Emperor Augustus insisted on bringing down the Celts onto the coast and into the valleys of the North. The Romans greatly feared the marauding raids of the hill dwelling Celts.

Viana, originally a small fishing village, had its golden age during the period of the Great Discoveries in the fifteenth and sixteenth centuries. Its sons became some of the most intrepid of the nation's voyagers, and it was the port of departure for many important voyages. João Velho was one of the first Europeans to visit the Congo while Goncalo Velho's 'discovery' of the Azores led to the islands being settled by the Portuguese.

The intrepid journey that has had, perhaps, the most abiding effect on the culture of the whole of the North was that of a certain João Alvares Fagundes. He it was who 'discovered' the lands of the North West Atlantic and, more importantly, their surrounding fishing grounds. The almost uniformly poor soil of Portugal has always meant that fish has formed an essential part of the national diet. Fagundes attempted to start a settlement in Newfoundland and though this failed large fishing fleets still set out from Viana to harvest the sea — in particular the cod, known as *bacalhau*, that is the ubiquitous dish of northern Portugal. It is said that there are as many different ways of cooking *bacalhau* as there are days in the year. In general though, to the foreign palate, the dish is exceptionally salty, a feature that has its roots, of course, in the preserving of the returning fleet's catch in salt before the days of refrigeration. The departure of the fishing fleet, after they have been blessed at the quayside by the city's bishop, is still an important event.

Viana was also the first point of export for the Port wine produced along the River Douro in the eighteenth century. As trade expanded the town had to be defended and hence was built, firstly, the Tower of Roqueta, and subsequently, extending the tower, the Castle of São Tiago da Barra, which is found to be along the estuary of the River Lima to the west of the town centre. The tower was built in the reign of Dom Manuel at the beginning of the sixteenth century, and the additions were made in the reigns of Kings Sebastian and Philip of Spain at the century's end. The town was raised to the status of a city in 1848 after it had fought resolutely on the side of the victorious Maria II, during the War of the Sucession. The title, 'do Castelo' meaning 'of the Castle', was then officially added to the town's name.

Fortunately for the visitor this golden age is not merely of historical interest, but has left its mark on the city with some beautiful Manueline and Renaissance houses. That there should be such a concentration of exceptional houses in such a small area bears some explanation. It was in the sixteenth century that Afonso III's charter of 1258, by which nobles and rich men were not allowed to settle in the city, lapsed. Hence the great families of the town, the Velhos, the Tavoras, the Lunas, the Alpoins and the Costa Barroses all settled together around the Rua de San Pedro, located in the centre of town between the cathedral and the waterfront. It was also at this time that a colony of Jews, some of whom at least were skilful merchants, fleeing from persecution in Spain, settled in the town.

A very useful map of the city can be obtained from the tourist office in the Praça de Erva, just off Viana's attractive central boulevard, the Avenida dos Combatantes de Grande Guerra. Just beside the tourist office in the Rua de Hospital Velho is the Old Hospital. Though it was remodelled in the seventeenth century the building was originally a hostel for pilgrims on their way to the great medieval pilgrimage site of Santiago de Compostela in Galicia.

To the right of the Praça de Erva along the Rua do Poco is situated the cathedral. This was originally simply the parish church and was dedicated, like other churches on the pilgrim's way, to Santa Maria Maior. The Galician influence can clearly be seen in the characteristic H-shape of the façade. The main body of the building was re-built in the fourteenth and fifteenth centuries in a Gothic style, but the twin towers are Romanesque, equivalent to the style in Britain known as Norman. The doorway has a number of arches resting on statues of St Andrew, St Peter and the Evangelists.

Opposite the cathedral is the house of the nobleman, João Jacome de Luna, dating from the middle of the sixteenth century and built in an early Renaissance decorative style. The front of the house facing the Rua do Poco has a series of corbels ending in animal-like figures that must probably have belonged to the eaves of a house formerly standing on the site.

To the right of the cathedral as one leaves it is another fine house. This is the former house of the navigator, João Velho. Its fifteenth-century Gothic arcade again shows the influence of Galicia and may have been part of an arcade that originally extended around the whole square. On the far side of the cathedral in the Rua de São Pedro is the church of Costa Barros which has the loveliest Manueline window to be found in Viana.

The town's other main permanent attraction is one of the most beautiful Rennaissance squares in Portugal, the Praça de República, at the end of the Rua Sacradura Cabral. In the centre of the square is a beautiful sixteenth-century fountain, the work of the Viana stone-mason, João Lopes the Elder. Constructed in 1553, its baroque shell-basins are skilfully decorated with birds and leaves. It is topped by an armillary sphere and a cross of the Order of Christ. This fountain was the model for many very similar fountains to be seen all over the country.

Forming the north end of the square is the Paco do Concelho, or town hall. Originally built at the beginning of the sixteenth century in a Gothic style only the façade retains its original appearance. Its arched arcade on the ground floor was in the past used for the sale of bread while the town council would meet on the second floor via a staircase at the rear which can still be seen today. Above one of the windows is displayed the town's coat of arms which includes a caravel, the elegant and sturdy wooden ships in which the great Portuguese navigators set sail. It is another reminder of the town's contribution to the 'Discoveries', that brought back to Europe among other things spices such as pepper, curry, saffron, ginger, coriander and paprika. Viana merchants made their fortunes from the Orient bringing back rice and tea, from the New World with pineapples, peppers, tomatoes, and potatoes, as well as coffee and peanuts from Africa.

Overlooking the fountain, too, on the corner of the Rua Candida dos Reis is the Misericórdia Hospice, or almshouse. Originally de-signed by João Lopes the Younger, its construction was started in

1520 and continued through more or less the rest of the century. The main façade is in three tiers, the upper verandas being supported on classical columns and figures. The church adjoining the hospice was rebuilt in the eighteenth century designed by Manuel Pinto de Vilalobos. The real treasure lies within, with the decoration of the church with some of Portugal's finest tiles. These ceramic tiles, produced in the Lisbon workshop Policarpo de Oliveira in 1720 depict scenes from the Bible and energetic little demons with great life.

Viana is one of the most famous areas in Portugal for the production of quality ceramics with a tradition in the craft that goes back for hundreds of years. This is reflected in the Municipal Museum, housed in the former eighteenth-century palace of the Barbosa Macieis family, which was again designed in the eighteenth century by Pinto de Vilalobos. The interior walls are decorated with fine tiles painted by Policarpo de Oliveira Bernardes in 1721. The museum also contains some fine eighteenth-century glazed ceramic earthenware from Coimbra, Lisbon, and Viana itself.

Viana is also an elegant modern resort as well as a town of great antiquity. There is a good range of hotels and restaurants and the tourist office has details of trips by boat up the River Lima and tours of the local *vinho verde* cellars. As elsewhere in the North there are also organised trips from here in the autumn to watch and sometimes assist with the grape harvests.

Much the best time to be in the city is, undoubtedly, for the festival of singing and dancing that has grown up around the religious festival of Nossa Senhora de Agónia, on the third weekend in August. Local shops cater for the many visitors selling a wide range of the traditional handicrafts, such as decorative lace and jewelry that will be on display in the celebrations.

The festival begins on late Friday afternoon when there is a solemn procession through the streets with statues and crucifixes taken from the churches of the town. All the statues are taken to the small baroque chapel of Nossa Senhora de Agónia on the western edge of the town. The mood is rather subdued in comparison to what follows, but there is much to enjoy in the colourful costumes of the cavalry men on their magnificent Lusitanian horses who precede the main procession and in the costumes of the local schoolchildren who dress as fishermen, farmers, angels, saints and bishops. Each of the parishes of the city and district of Viana is represented. As the visitor

*The Festival of Nossa
Senhora de Agonia
in Viana do Costelo*

*The traditional
women's costume of
The Alto Minho*

admires the garlands hung across the streets and the colourful bed-spreads hung out of the windows in welcome there is a sense of civic pride and tradition

One young woman, dressed as Our Lady, walks throughout the procession with her arms outstretched in what seems like an attempt to re-enact the physical suffering of the Virgin. The statues of Mary and other saints are borne shoulder high on biers by six and more men, sweating in the heat, and several statues are, rather bizarrely, bedecked with flowing hair and costumes. The moment at which the statue of Our Lady of Sorrows passes by is normally accompanied by a hush of what can only be described as veneration. Frightening or impressive as that might be, there is no denying the power that the spectacle evokes to the onlookers. Before the singing and dancing in the evening the end of the period of solemnity is signalled by small troupes of young drummers who march around the streets beating up a storm. Loudly banging fireworks are let off too as at festivals throughout the North. Their main purpose is to frighten off evil spirits.

Portugal, and particularly the North of the country, has a rich heritage of dance and song. During the festival the premier folklore competition in the country takes place on two improvised stages among the gardens of the waterfront. Each village or small town in the area sends a team of singers and dancers. Their costume is the traditional one of black dresses and suits. The women's dresses are decorated with intricate lace embroidery and gold and silver chains, often in the shape of hearts.

The traditional, hierarchical nature of these agricultural commu-nities is recognised in the organisation of the teams whereby the most richly dressed person, representing the local aristocracy, will merely observe while the others, including men dressed in very simple coarse trousers and shirt, representing the small farmers will dance the exhausting series of turns, spins and circles that make up the dance.

The singing that accompanies the dances, too, is as extraordinary in its way as the *fado* of the south. It is usually a duet of male and female voices in which the female voice is a little piercingly, but not uncomfortably, pitched slightly high. The whole group normally sings the chorus. The crowds are always large and appreciative and, though the competition may run, especially on Saturday night, until after midnight, they are always good natured. The vigour and energy of the dancers is infectious and this is useful since there is much else to be seen.

Walking away from the estuary towards the sea leads to the oldest part of the town, where the fishing community still lives. Their contribution to the spectacle is to hang nets from their windows and to decorate the narrow streets with a carpet of differently coloured flower petals arranged in intricate patterns.

Beyond the fishermen's quarters a huge street fair is held in the town's market place. As well as modern rides there are church-fête like stalls of hoopla and shooting galleries. For the courageous there is a very rickety wooden motorcycle 'wall of death'.

The festivities are rounded off on the Sunday evening with a tremendous firework display whose climax is the lighting up with fireworks of the iron road and rail bridge over the River Lima. The entire festival population lines the waterfront as they cascade from the bridge into the river. Quite often the display coincides with the crossing of the bridge by a hooting train. The bridge, incidentally, is one of the lesser known works of the famous French architect, Gustave Eiffel.

The Festival of Our Lady of Suffering is not the only one held in this area during the summer. In May the Festival of Our Lady of the Roses is held near Viana in **Vila Franca do Lima**, a small village south of the River Lima off the N203. Also in May is the Festas dos Andores Floridos in **Alvarães**, a village again on the south side of the Lima, this time off the N308. The streets are again carpeted with flowers and floats are covered in spring blooms. Viana itself has another festival at the beginning of August, the Festas de Santa Cristina, with a great parade of floats showing off the industries and crafts of the region.

As a resort popular with the Portuguese the nightlife of Viana is exciting and varied throughout the summer. The cafés and bars around the central Praça de Republica are full on most summer evenings and to sit and watch the world go by is often sufficient entertainment in itself.

For more active pursuits the short ferry across the River Lima takes visitors to a large party held two or three nights a week throughout the summer in the village of **Darque**, with food, wine, processions and dancing all included in the entrance fee. Like Povoa de Varzim and other modern resorts on this coast Viana also has its complement of nightclubs and discotheques.

Viana has many fine restaurants to sample. Those which may be found in the narrow streets to the right of the upper part of the main street, the Avenida dos Combatantes da Grande Guerra, are good and inexpensive while those around the Praça de República are more expensive and more atmospheric in so far as waiters wear the traditional costume of the region and folk singing or dancing may accompany the meal. Three things must be sampled to say one has really been to the Alto Minho: the *vinho verde*, the salted cod dish known as *bacalhau* cooked in an enormous range of different ways, and the green cabbage soup known as *caldo verde*. The latter, actually much more delicious than it sounds, is made up of green cabbage shredded very thinly and cooked in a stock of potatoes and pork sausage, both thinly sliced.

North of Viana do Castelo along the coast are situated some of Portugal's finest beaches. Apart from pleasant campsites at Ancora and just beyond the small town of Moledo there is very little tourist development. Mile upon mile of largely deserted beach stretch along the coast, backed by dunes and pine woods.

Some of the beaches are indeed still used as an integral part of the local economy. Like the rather better known customs of the fishing communities further south around Aveiro where the men drop the nets offshore and the women haul the nets and catch back to the beach, the fisher folk of the Minho still, often out of economic necessity, maintain their ancient traditions. Local people, usually women and children, harvest seaweed from the sea on relatively calm, usually misty days. The seaweed is loaded onto wooden carts pulled by cattle and is then spread onto the beach to dry a hundred metres or so from the water's edge. The seaweed is then dug into the sand and its nutrients increase the fertility, so that crops such as maize can be planted during the summer months. It is backbreaking work and is endured from sunrise to sunset. It is, perhaps, the most remarkable example of how the Portuguese ingeniously make fertile the almost universally poor quality of the soil in their country.

There are many very attrractive fishing villages along the N13 coast road where small beaches will be crowded with brightly coloured boats and the fishermen are often to be seen repairing their nets. Some of the finest long beaches are found around the village of **Afife**, 11km (7 miles) north of Viana. Tradition has it, incidentally, that the women of Afife are particularly attractive because of interbreeeding with some of Napoleon's troops who achieved a

The main square and fountain in Caminha

foothold in this part of the Alto Minho at the beginning of the nineteenth century.

Vila Praia de Âncora is a picturesque village on the estuary of the River Âncora. In the middle of the estuary is a small fort where fishing boats are moored. This is, of course, one of the many forts established along this coast to defend against incursions by the Spanish, the French and by pirates from as far away as North Africa. Local legend recalls that the town got its name when the wife of one of the town's noblemen eloped with a Moorish prince. On being re-captured she was cast into the river and died, tied to an *ancora* or anchor. As a seaside base away from the city with good (mainly seafood) restaurants and cheap pensions Vila Praia de Âncora is well worth considering. Most of the holiday villas and hotels will be occupied by Portuguese holiday makers rather than foreigners. The Portuguese have long recognised the North as the most beautiful part of their country.

In September Vila Praia de Âncora celebrates the Festas da Senhora da Bonança, or 'Our Lady of Fine Weather'. In an extraordinary spectacle the fishing boats are blessed and a statue of the Virgin is taken out to sea in one of the fishing boats.

This area is one of the few parts of Portugal that is really suitable

The medieval clock tower in the main square, Caminha

for recreational cycling. The main coast road is new and has no more than gentle inclines for long streches making it ideal for cycling, with lots of interesting side roads to explore inland into the pine woods and along the coast amongst the fishing villages. Ask in the well resourced tourist office in Viana for bikes to hire. By bike or by car along the N305 that follows the Âncora river inland is a beautiful leafy route with the chance of a swim in an idyllic river pool and falls at São Lourenço da Montaria.

For those interested in fishing the area has a great diversity of possible catches. Trout are caught in the River Âncora, trout, salmon and scallops further north in the River Minho, while in the River Lima there are reserves for salmon, savel and trout. Along the coast to Caminha, sea bream, grey mullet and bass are caught. Again the tourist offices in Caminha or Viana are the best places for advice on where to hire a boat or equipment.

The first major town which is worth exploring is the beautifully situated **Caminha**. Just within the broad estuary of the graceful River Minho, at its confluence with the River Coura, this ancient town looks across to Spain. Surrounded by water on three sides, it was for centuries a town of strategic military importance, but now it is a fashionable resort with a sailing centre and a pleasant lighthearted atmosphere. Its large central terraced square, the Praça do Conselhiero Silva Torres, is full of cafés and restaurants. The white parasoled tables and the wrought iron balconies, many decorated with flowers, all around the square lend it considerable style. A pleasant hour could easily be spent here just drinking the small cups of strong Portuguese coffee, known as a *curto*, and watching the world go by. If one is feeling more adventurous the restaurants will probably be serving the local specialities such as the conger eels that are plentiful in the Minho. They are served steamed, and known as *eiroz*. Whiting and bream are also favoured dishes in Caminha.

The delightful crenellated clock tower on the north side of the square is very old, dating from the fourteenth century and originally formed part of the town's medieval fortifications. In the centre of the spacious square is a beautiful sixteenth-century fountain. The fifteenth-century Pitas palace, with its Manueline windows, and the town hall, with its attractive loggia, both give to the square its quiet elegance. The Misericórdia chapel, built in 1551, almost next to the clock tower has a beautiful carved doorway and a classic gilt baroque altarpiece inside, very typical of the strange mixture of exuberance and veneration that marks religious feeling in Portugal.

The restaurants around the square are excellent, often serving Spanish as well as Portuguese food to welcome the day visitors from Spain, mostly on shopping sprees, who they for so long resisted.

Quite the most attractive sight in the town, however, and now slightly neglected, is the parish church to be found just within the old town walls at the seafront. From the square the gateway beneath the clock tower on to the Rua Ricardo João de Sousa leads to the church. Look out for attractive sixteenth-century town houses along this road.

The large scale of the church and the solidity of its granite structure reveals its origins as part of the town's fifteenth-century defences. The Renaissance doorways are decorated with boldly sculpted sea demons and creatures, showing the deep influence of the sea on the community. The south doorway is also carved with statues of St Paul, St Peter, and the Gospel writers, Mark and Luke. Within the church there is a highly impressive ceiling in maplewood carved in the Moorish-influenced Mudejar style. On the right-hand side of the church is to be seen a statue of St Christopher, the patron saint of mariners.

Caminha has a couple of comfortable *pensions* off the main square on the Rua de Corredoura, and there is a campsite a couple of kilometres (1¹/₂ miles) inland along the N301 at the pleasant village of **Vilar de Mouros**, which has a medieval bridge and a watermill, and another a similar distance to the south opposite the island of Fortaleza da Insua. An enterprising local fisherman is normally on hand to take parties over who wish to visit the sandy island.

The road along the River Minho towards Valença is a very attractive one with pinewoods on the right-hand side rising to the foothills of the Serra de Peneda, and on the other the swiftly flowing tidal river. At **Vila Nova de Cerveira** there is a luxurious *pousada*, built by King Afonso III, and an *estalagem* with tennis courts and swimming pool. Vila Nova de Cerveira also has a ferry that runs every hour from the walled town to the Galician town of Goyan.

The most beautiful town on the Minho, however, is the old town of **Valença do Minho** that lies within its own fortified city walls. The new town that lies below it on the hill is generally unattractive. The complex Vaubanne-style fortifications hide the old town from view until one drives through the main gateway. Once within, however, the great charm of the balconied and tiled houses becomes apparent.

View from the fortress walls of Valença do Minho to the Galician town of Tuy

The cobbled streets are usually crowded with day visitors from Spain. Benefitting from cheaper Portuguese prices the Spaniards stock up on towels, sheets, plastic containers and all manner of hand-made craft products. But this adds to rather than detracts from the atmosphere of the place.

Whereas most walled cities are medieval, Valença is almost unique in that it dates from the seventeenth century. From the walls one can admire the ingenuity of the angled fortifications, designed such that any attackers could be fired on from at least two sides at any one time. The watchtowers, the defensive outworks sloping down the hill below and the huge north and south doorways piercing the town's defences are all still intact. That they should be so perfectly preserved is obviously a delight for the visitor though the sense of impregnability is rather belied by the town's history. In fact, on the last occasion that the walls were to be besieged the town's occupiers fell, rather ignominiously, victim to a wily Englishman's ruse.

During the War of Sucession in 1834 Admiral Sir Charles Napier was fighting in the service of the liberal Dom Pedro against his reactionary brother Dom Miguel for control of the Portuguese throne. Valença was defiantly held by the Miguelites, while liberal Oporto was besieged by them. Without informing his employer of

The old town of Valença do Minho

Quinta gateway on the road from Valença do Minho to Moncão

his plans Napier decided he would remedy the situation in both towns. Reaching Caminha he put ashore a largely symbolic, but mobile, force of 500 Portuguese and Englishmen. Having marched south to liberate Ponte de Lima he returned to the Alto Minho and marched his force towards the seventy cannon, mounted then — as many of them still are now — high on the town's walls. He had no artillery whatsoever, but immediately sent a letter to the garrison's commander demanding his surrender on pain of the storming of the fortress and the deaths of all within. He marched his tiny army into sight of the defenders, then had them march out of sight again only to re-appear further along the horizon as if they were another section of a much larger force. To this simple ruse the proud walls of Valença fell victim and the town surrendered. The siege of Oporto was lifted shortly after and so ended the civil war.

The River Minho narrows considerably here and there is a fine view of the frontier bridge over the river. Elegant old dredgers ply up and down the river and the fortifications of the Galician town of Tuy sit defiantly on the far bank, almost seeming to glower back at the walls of Valença. Even in summer the trees, the grass, and the vines are a reminder that we are still in the Costa Verde or 'Green Coast'. Walking along the river bank here is very pleasant as is a walk across the bridge and the border to visit Tuy. The narrow steep streets of Tuy sit on ancient Roman fortifications and the cathedral fortress built in 1170 is also worth a visit.

There are some fine restaurants in Valença and in the Bom Jesus square there is a statue of Portugal's first saint São Teotonio. Valença also has a Vintage Train Museum, whose prize exhibit is a steam locomotive built in 1875 by the English company Beyer Peacock. An excellent *pousada* within the fortifications and named after São Teotonio has a beautiful view of the river. On Thursdays a large market takes place below the old walls on the road that leads to the bridge across the border and next to the tourist office.

One of the finest views in the North of Portugal may be seen by taking an excursion from Valença a few kilometres (2 miles) inland to Monte de Faro. Rising quickly through pines the views open out ever more extensively over the Minho valley, the coastal plain and in the distance the mountains of Galicia. The summit, which can only be reached by foot, is 565m (1,853ft) above sea level.

Returning to the N101 eastwards along the Minho the road winds between woods of pine and eucalyptus, while at the river's edge the local farmers grow maize and the grapes that go to make some of the finest *vinho verdes* in the region. Indeed for the Portuguese the next major town on the map, **Monção**, is synonymous with its Alvarinho *vinho verde*. About 6km (4 miles) before Monção watch out for the Lapela tower, another remnant of the former enmity between Spain and Portugal. Near to the tower is a river beach.

The town is in many ways like a small version of Valença. It is, however, not so dramatic, but more purely Portuguese in that it does not have all the Spanish day visitors. It is again, partially, enclosed by seventeenth-century walls. Unlike Valença, though, Monção has a very proud tradition of stout resistance to attack.

The most famous of the town's defenders was a woman, Deu-la-Deu Martins. In 1368 during the siege of the town by the Castilian, Henry of Trastamara, when through starvation the people were about to surrender Deu-la-Deu used some of the psychological subtlety that seems to be the key to military success on the Minho. Taking the last scraps of flour she baked two cakes and sent them to the enemy telling them that there was plenty more where that came from. The crestfallen and gullible besiegers promptly took her at her word, raised their standard and went home. In the wide attractive main square dedicated to her a statue also stands to her memory. A

The statue of Deu-la-Deu Martins in the central square, Monção

much more fitting memorial, however, are the local speciality cakes, *paezinho de Deu-la-Deu*.

In the seventeenth century the town again distinguished itself when besieged by the Spanish, and again it was a woman who led the townspeople. The Countess of Castelo Melhor, Dona Mariana de Lancastre, rallied the defenders throughout the five months of the siege and she negotiated an honourable surrender. At which point the Spanish were astonished to find only 236 men within and that they had been kept at bay through the latter parts of the siege by women and children.

The parish church of Monção, on the Rua João do Pinho on the descent to the riverside, is Romanesque dating from the thirteenth century. It contains another monument to Deu- la-Deu Martins.

There is a delightful walk along the northern ramparts above the river where João Verde's verse, a native poet of the town, seems very appropriate with Galicia so near:

On seeing you so close, Galicia and the Minho,
One would say you were two lovers who the river keeps apart.

Monção is also an attractive spa town, well off-the-beaten-track, with a rural charm all of its own. The spa is to be found to the east of the town. There is a pleasant park to walk in and a free campsite by the river. The spa is quite popular with the Galicians, however, so it can become quite busy.

Monção's festival is that of Corpus Christi on 18 June, and is marked with a ritualised costumed combat between St George and the Dragon. The dragon is finally defeated when St George manages to pull off one of his ear-rings! The festivites are, of course, accompanied by the usual bunting, a brass band in the bandstand on the main square and much drinking and dancing.

From Monção there are two main routes to be followed. The N101 leads into the hinterland of the Alto Minho and eventually returns to the River Lima. Alternatively the N202 continues along the valley of the River Minho up to the border post of São Gregorio. The advantage of the Alto Minho route is that it gives easy access into the Peneda-Gerês National Park, one of the least appreciated of the Iberian Peninsula's nature reserves, and one of the most off-the-beaten-track areas of Europe that is still within relatively easy reach of civilisation. Having reached the almost frontier-like town of Castro Labreiro, however, there is no road across the reserve for cars. For experienced hikers there are some testing but rewarding routes south. The motorist though must return along the N202 road to Monção.

The journey into the park will be described here first and the journey south into the finest *vinho verde* country of the Minho will be described later.

The Minho valley between here and Melgaço is wild with pine forests on either side, only at the river's edge are there vineyards. Five kilometres (3 miles) out of Moncão look out for the Palácio de Brejoeira, a lovely nineteenth-century building which, unfortunately, is not open to visitors. In the palace grounds is produced one of the finest of the *vinho verdes*, named after the palace.

About a third of the way along the valley towards Melgaço, around 10km (6 miles) from Moncão is a turning to the tiny village of **Barbeita** and its nearby prehistoric hill town, known as the *Castro da Nossa Senhora da Assuncao*. Like other *castros* this windswept hilltown was almost certainly occupied by the Celts and gives an intriguing insight into the lifestyle of these people, about whom little is known for certain.

Here as in all parts of the Alto Minho the roadsides and hillsides are dotted with houses of recent construction that are half finished

A Minho farmer carrying sheep skins on his bicycle

and are apparently abandoned. These are the houses of the emigrants earning money abroad, often in France or in Brazil, who return each year to their home town, or *terra*, to add another stage to the houses that will eventually be their homes. Emigration has long been a feature of life in these northern communities. Most of the emigrants are male and it is for that reason that women are so often seen working in the fields. Having saved enough money many of the emigrants return so do not be surprised to find shop and bar owners who speak fluent French. The emigration has been made more tolerable by the fact that marriages still tend to be organised within the village communities. In August many of the emigrants return and the Minho is at its gayest. Long trains of honking cars, often Citroens or Peugeots, their aerials decorated with white lace, trail through the villages signalling that another emigrant has earned enough money to marry a local girl.

With the rapid industrialisation that has been going on throughout the Iberian Peninsula since Spain and Portugal joined the European Economic Community in 1986 the number of emigrants has slowly begun to fall. As 80 to 90 per cent of small businesses in Portugal are located in the North, it will be interesting to see how the future develops.

The point at which the River Mouro joins the Minho lies just beyond the turning to Barbeita. The Ponte do Mouro, or 'Bridge of the Moor', over the river at the village of **Ceviaes** is the location of a famous meeting in Portuguese history. In 1368 the powerful English nobleman, John of Gaunt, the Duke of Lancaster, met the Portugese king, João I and arranged with him that he should marry his daughter, Philippa of Lancaster. In this way was established the first and most important of Portugal's royal dynasties. The presence of John of Gaunt and his Lancastrian bowmen was also to be one of the determining factors in the historic defeat of the Castilians at Aljubarrota in 1385 which established the fledging Portuguese state's independence from its larger neighbour. A plaque on the bridge commemorates the meeting.

The delightful river beyond here is considered to provide some of the best trout fishing in the country. Two points at which it may be worth considering a pause are the tiny spa town of **Peso**, 5km (3 miles) outside Melgaço, and just off the road to Melgaço, the village of **Paderne** which has a beautiful Romanesque church. As accommodation can be difficult to find in this remote area a stay at the Peso spa or the *pensions* nearby is worth considering. Peso also has an idyllic campsite near the river.

South of Melgaço on the N202 lies the Gerês National Park and within it the 'forgotten' village of Castro Labreiro, which will be described later in this chapter.

Melgaço is an ancient town built around its medieval castle. The twelfth-century castle is presently being repaired but the view from the battlements is still impressive and the surrounding narrow streets are very pretty. As at Moncão the castle was the occasion for the martial virtues of women to be displayed.

After their crucial victory over the Spanish at Aljubarrotta John of Gaunt and João of Avis laid siege to the castle of Melgaço which was stoutly defended by 300 Galicians. With preparations being made after fifty-one days for the final and, inevitably, bloody confrontation, a woman within the walls, known as 'La Renegada', knowing there to be a woman in the Portuguese ranks, Ines Negra, challenged her to single combat. Renegada emerged from the encounter, almost without hair, her nose bloodied, and defeated. Feeling that their sense of honour had, nonetheless, thus been appeased the Galicians retired and handed over the castle to the new king.

Melgaço also has a fine example of a provincial Romanesque

A religious procession at a hillside village in the Alto Minho

The parish church at Caminha, Alto Minho

Guimãres castle, Costa Verde

A roadside shrine,
Vila do Conde, Costa Verde

A quiet corner of Melgaço

parish church dating from the thirteenth century, situated near to the castle on the Alameda Ines Negra. It is most remarkable for the low-relief carving of a rather fiendish wolf above the lateral doorway. The locals have long believed the wolf to be a symbol of the Devil. The town has a couple of good restaurants and pensions.

There are also a couple of excellent river beaches in this area to which the locals are willing to direct the visitor, though they can still take some finding up and down the twisting valley roads. The River Minho is so narrow here that it is possible for even the average swimmer to swim back and forth between Spain and Portugal with ease.

Melgaço is an excellent spot from which to begin an exploration of the northern section of the Peneda-Gerês National Park. The N202 is a pleasant scenic route and just before the village of **Lamas de**

Mouro there is a delightfully green valley with a Roman bridge and an old aqueduct and watermill. At Lamas de Mouro itself there is as tranquil and off-the-beaten-track a camp site as one could wish. Just within the national park is the sanctuary of Nossa Senhora da Peneda. From here there is a walk to the peak of Penameda, 1,285m (4,215ft) above sea level, which has some delightful views of the national park.

The **Peneda-Gerês National Park** is the largest nature reserve in Portugal and, though it is well known to the Portuguese, its beauties have recieved little attention abroad. Covering over 70,000 hectares (270 sq miles) it is divided into two halves by the River Lima. The northern section, bounded by the Spanish border, is dominated by the Peneda mountain range and Melgaço is the best point of entry into it. The Peneda area is, if anything, the lesser visited of the two areas. As the road from Melgaço rises steeply the terrain becomes wild and arid, with huge boulders dominating the landscape.

Despite this harshness of terrain the park has been inhabited for thousands of years. The dolmens erected at Castro Labreiro, Pitoes, and Paradela are thought to be as much as 5,000 years old. The Celts also have left their mark especially around Calcedonia, as have the Romans. Over a hundred Roman milestones that marked the route from Braga to Astorga in Spain can be seen in the park. The inscriptions on them give notice of the honours bequeathed by Caesar on his generals in Iberia and Lusitania.

Above all though it is the unique flora and fauna of the park that should entice the traveller. Deer, horses, wildcats and wolves (at least in special reserves) reside in the park. There are also Luso Galician wild ponies that are only found here. For the birdwatcher there are over a hundred different types of birds to be seen, including eagles. For the amateur botanist, as well as the abundant woods of cork oaks and firs that the highest annual rainfall in the country provides, there are also several plants, such as the Gerês juniper and the Gerês iris that, again, are only found here. Needless to say the picking of flowers in the park is forbidden as is the lighting of fires. Many hundreds of acres of woods are lost in fires throughout northern Portugal every summer, usually through visitor's carelessness. There is some suspicion too that older woods are deliberately burnt down in order to plant the faster growing and therefore more profitable eucalyptus trees that are becoming such a prominent feature all over the country.

A swimming place on the River Minho, with Spain on the far bank

The area around **Castro Labreiro**, 950m (3,000ft) above sea level, is made up of high rocky hillsides. The village has been rather spoilt by the unrestricted building of new and rather unattractive houses. However, there is an exciting walk along an exposed ridge to reach the fortress itself. It was built by the first king of Portugal, Afonso Henriques. The reasons for the building of the fortress and what it sought to defend still remain unclear. It was partially destroyed when a bolt of lightning struck its store of gunpowder. The views over the national park are tremendous and the game of giving names to the extraordinary rock formations all around, such as the tortoise, the dragon, or the boar, can be enjoyed by foreigners as much as it has been for centuries by the local people.

Should the village be deserted this may well be because the local people have followed the ancient custom in the mountains and have moved up to spend the summer with their flocks of goats and sheep in the high peaks. The villagers only return to their winter houses in December. These winter houses are known as *inviernas* while their summer homes are known as *brandas* or soft houses, and are little more than improvised shelters.

Castro Labreiro has also given its name to a particular breed of hardy muscular working dog, used to herd sheep and goats and to

An old irrigation system near Lamas de Mouro

protect them from wolves and which can still sometimes be seen in the village. Castro Labreiro has a single *pension*.

For the serious walker who wishes to try the two-day trek across the Park to Lindoso, 25km (15 miles) to the south, there are great delights in following the course of, first the River Peneda and then the River Labreiro. However fog can often settle here for a whole day at a time and the temperature can drop quite rapidly so it is important to be properly equipped. An additional problem is that the survey maps that are really essential for the trip can be difficult to obtain. Should the idea nonetheless still appeal it is best to contact the National Tourist Office in Lisbon in advance, or try specialist map shops, such as Stanfords or McCarta in London.

Returning on the N202 to Monção, the N101 heads south from the spa town into the heart of the Minho's *vinho verde* country. Monção is famous throughout northern Portugal for the quality of the unusual and increasingly popular *vinho verde* that is produced there, and it is, perhaps the best place to sample the wine and to consider the unusual methods by which its distinctive flavour is produced. It is a light wine low in alcohol and it has been grown in this region for centuries. The distinctive taste of the wine derives largely from the preponderance of granite in the soils and in part

The village of Castro Labreiro in the Peneda-Gêres National Park

from the particular character of the vines. The vine is, as can be testified to by anyone who has spent any time in the area, a creeper, to be seen hanging from granite columns along almost any roadside.

In the past the vines were trained to grow up the trunks of trees. This can still occasionally be seen and is believed to have been first introduced into the province by the Romans, who knew the vines as the *ulmisque adjungere vites* or 'the vines that grow up trees'. The problem is that as the vines can reach heights of 5m (16ft) or more, conventional methods of cultivation would make picking or pruning very difficult. Hence the use of granite columns, or even more attractively, the use of leafy arbors, occasionally forming a roof over a road or a drive on a large estate. The Atlantic influence, with its resultant coolness, prevents the grapes from fully ripening and leaves an unusually high level of acidity in the grape — this is the determining factor in the character of the wine.

After harvesting in the late autumn, the wine is fermented for just forty-eight hours before being stored in casks through the winter. It is bottled from January through to March. It then undergoes a second fermentation, called a malolactic fermentation, in the bottle in the natural heat of May and June that converts the harsh malic acid into lactic acid and carbon dioxide; hence the tiny sparkling bubbles in the wine. The bottle must be kept horizontal and the cork wet or the gas escapes and the wine becomes flat. It is best drunk after two years in the bottle and, again, must be drunk straightaway once opened or the wine's flavour will be impaired.

The *vinho verde* region was demarcated in 1908 and it represents 15 per cent of the wine producing area of Portugal and 20 per cent of its production. Both red and white wines are produced but the people of the Minho have such a prodigious appetite for them that 85 per cent of the production is consumed within the region.

Only a few of the white wines reach the export market. The best known of these is the very dry, sparkling 'Gatão' wine that is produced near Amarante. The best of the grapes for the red variety are Vinhão, Borracal, Espadeiro, and Azal Tinto. The Minho people themselves normally drink red wine. The finest of the white wine grapes are the Azal Branco, Loureiro, and Alvarinho. The Alvarinho is the best of these giving a higher alcohol level of 11 or 12 per cent, in comparison to an average of 8 or 9 per cent, and with a lower level of acidity. It can only be grown by government decree in the region of Monção. Other areas producing particularly fine *vinho verde* are Santo Tirso and Terras de Basto.

The Minho also produces a unique brandy known as *aguardente*, and appropriately nicknamed 'firewater'. The stalks, pips and skins of the grape are all apparently used in the distilling of the brew. It should be tried once — but perhaps once only.

From Monção the N101 runs to the south through the heartland of the Minho and enables the visitor to see the life and work of the province at close quarters in the small villages that line the route. The most attractive of these villages are those that are sited above the River Vez, such as **Aguia**, with its attractive mansion of Solar de Torre, and the unlikely named Aboim das Chocas.

At the village of Extremo it is worth considering a turning to the old and very much off-the-beaten-track village of **Paredes de Coura**. There is excellent trout fishing in the nearby River Coura and remains of Celtic, Roman, and Suevian occupation are to be found in the surrounding countryside. It is also a traditional centre for the production of cotton and woollen blankets and so is a good spot to look out for a bargain. Codfish, cooked in the 'Miquelina' style, one of the 365 different ways of cooking *bacalhau*, is the town's speciality.

$8^1/_2$km (5 miles) beyond Parades de Coura following the N301 along the course of the River Coura towards Caminha is the turning to the small village of **Rubiaes** a kilometre or so north along the N201. Though a slight detour from the route it is worth considering as the parish church has one of the impressively carved Romanesque doorways for which the North is justly famous.

Returning to the N101, the first place at which good restaurants and *pensions* are available lies 40km (25 miles) to the south of Moncão at **Arcos de Valdevez**. Set on the banks of the River Vez there is a picturesque low bridge, a pillory bearing the arms of Dom Manuel, and no less than six churches. The finest of these are the Romanesque Chapel of Nossa Senhora de Conceição de Praça, and the baroque church of Nossa Senhora de Lapa. This latter church was built in 1767 and is unusual in having an octagonal shape. The interior is sumptuous and is the work of the sculptor Brother Antonio Vilaca. There is also a pleasant walk through the public gardens along the bank of the river.

Near to the bridge is the manor house of Casa de Requeijo, which is open to visitors and recieves guests. A second manor house, the Paco da Gloria, is an eighteenth-century building with an imposing three-storey tower. It too offers accommodation and has a swimming pool and lovely gardens. There are a couple of other *pensions* in the town and some good value restaurants.

Like many of the other towns of northern Portugal Arcos de Valdevez really comes alive with the return of the emigrants in August. *Festas* take place during three days in the middle of the month, beginning with the usual loud firecrackers to frighten off any evil spirits. This is followed by brass bands, costumed characters, dancing and innocent fun that marks out the Minho even from other regions of Portugal.

Just $4^1/_2$km (3 miles) to the south lies one of the most beautiful river valleys in the country, that of the River Lima. The Lima, of course, runs into the sea at Viana do Castelo where our tour of the Minho began. In the period prior to the Roman conquest of northern Portugal this river had served as a tribal frontier. Its magical qualities derived from a legend originating from this time that a group of Celts from the south had marauded across this natural frontier but had never returned. When the Romans under Decius Junius Brutus marched north in 137AD the legionaires refused to cross the river believing it to be the legendary Lethe, or River of Forgetfulness. The soldiers feared that if they crossed they would lose their memories and so never return home to their families. Brutus only managed to persuade them to cross by fording across alone on horseback. From the far bank he called the soldiers over individually by name to show that he had not lost his memory.

Ponte de Barca is an attractive little town on the north bank of the meandering river. The gracefully arched bridge that dominates the scene was built in the sixteenth century. The town's present name is relatively new. It was originally known as *Castelo de Nobrega* or *Terra de Nobrega*, that is the 'Castle or Land of Nobrega'. It became known as Ponte da Barca, or 'Bridge of the Boat', when a pontoon bridge was used for fording the river. Its early good fortune was to lie at the crossroads of the two medieval pilgrim routes, from Braga to Santiago, and from Ribeira de Lima to Orense in Spain, which brought it wealth by catering for the needs of the pilgrims.

The town has an interesting parish church which was built largely in the fifteenth century, though local wealthy families have added side chapels without too great a regard for artistic harmony. It was reconstructed in 1714 by Manuel Pinto de Vilalobos, the architect of the Misericórdia church in Viana de Castelo at the mouth of the River Lima.

The town hall, preceded by a granite staircase and the market hall alongside the bridge are both imposing buildings built during the dictatorship of the Marquess of Pombal in the eighteenth century. On Wednesdays a much larger market takes place on the wide sands of the river bed.

The best way to enjoy the town though is simply to relax and savour the beauty of the setting. This beauty is, perhaps, the reason for the many stories of enchantment that have grown up around the town. An ancient tradition that is still reputed to be practised is the *baptizado de meia noite*, or midnight baptism. Pregnant women of the town go down to the river at midnight to have their unborn children baptized. Thus baptized in the mother's womb the child, it is believed, will be born healthy and strong. As the bells toll midnight the child's godparents must be the first people to cross the bridge.

The best places to stay in Ponte de Barca are the combined *pensions* and restaurants that overlook the river. A meal taken on a verandah or a terrace in the long summer evening is an unforgettable experience, even more so if it coincides with the flash thunderstorms that are quite frequent in the Minho. More expensive but elegant accommodation is to be found in the eighteenth-century manor house, the Paço Vedra, located a couple of kilometres outside of the

A religious procession in one of the hillside villages of the Alto Minho

town in its own estate. Ask in the tourist office near the bridge for directions. The office can also advise on the best place to hire boats and to go swimming in the river. In the summer months especially the water level can drop quite dramatically.

Ponte de Barca's festival is that of São Bartolomeu in late August when among the music and dancing there are displays of local crafts, such as linen work.

From Ponte de Barca the course of the Lima can be followed either west to Bravães, Ponte de Lima and a return to Viana or east to the Peneda-Gerês National Park and the town of Lindoso.

The N203 from Ponte de Barca to Lindoso is a scenic route through pine trees along the wooded foothills of the Serra de Soajo. The Serra do Gerês can be seen to the south of the river. There are a good number of attractive places along the route at which to stop to fish or to swim before reaching the village of Entre Ambos os Rios where there is an official campsite.

From here the road rises as it enters the national park. Just after the turning to Soajo to the left the meandering river below has been enlarged by the construction of a hydro-electric dam. At a second dam just below Lindoso it is possible to walk across the river and it is a good place from which to begin a hike in the national park, following initially the course of the River Labroeiro. Lindoso is alternatively a fine spot from which to hike in the opposite direction to the town of Gerês across the Serra Amarela. Like those from Castro Labreiro, these testing walks across the mountains — where the weather can change dramatically within minutes — should only be attempted by experienced walkers with good survey maps.

The first sight of **Lindoso** from the N203 is its thirteenth-century castle fortified by Dom Dinis. Facing the frontier with Spain it was attacked on several occasions by the army of Philip IV during Portugal's War of Independence in the seventeenth century. It has now been substantially repaired and houses information on the national park. The views from the surrounding walls and watch towers over the Lima valley and the national park are superb.

At the foot of the castle are arranged together sixty granite *espigueros*, used for storing maize. These granaries are found throughout the Minho and the usual placing of a cross on their roofs indicates the religious feeling that motivates their careful construction. The sight of so many of the granaries together and their obvious resemblance to a graveyard invites some explanation as to their significance. The word *espigueiro* is derived from *espigo* meaning corn cob. They appear to be quite ancient but, in fact, the growing of corn was only introduced into the Minho in the seventeenth century. Its introduction transformed the small holdings of the area as it was discovered that from the maize a staple food, bread, could be made. Maize bread is called *broa* by the country people. This accounts for the importance of the granaries and also, as the bread was often used during Mass, for its religious significance. The harvesting of the maize and the de-leafing of the cobs is one of the great social occasions of the year in villages throughout the Minho.

The granaries are also known as *canastros*, and being raised from the ground serves the practical purpose of protection from flooding and rats. The *canastros* at Lindoso date from the eighteenth and nineteenth centuries. The maize bread should be tried in combination with a glass of the local *vinho verde*. There is an example of a traditional oven used to bake bread in the castle of Lindoso.

Returning from Lindoso along the N203, after about 10km (6km) is the turning to the village of **Soajo**. This is a tiny village isolated among hills and the highlight of a visit is again the collection of *canastros* sitting together on a rocky platform. The reason for their being placed together, as at Lindoso, is the traditional methods of collective farming practised as a matter of survival by the village community. Even today herds of sheep and goats are said to be held in common by the people of the village.

A source of income for the local people has also long been hunting. The men of Soajo were given privileges by the former kings of Portugal, the Braganças, deposed at the beginning of the twentieth century, to hunt the wild bears, wolves and boars that once lived in the mountains. The people of these remote villages still have a great pride in their independence and self-reliance. The only accommodation in Soajo is in rooms above the village café.

Taking up the route previously mentioned to the west of Ponte de Barca along the N203 quickly brings the traveller, in just $3^1/_2$km (2 miles) to the village of **Bravães**.

This tiny village is home to one of Portugal's finest Romanesque churches. Set among the hanging vines producing grapes for the local *vinho verde* wine, the church of São Salvador is a very simple, yet impressive, rectangular structure in granite. It was built during the reign of Afonso VI at the end of the eleventh century by a local nobleman, probably at the instigation of the Cluniac monks of Santiago de Compostela who brought the beautiful carving typical of their cathedral south along the pilgrim's way to Braga. It then passed into the hands of the Benedictine order of monks and from them to the Augustinians.

Its most remarkable feature is the elaborate and exuberant carving to be seen in the main doorway. Amongst the figures can be discerned doves, monkeys, and two bulls' heads at either side of the doorway modelled on the local long horned *gado barrosoa* cattle, so important to the region's economy. In ways that echo the treatment of cattle in India and parts of sub-Saharan Africa these cattle can often be seen leading religious processions in the Minho.

A low relief of the the Lamb of God is to be seen, supported by two griffins, decorating a side doorway. The interior contains two medieval murals of Our Lady and St Sebastian. Sebastian is often depicted in paintings and statues in Portugal, typically tied to the stake and pierced by arrows during his martyrdom, as it was believed he visited the country in the Middle Ages. Like several other fine monuments in the country, the church was substantially restored in the 1940s.

Ponte de Lima, the largest town of the area, lies 14km (9 miles) beyond Bravães through attractive villages and woods of pine, chestnut and eucalyptus, ideal for a stroll and a picnic. It is a pleasantly spacious town in which to spend a day or even longer. It has a good number of hotels and is a centre for the development of, what the Portuguese call *Turismo de Habitação*, or manor house accommodation. Their offices are combined with the tourist office in the Praça de República in the town centre. They offer accommodation in the homes of wealthy Portuguese families, and while usually very attractive, they can often be very expensive. Most are dotted around the countryside to the north-west of the town. The manor house owners often organise small-game shoots in their areas.

The origins of the town are very remote. It may have been originally inhabited by a Celtic people known as the Limicos. Archaeological remains of celtic *castros* found here date back to 150BC. The Romans knew the town as *Forum Linicorum* and it was they who first made it into a place of some importance as a centre for trade along the main Braga to Astorga road and as a point of defence along the Lima. They constructed a stone wall to surround the town and constructed a bridge over the river, a portion of which stands to this day on the north bank of the Lima. The changing course of the river necessitated an extension to the bridge in 1355 when the town recieved a royal visit from the king Dom Pedro.

The remains of the Roman bridge and the medieval bridge, towers and a portion of the town wall give to the town its distinctive character. The bridge is of particular architectural interest as it is unusually made up of a combination of fifteen semicircular and twelve pointed arches. The solitary medieval keep still standing is that of São Paulo and stands on the south side of the Lima overlooking the bridge. The rest of the medieval defensive wall was destroyed to allow for the expansion of the town.

The sands of the river bank are used six times a year for the oldest recorded market in Portugal. Proof of this can be found within the old prison tower where the municipal library is located. On request the librarian will bring out the original Royal Charter granted to the town in 1125 by Queen Dona Teresa.

The north side of the riverbed is used during the markets for the selling of cattle and the long horned *gado barroso* oxen still used to plough the narrow, steep slopes of the hills of the North where modern machinery cannot cope. Below the bridge snacks of sardines and cakes are for sale to be washed down, of course, with *vinho verde*. Craftspeople also bring their wares from the surrounding districts and villages. Embroidery from Correlha, basketwork from Rebordoes and Facha, furniture from Arcozelo, wooden barrrels from Fornelos and tin work, lace work and wooden clogs from Ponte do Lima itself. Prices are very reasonable and it is worth haggling.

By the south bank entrance to the bridge is a small but neat square, the Praça de Camoes, in the centre of which is a seventeenth-century baroque granite fountain. The winding streets around the square are fun to explore and the traveller is almost certain to find some of the fortified sixteenth-century doorways, emblazoned with coats of arms, that are dotted around the old town. Ponte de Lima was the original home of some of the great aristocratic families of Portugal in the Middle Ages, as the great number of manor houses in the region still testifies. It is said that some of these families were established before the country itself was. Merchants, generals and explorers all came from here. The most famous was Ferdinand Magellan, the first man to circumnavigate the globe. The eighteenth-century mansion of the Counts of Aurora is probably the finest of these houses.

The most interesting church to visit is also to be found on the riverfront. The church of St Francisco has been converted into a museum. Its finest exhibits are a splendid Rococo altarpiece in the chancel, two beautifully sculpted pulpits, and several ancient statues. The church of Santo Antonio dos Capuchos next to the church of St Francis has also been secularised and dates from the fourteenth century. It houses some rare and attractive Hispano-Arab glazed tiles, as well as a series of temporary exhibitions.

Ponte de Lima is particularly lively in early June during the Festas de São Jorge, when there is a medieval costumed procession including St George himself. In September the town is host to the inappropriately named 'New Fairs', which began in the twelfth century. Underlining Ponte do Lima's long established role as the market town for the surrounding area it is essentially an agricultural fair. Everything relating to small-scale farming is sold here.

The essential reason for being in Ponte de Lima as a visitor, however, at any time of the year is always the same. It is, as in its long time civic rival further upstream, Ponte de Barca, to sample the particular leisured and graceful atmosphere of the town and its setting. The finest part of the day is the evening which may be spent, perhaps, walking beneath the *alameda*, or avenue, of plane trees that line the river and sampling the local wines served straight from the barrel in the traditional taverns, or *tascas*, in the medieval streets of the town.

Should the Romanesque church at Bravães have been particularly enjoyable a $12^1/_2$km (7 miles) journey south along the N201 leads to the turning along the N308 to **Rio Mau**. This village also contains a very fine Romanesque church.

Following the N202 for the final 20km (12 miles) or so west to Viana do Castelo our point of departure in the region, a brief detour to the right after the village of Santa Comba to **Estarãos** provides an opportunity to see perhaps the most interesting of the manor houses of the region. The Moinho de Estaraos is a converted mill built in the seventeeth century and extensively renovated in the nineteenth. It is near to a three-arched Roman bridge over the River Estarãos.

Just beyond the turning to Estarãos is the manor house of Bertiandos. The mixture of architectural styles in the house reflects the long animosity of the two branches of the family that occupied the two wings of the building. A further manor house, the Solar dos Almadas is situated near Lanhezes. Our final destination of Viana do Castelo lies just 15km (9 miles) further down the Lima valley.

Further Information

— Alto Minho —

Tourist Information Offices

Arcos de Valdevez
☎ 058 66001

Caminha
Rua Ricardo Joaquim de Sousa
☎ 058 921952

Melgaço
Largo do Loreto
☎ 051 652757

Ponte de Barca
☎ 058 42104

Ponte de Lima
Praça de República
☎ 058 942335

Valença do Minho
Posto de Fonteira
(on the main Estrada N13)
☎ 051 22182/23374

Viana do Castelo
Praça de Erva
Rua do Hospital Velho
☎ 058 22620/24971

Vila Nova de Cerveira
Praça da Liberade
☎ 051 95787

Information on Peneda-Gerês National Park
Arcos de Valdevez
☎ 058 65338

Caldas do Gerês
☎ 062 65181

Places of Interest

Melgaço
Peso Spa
Open: June to mid-October

Monção
Spa
Open: mid-June t0 October

Viana do Castelo
Municipal Museum
Largo de São Domingos
☎ 058 24223
Open: 9.30am-12.30pm, 2.30-5.30pm. Closed Mondays and holidays.

Museum of Sacred Art
Largo de São Domingos
☎ 058 22508

Markets

Darque — Sunday

Melgaço — Friday

Monção — Thursday

Valença do Minho — Thursday

Viana do Castelo — Monday

Festivals

Moncão
Corpus Christi
June 18

Nossa Senhora das Dores
September 19-22

Ponte de Barca
São Bartolemeu
Late August

Ponte de Lima
São Jorge
Early June

New Fairs
Late September

Viana do Castelo
Nossa Senhora de Agónia
Weekend nearest to 20 August

A fishing village near Vila do Conde, Costa Verde

A bathing spot on the River Cavado, Costa Verde

The Dom Luís I bridge and barcos rabelos *boats, Porto*

The parish church at Luzim, Douro Valley

2 • The Costa Verde

This region of northern Portugal contains some of the most beautiful, unspoilt coastlines in Europe and some of the country's most important historical sites. Indeed it is in this area at Guimarães that the the present independent nation state had its beginning. It is a conservative, traditional part of the country in both religion, as we shall see in the great pilgrimage centre of Braga, and economically as evidenced by the continuing presence of many people still farming their small plots in ways that have not changed for generations. This traditional attitude to life abides, too, among the fishing communities who still go out in small boats onto the Atlantic, who still produce large wooden vessels at Vila do Conde and whose women and old men still harvest seaweed to make the sand of the beaches bear crops.

The easiest place from which to begin a tour is the ancient town of **Braga.** It can be reached very quickly from the second city of Porto on the recently completed and fast N3 road. This road goes over twisting, rolling hills to within 13km (8 miles) of the city. The final part of the journey on the N13 is a delightful drive through pine woods, fertile farms and vineyards producing the famous local *vinho verde* from vines growing on granite columns. The aptness of the adjective green to describe the region is immediately apparent.

Braga is the third most important city in Portugal and though not very well known to foreigners this does not prevent it having all of the traffic and congestion problems that are associated with a modern city. It is, nonetheless, a bustling, beautiful city full of baroque façades, art nouveau cafés and neon signs above the shops, that are rather reminiscent of London in the 'sixties. All that could be required in terms of hotels and sports facilities is available here, as are several late bars and night clubs.

Though Braga is a busy industrial city, producing leather goods, textiles, bricks and light engineering, its centre has one of the largest

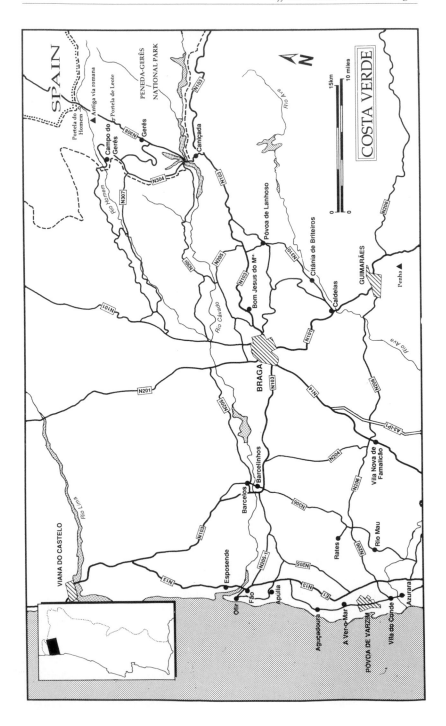

concentrations of historical buildings in Portugal, and a plethora of churches reflecting its ecclesiastical importance over the centuries. It has even been referred to as the 'City of the Archbishops' and the 'Portuguese Rome'.

The earliest settlement here was probably a Celtic tribe, the Bracari, from which the name Braga is derived. Conquered by the Romans in 250BC, Braga was an important town, and as the empire began to contract *Bracara Augusta* was taken over by the 'Barbarian' people, the Suevi, who made it into their capital. The town was subsequently conquered by the Visigoths and later, the Moors. Its prosperity and its 'Golden Age' began with the Christian reconquest. The town was liberated by Ferdinand, the King of Leon, in 1040. Soon after it became the seat of an archbishop's see and its ecclesiastical influence grew, at a time when bishops were politically as powerful as the nobles. Its apogee of influence was in the thirteenth century when the Bishops of Astorga, Tuy, Logo, Orense, and Mondedonho as well as Viseu, Coimbra, and Porto were within its archdiocese. The most influential of the bishops was Dom Diego de Sousa, who in the sixteenth century dedicated himself to improving the architectural heritage of the city.

The central attraction in the city centre as elsewhere in the northern towns is the cathedral, in effect, the religious centre of the whole country, as it was once the religious centre of the whole peninsula. It houses the remains of Henry, the first Duke of Portucale, and his wife, Teresa. It was they who constructed the first basically Romanesque church on the site. Unfortunately little remains of the original and the different stylistic additions, Gothic, baroque, Renaissance, made by the succeeding prelates have, in the opinion of some, destroyed any overall sense of artistic unity in the building. It remains very impressive and certainly exudes authority, but it is not, as surely any ecclesiastical building should be, uplifting.

Nonetheless a great number of individual sections of the structure and individual aspects of the interior are very beautiful. The massive ornate main façade, initially unattractive, illustrates the point. The arching over this main doorway is one of only two Romanesque features remaining, and in its illustration of the medieval story of Reynard the fox, is fascinating. The portico before this archway is supported on contrasting Gothic arches which viewed on their own terms are very attractive too. They were constructed by sculptors from the Bay of Biscay brought to Braga by Diogo de Sousa. The other

The façade of Braga cathedral

Romanesque remnant is the south door. At the opposite end of the
church adorning the exterior wall of the chancel is a fine sculpture of
Our Lady Suckling the Holy Child, said to be by the Rennaissance
sculptor, Nicholas Chanterene.

The interior of the cathedral is surprisingly dark and initially
rather confusing as two side chapels are immediately apparent to left
and right. Walking forward into the main nave, however, the inad-

visability of placing ornate baroque decoration on the simple structure of an early Gothic, sixteenth-century structure is evident. It has
the effect of annulling the grace of the soaring granite vault; a fine
development of his craft by the master architect of his day, João de
Castilo.

Viewed from a different angle, however, from the choir looking
down onto the baroque decoration of the nave rather than up at it, its
individual, independent attractiveness is plain to see. The eighteenth century twin organs are, indeed, a *tour-de-force* of rococo exuberance; its gilt trumpets seeming to multiply before the eyes. The
choir stalls, made of wood imported from Brazil in the eighteenth
century, are intricately carved and delicately inlaid.

Each of the three chapels within the cathedral are worth visiting.
But undoubtedly the most important of them is the Capela dos Reis,
the Chapel of the Kings. Here are buried in sixteenth-century tombs
the bodies of Henry of Burgundy, the first independant ruler of the
Dukedom of Portucale and his wife, Dona Teresa. Teresa was the
daughter of Afonso IV of Leon and Braga actually formed part of her
dowry. Set beside them is the mummified body of Dom Lourenço de
Vicente, an Archbishop of Braga, who fought at the Battle of
Aljubarrota, alongside the establisher of Portugal's second ruling
dynasty, João of Avis. The Gothic vaulting of the chapel rests on
beautifully sculpted stone in the shape of human heads. To the right
of the main nave and chancel are situated the Gothic chapel of St
Gerald, decorated with painted tiles depicting the life of the saint,
and the Chapel of Glory, decorated with fourteenth-century wall
paintings.

The chapel of Nossa Senhora de Piedade was ordered to be built
by Diogo de Sousa in the sixteenth century to house his tomb. The
high altar within is a fine Renaissance work and the reclining figure
of the archbishop himself is again attributed to the Renaissance
sculptor, Nicholas de Chanterene.

The cathedral also houses to the left of the main doorway one of
the finest collections of religious art in Portugal. It contains precious
reliquaries of solid gold and silver from the tenth to the eighteenth
centuries, and an impressive array of religious vestments with a
surprising range of styles and designs. There is also, appropriately,
a range of the badges of the Bishop's office, the mitre and the cope.
There is also an iron cross said to be the one before which Mass was
said for the first time in Brazil by a Brother Henrique after the arrival

Capela dos Coimbras, Braga

of the explorer Pedro Alvares Cabral in 1500. Also on display are a pair of the platform-soled shoes worn by the Archbishop Rodrigo de Mouro Teles who was so short that he could not reach above the altar table without them.

Across the Rua Do Souto, that runs along the north face of the cathedral lies the beautiful courtyard of the former archbishop's palace. At the centre of it is a delightful baroque fountain, dating from 1723. It was constructed by the Archbishop Dom Rodgrigo de Mouro Teles and bears his coat of arms. The surrounding large complex of buildings now house the Public Library, the District Archives and the Dom Diogo de Sousa Museum. The oldest part of the palace is, at the rear, on the north side that looks onto the lovely Garden of Santa Barbara. This fourteenth-century wing was built by the Archbishop Don Goncalo Periera. The garden also contains some picturesquely ruined gothic arches, and another seventeenth-century fountain.

Turning back to the palace complex from the garden the seventeenth and eighteenth-century additions that lie to the right house the Public Library with over 250,000 books, the second largest collection in Portugal. The reading room is worth trying to visit to see its coffered ceiling. The Dom Diogo do Sousa Museum has not yet been fully opened, but some remnants of the Roman occupation, such as inscribed milestones can already be viewed.

Though the palace, which at one point in the Middle Ages covered a tenth of the area of the city, and the cathedral, with their stolid monumentality can create a rather sombre atmosphere some of the finest sights in the city are, however, much more low key and best discovered by exploring in a casual way the many backstreets and small churches in the city. The tourist office on one of the corners of the Praça de Republica has a selection of city street maps.

One of the most striking churches is, for example, the Church of St Lawrence on the Rua de São Vicente, north from the central Praça de Republica along the Rua dos Chaos. It is a small church with a typically ornate baroque altar. Built in 1565, and restored in 1691, it was sited where a Visigothic chapel had once stood in the seventh century. In the sacristy there is a stone believed to date from that period. It is inscribed with words which translate as:

Here lies Remismuera since the first of May, 618, Monday, in peace. Amen.

The walls are entirely covered with tiles depicting the life and death of the third-century saint and the removing of his remains to Lisbon. Above the doorway the organ and choir are decorated with finely carved figures. The churches of Saints Vitor, Francis, and most famously, Sebastian all contain similar depictions in tiles of the lives of the saints. The latter contains, perhaps, the finest work.

A chapel that is in contrast to these is the Capela dos Coimbras off the Rua de Afonso Henriques. This is a small Renaissance chapel built unusually in the form of a square crennellated tower. The statues are in Anca stone. Next to it stands the house of the Coimbras which possesses exquisite Manueline windows. These are in fact all that was rescued from the original building when it was demolished in 1906.

The final architectural aspect of Braga's heritage to consider are the town hall and the Raio Palace; considered to be two of the finest secular baroque buildings in Portugal. The beautifully proportioned town hall was designed by Andres Soares. It was begun in 1753 but was not finished until 112 years later. Above the main doorway is a statue of Our Lady of Relief. The assembly room within has some attractive historical oil paintings of the city which are worth seeing.

In the square before the town hall is an attractive baroque foun-

Bom Jesus do Monte

The pilgrims' stairway at Bom Jesus do Monte

tain known as the Fountain of the Pelican. The fountain, which is illuminated at night, was originally part of the Archbishop's garden.

If anything, however, the Palacete de Raio, or the 'House of the Mexican' as it is more usually known in the city, is an even finer example of the elegance of early eighteenth-century Portuguese baroque. It is to be found behind the post office on the Rua de Raio. The graceful curves of the façade are accentuated by the facing of tiles and above them sits an imposing balustrade. The quality of the buildings of this time have in fact given rise to a creation of a sub-section of the baroque, 'the Joanine', named after the king who reigned during their creation, João V.

A third elegant mansion, the Casa Dos Biscainhos, west of the town hall on the Rua dos Biscainhos, now houses a small ethno-graphic and architctural museum. This seventeenth-century noble-man's house itself is delightful, with its balustraded stairway and passageway through the façade, very similar to the famous Palace of Mateus at Vila Real, which was used to allow horses to pass directly through to the stables.

Another fine place to visit in the central shopping area of the town and, quite unexpected there, is the workshop of the saddle makers, Clemente's of Braga, in the Rua dos Chaos. From the shopfront this appears to be merely another general leather store; a request, however, mimed if necessary, to see the saddles being made should lead you through the back of the shop into the workshop. Saddles have been produced here for over eighty years and they are still hand made in the traditional manner, in particular for the royal horses of Alter de Chao in the Alto Alentejo. The mini-tour goes through all the stages of the saddle's manufacture, taking the visitor through tiny corridors and stairways until all sense of direction is lost, and one re-emerges back in the shop. The tour is usually com-pleted by the proud displaying of photographs of the many famous people who have requested saddles from 'Clementes'. There is, however, never any pressure to buy.

At the nearby village of Galego St Mary there is a ceramics workshop belonging to Julia Ramalhos, a member of one of the most famous artisan families in Portugal. Several other of the country's finest craftsmen work in or near Braga. Jose Freitas de Carvalho maintains the long tradition of woodcarving and Domingos Machado makes the small, guitar like, four stringed instrument, the *cavaquinho*. Pottery and weaving are also traditional industries. Ask at the tourist office for details of when it is possible to visit any of these workshops.

Almost opposite the tourist office on the Praça de República is the Café Vianna, an excellent place to relax with a coffee or a light meal. The art deco interior is worth seeing.

As one might expect Braga has many religious festivals throughout the year, the most important being those of Holy Week. The whole town is decorated, windows being adorned with colourful bedspreads and many in the processions will be hooded and barefoot in penitence.

The more secular fesitivites are around the feast of St John from 16 June to 25 June. There are the usual Minho festivites of singing, dancing, and fireworks. There is also the custom of presenting friends and relatives with the herb basil in a clay pot. Two rules must be followed on recieving this gift. Its fragrance must not be smelt directly but only by smelling one's fingers having caressed the plant and it must only be watered by moonlight. If these rules are not followed then tradition has it that the plant will die. Braga's weekly market is held on Tuesdays.

Braga is most celebrated within Portugal, of course, for the pilgrimage church at **Bom Jesus do Monte** that lies just a few kilometres outside of the city along the N103, and which can be seen dominating the landscape to the east of the city. The church itself is a beautiful neo-Classical building designed by the Braga-born architect, Carlos Amarante. But the uniqueness of the place resides in the succession of staircases that rise up the hill to the church's main façade.

The essential way to appreciate Bom Jesus is to ascend the 'Via Dolorosa' of the baroque staircase. For those visitors who wish to follow the pilgrim's path here is a more detailed description.

The summit of the hill was a site of devotion from at least the fourteenth century, when it was known as the Holy Cross of Monte Espinho. It was in 1772 that the plan for a new sanctuary was devised, instigated by Archbishop D. Rodrigo de Moura Teles. The arched portico at the base of the steps with which the Via Dolorosa begins bears his coat of arms. The intention was to provide an alternative Way of the Cross for those pilgrims who could not afford to visit Jerusalem. The sanctuary was finally completed in 1811, though it was not consecrated until 1857.

Beyond the portico, as the steps ascend a succession of chapels

Statue of the Prophet Jeremiah on the main façade of Bom Jesus

appear to either side. In each of them are groups of life-size, and remarkably life-like, terracotta figures. The chapels of the first flight show Christ's Last Supper and then the beginning of his Passion in the Garden of Gethsemane. Subsequently they depict his Whipping, the Crowning with Thorns, Simon of Cyrene assisting Christ with the Cross, and his being nailed to the Crucifix.

Above the next wide terrace begins the double stairway of the Five Senses. It comprises six fountains the first of which represents the Wounds of Christ. At the top of the first flight is the second fountain, dedicated to sight. Each of these fountains represents for the devout pilgrim a point of spiritual repose, a chance to drink from 'the Water of Life'. It is crowned by the statue of the Prudent Man, his decorative eagles symbolising his spiritual insight. The Sun, symbol of Divine Light, is placed between the statue and the fountain. To the right and left of the fountains are statues of Jeremiah and Moses respectively.

The third fountain represents hearing. The main figure holds the ancient musical instrument, the *cithera*, which in classical mythology Orpheus used to silence all of nature. The bull's head represents the power of God's call to devotion. The side statues are the Spouse of Song, again bearing a *cithera*, and King David with his lyre.

The fourth of the fountains represents the sense of smell. The central figure is that of a wise man holding a hyacinth. Three dogs, who have a keen sense of smell, are represented amongst the figures. These represent the faithfulness and loyalty of Christ. The nearby statues are of the Biblical figures Noah and Abishag. The inscribed tables relate these two figures to the sense of smell.

The fifth fountain represents taste and is crowned by the figure of Joseph of Egypt carrying in his hands a chalice and fruit. The presence of monkeys amongst the figures alludes, apparently, to their keen sense of taste. The figures to left and right are Esdras, and Jonathan, Son of Saul. The Old Testament figure of Esdras bears a chalice and loaf referring to the Last Supper of Christ and Jonathan holds a honeycomb in his right hand with a beehive at his feet.

The last of the fountains, topped by a statue of King Solomon and depicting touch, also shows a youth pouring water from a jug. The creature that figures on the basin's pedestal and elsewhere is the spider. His webs are a symbol of the connections between humanity and its Creator. To either side of the fountain are Isaac and Isaiah. The tablets, again nearby relate the figures to the sense of touch.

At the top of the stairway, and before the Stairway of the Three Virtues, there is a spacious courtyard with stone benches from which the view over Braga can be enjoyed.

The first fountain of the Three Virtues represents Faith, her head and eyes covered by a veil, and in her left hand a chalice and host. Her right hand points to her ear. Though Faith can no longer see Christ, hence the veil, she observes the sacraments and hears the Gospels. To the right of her is a statue representing confession, bearing the Ten Commandments. The left-hand statue is an extemely complex figure. She represents docility. The symbols on her shield are drawn from pagan as well as Christian iconography. The elephant represents Christ as the support of the world, the sand glass the passing of time, the serpent the crucified Christ, and the two mirrors the divine wisdom reflected in the Scriptures.

On the second terrace the fountain is topped by a figure representing Hope, resting on an anchor and bearing a dove. The fountain itself represents Noah's ark. The three figures on this level all refer to the Biblical story of Noah and his faith in God's promise that he and his family would be spared from the flood.

The third and last of the fountains is topped by the figure of Charity, bearing two infants in her arms. To her right is a figure representing Peace, bearing an olive branch, and to the left a statue embodying Benign Grace.

In the final courtyard before the sanctuary itself there are two further chapels that complete the Way of the Cross, The Raising of the Cross, and the Descent from the Cross. The Crucifixion itself is shown on the main altar of the church. The eight statues round the courtyard are of figures involved in the condemnation of Christ, such as Pontius Pilate, Nicodemus and Caiaphas. In the Evangelist's courtyard there are further chapels to the Resurrection and the lives of the Evangelists. However the ascent of the staircase has probably provided ample exposure to religious iconography. Should the visitor be out of breath by the end of the climb it is worth remembering that the faithful make the ascent on their knees!

For those visitors who are content to admire the views from the base of the staircase and from the church itself there is a funicular to the top or a steep twisting road to drive up. On the terrace around the church there are two hotels and a tea shop, and dramatic views over the surrounding countryside. The statues of historical figures that are arranged around the terrace are attractively stately and though there are many visitors the atmosphere remains that of a national shrine rather than that of a world-renowned tourist venue.

The main doorway of the church is flanked by statues of Josiah and Jeremiah, and is richly decorated. The interior, too, in a neo-Classical style somewhat unusual for the area, is well proportioned, though with too great and unnecessary prominence given to the central pillars. The altarpiece is quite extraordinary with its life-size representation of the scene at Calvary including the family of Jesus, Roman soldiers and sixteen figures in all.

The strangest sight in the church, however, is the preservation and display of a figure that is claimed to be the mortal remains of St Clement. The pinched, drawn figure, its skin tightly drawn across its bones, is bizarrely dressed in light blue and white cap and knickerbockers. On some of the side altars pilgrims leave votive offerings, often in the form of wax arms or legs, depending on the nature of the affliction for which intercession is sought. Pictures and photographs of loved ones for whom prayers are sought are also left.

In rather lighter mood there is a pleasant walk in the woods behind the church and, hidden amongst the trees, surprisingly, there is a boating lake and tennis courts.

Four kilometres ($2^1/_2$ miles) south of Bom Jesus do Monte on the even higher Mount of Sameiro, there is another sanctuary dedicated to Our Lady. It is the second most important centre for the Worship of Mary in the country after Fatima. The church itself built in the late nineteenth and early twentieth century is not particularly attractive, however, and the main thing to enjoy from a visit is the spectacular panoramic views over the Minho, and across to the Serra de Marão and the Serra do Gerês.

From Sameiro, it is a short drive of about 10km (6 miles), along the N309 to the most important archaeological site of Celtic occupation in the country, the *Citânia de Briteiros*. This is a remarkably complex site comprising in effect an entire settlement of primitve houses, streets, social areas, burial chambers and, even, what some experts believe are a prison and a courthouse. The road is well signposted from Braga and provides some delightful views as it rises onto the ridge of Monte Sameiro. The villages along this route, Lagoasa and Sobreposta, really feel off-the-beaten-track, the people still living and working in close proximity to their animals and land.

The Celts were, of course, hill dwellers. The Romans greatly feared their descent from the hills, and the *citânia* occupies a spectacular position on the high ground above the River Ave. The Celts were monogamous and patriarchal and each clan would build a defensive hillfort or *citânia* There are about seventeen *citânias* distributed around the area of Guimarães and Braga. A number of clans would sometimes join together to form a tribe and this seems to have been the case at Briteiros. From Roman descriptions of the time we know that they were a resolute people in warfare and greatly given to dancing and singing in peacetime. They were not a sentimental people, as they attempted to predict the future by an examination of the entrails of their prisoners!

There is a nominal entrance fee but in return one recieves a small map and guide to the settlement. Most of the smaller items have been removed to the Martins Sarmento Museum in Guimarães, but the scale of the site is in itself surprising and intriguing. Martins

Celtic huts at the Citânia de Briteiros *archaeological site*

Sarmento was the archaeologist who almost single-handedly excavated the site, beginning in 1875.

Within the outer defensive walls there is a rough stone main street that runs between the remains of a large number of houses. Along the street, too, there runs a shallow gutter that was used for the purposes of running off heavy rainfall. Around the site there is the original spring that provided water for the community, stone benches in communal areas and on the highest point two huts have been reconstructed to approximate as closely as possible to the Celts' own. There is also the controversial 'funerary tomb', located a little way down the hill from the main settlement, about which there is still considerable academic dispute. The *citânia* is a fascinating place, little known, yet extremely valuable in granting an insight into the way of life of a people, often discussed, but about whom very little is known for certain.

Before leaving the environs of Braga, there remains one last ancient monument to consider. This is the Chapel of São Frutuoso de Montelios situated $3^1/_2$ km (2 miles) north-west of the city, taking the right-hand turning off the N201 at São Jeronimo Real. This eleventh-century chapel, one of very few Byzantine buildings left in Portugal is incorporated in the eighteenth-century church of St Francis.

The rugged landscape of the Peneda-Gerês National Park near Caldas do Gerês

São Frutuosus was from 653 to 665 the Bishop of Braga, and a Visigothic nobleman. He established several monasteries and had the original church built as his mausoleum. The building fell into the hands of the Moors in later years, and there is considerable academic debate as to how much of the original remains and how much was newly constructed in the eleventh century, after the Christian reconquest. Certainly it is a very ancient and atmospheric place, built in the form of a Greek cross. The central chapel is lit by four small windows and the four arches below are supported on marble pillars. The capital of each pillar is beautifully carved.

Two equally attractive routes now present themselves. To the south of Braga along the N101 is the birthplace of the Portuguese nation, Guimarães, while to the north-east, along the equally scenic N103 is the most beautiful of the country's national parks, Peneda-Gerês, and its most attractive town, Caldas do Gerês, approximately 40km (25 miles) from Braga.

The national park is entered along the N304, passing the beautifully situated São Bento *pousada* and a tremendous view of the Cavado Gorge, at the point at which it crosses the confluence of the Rio Cavado and its tributary, the Rio Caldo. Both rivers have been turned into reservoirs by the Canicada dam at their western edge in

A group of Roman milestones in the Peneda-Gerês National Park

order to produce hydro-electric power. It is a mere $6^1/_2$km (4 miles) from here to Caldas do Gerês.

Peneda-Gerês, covering over 70,000 hectares (270 square miles), is the largest nature reserve in Portugal. The northern mountains, the Peneda range, are best visited from the Alto Minho (see Chapter 1). The more popular areas around the spa town of Caldas do Gerês are well visited by the Portuguese at weekends but are normally quieter during the week. The park has a unique flora and fauna. Deer, horses, wildcats and wolves (at least in reserves) reside in the park. There are also Luso Galician wild ponies that are only found here. For the amateur ornithologist there are over a hundred different types of bird to be seen, including eagles. For the amateur botanist, too, as well as abundant woods of cork oaks and firs that the highest annual rainfall in the country provides, there are several plants, such as the Gerês juniper and the Gerês iris that, again, are only found here. Picking flowers and lighting fires are, of course, both forbidden in the park.

The spa of **Gerês** is an elegant and tranquil town outside the busy summer weekends and, with its row of Victorian hotels, is a good base from which to explore the park. The spa season is from May to October and the waters are believed to be good for liver complaints and, like so many other Portuguese spas, digestive problems. The town's position at the bottom of a wooded gorge makes it a pleasant place to stroll and in the elegant courtyards of the old hotels on the main streets, should you have an inclination for improved health but no desire to 'take the waters', the local therapeutic herbal teas are served.

A remarkable day trip from Gerês into the park is to the reservoir created by the damming of the River Homem, with the resultant submerging of the village of Vilarinho das Furnas. The route can be found by returning to the south of Gerês and taking the road after a kilometre ($^1/_2$ mile) or so to Campo do Gerês. The reservoir has many places from which to swim and there is a strenuous but rewarding walk to the submerged village on the far side. While driving or walking along the reservoir look out for the collection of Roman milestones that have been brought together, that used to border the nearby Roman road from Braga to Astorga in Spain. The milestones are inscribed both with directions and distances and with notice of honours bequeathed on local commanders by the Emperor.

Returning to *Citânia de Briteiros* the road goes south to join the N101 at the pretty spa town of **Caldelas**, which, like all spa towns, has a couple of fine hotels. After what may have been a rather heavy schedule of ecclesiastical and historical monuments around Braga its boating lake and swimming pool provide a pleasant break. It also has a camp site. The bridge over the River Ave just to the south of Caldelas is a good place from which to walk or to swim. The only other people likely to be around will be local women doing their washing in the river.

Just 7km (4 miles) from here is the original capital of Portugal, **Guimarães**. As the huge sign in the centre of the town proudly announces, Portugal was born here, and it was born even more precisely in the medieval castle that still stands on a hill to the north-west of the city.

In 1095 the King of Leon and Castile, Afonso IV, granted to his son-in-law, Henry of Burgundy, the County of Portucale. Henry then erected the seven towers around the central tower and installed his wife and court within. The tower had been built after an invasion of Normans in 996 by a local noblewoman, Mumadona.

It was here that in 1110 the fonder of the Portuguese nation, Afonso Henriques was born. He succeeded his father in 1112. As his mother, Teresa, acting as regent, was meddling in the affairs of her

Guimarães castle

half-sister's kingdom of Galicia, and having an affair with a Galician nobleman, Afonso eventually rebelled against her regency and defeated her in battle at the nearby village of São Mamede in 1128.

From that time on Afonso worked constantly at the expansion and consolidation of his kingdom. His most glorious moment was at the battle of Ourique, when he decisively defeated the Moors in 1139. From that time on he was known as the King of Portugal. This was recognised by his cousin, Alfonso VII of Castile, in 1143. Four years later he had captured Lisbon from the Moors. There were many English Crusaders whose help was enlisted by Afonso against the Infidel, and one of these, Stephen of Hastings, stayed in Portugal and eventually became Lisbon's first archbishop. Afonso continued to fight the Moors throughout the remainder of his life at innumerable battles. The Portuguese are enormously proud of their nation's founder and are to be seen having their photograph taken at the foot of his impressive statue near the castle every day.

The castle itself is simple but marvellously evocative of its history. Its round bailey and huge central keep seem to rise out of the rock that in places does indeed form part of its fabric. The simplicity of the medieval castle, designed above all for safety from attack, is a reminder of how harsh life was for even the most noble at this time.

The cloister of the Palace of the Braganças, Guimarães

However, there are signs in the stones that jut out of the bailey wall and once supported a floor and in the window seats that this was at times a place of relative luxury.

In front of the castle is to be found the remarkable twelfth-century church of St Michael. It is a beautifully simple single-nave Romanesque structure. It contains within it the font in which the young Dom Afonso was said to have been baptised by the Bishop of Braga. There is also a ninth-century statue of St Michael and a twelfth-century crucifix. The main use to which the church was put, however, was as a burial place for knights who had died on the Crusades. On the walls there are crosses of the crusaders and in the main part of the church forty-two knights are buried.

Below the church stands the impressive bronze statue of the resolute founder of the country himself, Afonso Henriques, cast at the end of the nineteenth century by the sculptor, Soares Dos Reis.

To the right of the statue is a palace of the last royal house of Portugal, the Braganças. It is on a very large scale but is rather unsuccessfully modelled on an imported Flemish style. Much of the building was reconstructed in the 1930s. Nonetheless it is worth visiting for the Gothic cloister within and some fine seventeenth-century Dutch wall tapestries. Several of the larger rooms have upturned caravels for ceilings — caravels being the small but sturdy ships in which the great Portuguese explorers of the fifteenth and sixteenth centuries set sail. The chapel was entirely rebuilt in 1935 in a fifteenth-century style and has attractive stained glass windows. The upper floor of the palace opposite the chapel is reserved for visits by the President of the Republic, the socialist Mario Soares.

Guimarães is not just a historical city, however, it also has a bustling commercial centre, fine hotels and cinemas and on the high point of Penha there is a campsite with spectacular views of the city and beyond to the mountains of Gerês.

Penha is one of the sacred mountains, like Bom Jesus do Monte, that are such a feature of the North of the country. Its pilgrimage church, Nossa Senhora de Penha is dedicated to travellers. The summit is crowned by a monstrously huge statue of Pope Pius IX, apparently the last great champion of papal infallibility. It is probable that the hill was originally the site of a celtic *castro* of the type that can be seen above Viana and at Briteiros, near Braga. When the present roads to the summit were being laid many signs of human habitation were found dating back to Neolithic times. Most of these are now to be seen in the heart of the town in the Martins Sarmento Museum, one of two very fine museums in Guimarães. On one of the huge boulders that are littered around the summit it is also worth looking out for an engraved memorial to Sacadura Cabral and Gago Coutinho, two Portuguese airmen who pioneered trans-Atlantic flights. The campsite near the summit is beautifully located, with a swimming pool and with tremendous views nearby, particularly at night when the lights of Guimarães are far below.

The Martins Samento Museum is to be found near to the centre of town on the Rua Dr A. Pimenta, housed in the former convent of São Domingo. It was named after the man who made his life work the excavation of the Celtic settlement at *Citânia de Briteiros*. The façade has unusual semicircular alcoves and the three words 'Archaeology, Ekthnography, and History' above the doorway. The place gets relatively few visitors even in high season so often there is a personalised tour by one of the university students who earn some extra money working in the museum over the summer. The exhibits have been collected from the Roman settlement at Braga, and the Celtic sites at *Citânio de Briteiros* and *Castro Sabroso*. As well as practical items, such as arrowheads and coins, one piece of sculpture stands out among the exhibits from *Briteiros*. This is a delicately carved cart pulled at both ends by oxen and men carrying tools. There is also a model of the controversial 'funerary tomb' that can still be seen at *Briteiros* and in the cloister below is a large stone slab believed to have been used to seal the entrance to this tomb, known as a *pedro formoso*. The tomb is believed to have been communal and after cremation the ashes of each individual would be put in a sarcophagus and pushed through the small entrance at the foot of the stone. An example of such a sarcophagus is exhibited near to the stone. Martins Sarmento believed the *pedro formoso* to have been a slab on which sacrifices were carried out, while others believe it and the 'funerary tomb' to have been some kind of primitive sauna.

Engraved on several of the Celtic stones are stars. Stars of three points are believed to have represented the sun god and stars of five points the weather god. Axes and tools have also been carved on some of the tombs, representing the work of the person interred.

Interesting insights into Roman culture are also to be gained here. For example, models show how they constucted their roofs and how the builders would carve into the stone an animal's paw, such as a that of a sheep or a cat, as a means of identifying themselves as the builder. The tiny tear-shaped glasses in the display cases were used to collect a person's tears prior to their death or emigration and were given as a gift and memento to friends or family. Other of the tiny glass vessels were used to keep juices from flowers to use as a perfume after a visit to the baths. They were, apparently, used much more often by men than by women.

In the cloister below there is a very large Roman standing stone carved with pictures of a young girl and an old woman. This was from a young girl to her grandmother, in effect, a kind of greetings gift. The museum's most striking exhibit, however, and probably its most valuable, sits in the small garden just next to the cloister. This is the Collosus, a prehistoric figure dating from around 910BC, which stands around $4^1/_2$m (15ft) high and is remarkably full of life despite its curious shape. Discovered at the *Briteiros* site in 1930 it took twenty-four pairs of oxen to drag it to the museum.

This is an appropriate point at which to leave a museum that gives one a great sense of the prehistory of the Portuguese state, and to visit the other fine museum in Guimarães, that was originally a monastery, intimately involved in the setting up of the new state. The first construction on the Alberto Sampaio Museum site was a tenth-century Benedictine monastery, ordered to be built by Mumadona, a local noblewoman. Nothing of the monastery remains but it was, perhaps, the reason why the young Dom Afonso chose the town as his first stronghold. The oldest part of the museum is the thirteenth-century Romanesque cloister that lies just within the main doors. The small cloister is incomplete but was carefully restored in the 1930s and the decorative carving on each of the capitals is worth examining.

In the left corner of the cloister is a fascinating fifteenth-century Gothic mortuary chapel. The tomb in the centre of the chapel is that of the First Duchess of Bragança, one of the founders of the royal line that was eventually to rule Portugal for hundreds of years. She married an illegitimate son of João of Avis, and was the daughter of Nun Alvares Pereira, the king's first adviser and a brillaint military strategist. That her tomb is so simple and that she was buried in the habit of a nun testifies to the power of the medieval church. She believed that by being so dressed her acceptance into heaven would be speeded. In the tombs set into the walls the founder of the chapel, Goncalo de Frietas, and his wife are also dressed as a monk and a nun respectively.

As one proceeds around the cloister there are some fifteenth- or sixteenth-century Hispano-Arab ceramic tiles which were probably produced in Sevilla or Valencia. A fine contrast of Gothic and Romanesque statues then follows. St Bartholemew, with his axe bloodied from slaying the devil at his feet, and the pregnant St Margaret, to whom local women still come to seek intercession, are both beautifully crafted pieces of Romanesque art which communicate great solemnity. The Gothic statue beside them, however, Nossa Senhora Formosa, evokes more emotional expression of religious feeling.

On the first floor of the museum is the Chapel of Santa Clara. This part of the building was once used by an order of reclusive nuns. The chapel was consequently utilised by local noble families as a place to isolate their daughters from the world should they have become involved with someone of whom they disapproved. There are also some very fine ceramics from Coimbra and Viana do Castelo, dating from the seventeenth and eighteenth centuries respectively.

On the second floor are to be found some of the finest examples of Portuguese art from the late middle ages. At the top of the stairs is a fifteenth-century fresco. An alabaster sculpture of the Virgin, dated around the thirteenth century, is believed to have come from the English town of Nottingham, a great centre for the production of alabaster religious figures between the twelfth and fifteenth centuries. The room also contains a remarkable historical curio, the battle smock worn by João I, at Portugal's most famous battle, their victorious confrontation at Aljubarrota with the King of Castile in 1369. It is very threadbare but authenticated as the original. On the wall nearby are portraits of the king himself and of his adviser, Nun Alvares Pereira.

The most exquisitely beautiful of the exhibits in the whole musum, however, is the silver gilt Gothic triptych depicting the Visitation, the Annuncaition, and the Nativity. The item, crafted in the north of Portugal, was given to the monastery by João I after the famous battle as he had prayed for victory in the monastery. The story of the triptych having been recovered from the tent of the King of Castile is apocrophyl. In addition this fine museum contains many other precious examples of religious art.

Though Guimarães is, undoubtedly, the highlight of the region in terms of history the Costa Verde still contains much else of interest for the visitor. This includes the largest market of the region, if not of the whole country, that takes place at Barcelos on Thursdays.

The best way to reach Barcelos from Guimarães is to take the N206 through the interesting town of Vila Nova de Familicão. As the road winds its way through villages that do not seem to end before the next one begins, just how densely populated the area is becomes clear. Old country houses, with their *vinho verde* grapes trellissed on to granite posts overhanging the roadside, sit next to new large properties, many of them still incomplete, built in stages by the emigrants when they return each summer from France or Brazil. Every inch of cultivable land is used and driving is hazardous with all types of hand- or oxen-drawn carts liable to be around the next corner. The people work extremely hard and do not return from the fields until twilight.

Barcelos is a very attractive town, built picturesquely on the north bank of the River Cavado. To the south of the river is Barcelinhos.

Barcelos is renowned for its market, but its well kept gardens and lawns and its mature chestnuts and elms make it a pleasant place to be any day of the week. The medieval castle keep in the centre of the town doubles as the tourist information centre and as a display centre for local crafts. Barcelos can realistically claim to be one of the

Shoe cleaners in Barcelos

prime areas in the country for the continuance of traditional handicrafts. The most important of these is pottery, which is produced in great quantity and in all shapes and sizes. Baskets, straw hats, ox yokes and cartwheels, furniture, lace and linen are all produced in the villages of the borough. The tourist office will happily inform the visitor of where each particular craft can be seen being practised. The most famous craft family in the country, the Ramalhos, still work in the area. Their reputation was establishd by the late Rosa Ramalho who depicted and satirised her fellow countrymen and women in distinctive ceramic figures. These can still be bought in the shops and market stalls of Barcelos today.

If a trip into the countryside to find a workshop does not appeal, however, all the local producers bring their wares to the largest and most celebrated fair in the Minho which is held in the huge Campo de República in the centre of Barcelos every Thursday. Its dimensions are 150m by 200m (500ft x 650ft), but its grandeur is really owed to its setting.

Next to the medieval tower is the lovely seventeenth-century Igreja das Cruzes. Before it are lovely eighteenth-century gardens, the Jardim das Obras. Looking anticlockwise around the square one then sees the old monastery of the Capuchin Fathers which is now

Portuguese souvenirs include the cockerel, now the national symbol

the Misericordia Hospital. The attractive façade was built in the Joanino development of the baroque style. Lastly on the far side of the square from the tower is the former convent church of the Bendictine sisters, now known as Our Lady of Terco, which contains some beautiful eighteenth-century tiles depicting the life of St Benedict. Though little known, this square provides the visitor with an unforgettable setting in which to seek out some of the finest craft work in Portugal.

Barcelos is, of course, a very old town and remnants of the old walled citadel still survive and are to be found by the river. The old quarter is dominated by the granite manor house, the Solar dos Pinheiros, with its remarkable Romanesque doorway, and, best of all, the remains of the old Ducal Palace. The palace originally extended to the fifteenth-century bridge that still stands below. The road from it once passed beneath its arches. Falling into disrepair in the seventeenth century, it was damaged badly in the famous earthquake of 1755 which caused so much destruction in Lisbon. The ruins are now the setting for an agreeably haphazard archaeological museum. Beautifully carved tombstones of crusaders lie next to Roman and medieval inscribed stones and columns. It also contains the original statue of the cockerel that has come to symbolise Portugal, the fourteenth century, Cruzeiro do Senhor do Galo.

The medieval story with which the cock is associated cannot be given much credence as, with its intimate association with Santiago de Compostela, it also occurs at other towns along the pilgrim's route in Spain. Nonetheless it is a good story and bears repitition. A pilgrim was making his way to Santiago when he was accused by a local nobleman of having stolen his silver. The pilgrim could offer no defence, and was about to be summarily executed by hanging when he prayed for the help of St James. At that moment, with the rope about his neck, he saw the cooked cockerel that lay on the rich man's table. He claimed that if he were innocent then the cock would crow. Sure enough the cock crowed and the man was saved. Regardless of the merits of the story, the monument is a fine low relief crucifix, carved with figures of the pilgrim, St James, the hanged man and the cock. The cross originally came from a place called Forca Velha across the Cávado in Barcelinhos.

The area surrounding the town as well as containing some fine workshops also has some interesting historical sites that reflect the long history of the borough. Four miles to the east, off the N103, taking the turning to the village of **Areias de Vilar**, is the ancient Benedictine monastery of Vilar de Frades. Originally built in the eleventh century, only one beautifully carved doorway remains from that period. The main part of the present building was built in the sixteenth century, and beautifully embellished in the eighteenth with carvings of the saints. It is now used as an idyllically situated psychiatric hospital. The convent church, though, can still be visited and it contains a delightful interior with mid-eighteenth-century tiles. The monastery stands very close to the picturesque River Cávado, and it is a pleasant place for a stroll far from the tourist trails.

About 5km (3 miles) north of Barcelos off the N306 is a fine Romanesque church and defensive tower at the village of **Abade de Neiva**. The church of Our Lady was built in the twelfth century, and was restored in the 1940s.

Two routes from Barcelos to the distinguished coastal town of Vila do Conde now present themselves, firstly to the west and along the coast, taking in some fine beaches and old fishing villages, or to the south which takes the traveller with an interest in architecture and history to some fine monuments, this latter route is described first.

South of Barcelos following the small country road, the N306, through Barcelinhos are to be found a number of fine remnants of the area's long history of habitation. The first village is **Pedra Furada**, whose name means 'stone with a hole'. This is a largely unremarkable village apart from the fact that in the village churchyard is a large ancient, round shaped stone, with a hole in it, that is older than the village itself and almost certainly Celtic in origin, possibly part of the type of burial chamber that is to be found in more complete form at the *Citânia de Briteiros*.

Continuing another few kilometres to the south a turning to the right at the village of Fontainhas leads to the village of **Rates**, and its fine Romanesque parish church of São Pedro (St Peter). It is a particularly fine example of the style, particularly in the quality of the carving over the doorway and the capitals, and was built in the twelfth and thirteenth centuries by Benedictine monks. Above the entrance is a low relief figure of Christ in an oval, with a figure to each side. Each figure is standing on a prostrate character, perhaps, as a representation of Christ's rising from the dead. The ancillary decorative carving is very similar to the kind of abstract Celtic decoration that is commonly found in Ireland. The capitals of the cylindrical pillars within the nave are similarly intriguingly carved and merit attention.

Turning beyond Fontainhas towards Vila do Conde, along the N206 leads to the village of **Rio Mau**, and another fine Romanesque church, that of St Lawrence. Rather plainer than St Peter's it too has finely carved capitals. Povoa de Varzim and Vila do Conde lie just a few kilometres further on.

To the east the road from Barcelos to the coast is very attractive and it is a pleasant area for walking in woods of pine and fir. On the coast, and at the mouth of the River Cávado, is **Esposende** a modern tourist centre catering primarily for Portuguese holiday makers. It has disadvantages in terms of a certain loss of atmosphere but advantages in that facilities such as hotels, discos and restauraunts are readily available.

The town has a long esplanade and beach, though these are usually both very crowded, and a small fortress looks out to the Atlantic. The beaches to the north to Mar and to the south to Apulia are particularly fine and unspoilt as they form a coastal zone protected from development. The main coast road, the N13, crosses the Cavado to the originally Roman town of Fao, which has now been, more or less, subsumed in the again, rather unattractive, tourist resort of Ofir. Nearby, however, are the remains of a Roman camp at Belinho.

Ofir has an *estalagem* and other grades of accommodation, as well as tennis courts, swimming pools and water skiing. The town's great landmarks are the distinctively shaped rocks just offshore that are known locally as the 'White Horse Rocks'. The legend surrounding them states that they were originally real horses belonging to King Solomon which were shipwrecked and petrified as they struggled ashore against the waves. The rocks are popular with snorkellers and underwater divers as is the calmer water of the Cávado estuary. Sailing boats, fishing tackle or rowing boats can all be hired in Ofir.

Between here and the largest resort on this coast, Povoa de Varzim, there are fine, unspoilt, dune backed beaches at Apulia and Agucadoura. This is a good area in which to walk and explore and tiny fishing villages remain, untouched by the tourist industry. Their small colourful fishermen's boats can still be seen on the beaches. At **A Ver-o-Mar**, just $2^1/_2$km ($1^1/_2$ miles) north of Povoa de Varzim, it is possible to see an agricultural curiosity, the ingenuity of which seems to be particularly Portuguese. For a distance of at least 4km ($2^1/_2$ miles) the local farmers have dug down into the sand dunes until moisture is reached. They then plant vegetables including maize, potatoes and cabbage, while the sides of the plot are shored up by vine trellisses. At the heart of this area is the Estalagem St Andre.

In marked contrast, **Povoa de Varzim** is the nearest the North of Portugal comes to an international resort. In addition to the facilities at Ofir it has a casino, a golf course nearby and a roller skating rink. There are public swimming pools and tennis courts and rowing boats and motor boats can be hired for inshore and offshore fishing. The monumental casino built in 1934 offers bingo and slot machines as well as roulette and also houses an impressive collection of contemporary Portuguese art.

The town is famous in Portugal as the birthplace of their best loved nineteenth-century novelist, Eca de Quieroz, the equivalent of the English writer Dickens. His best known translated work, was *Cousin Bazilio*, based on real life events in the English town of Newcastle upon Tyne. His statue can be seen in the main square.

The most interesting section of the town, however is certainly the 'Barrio dos Pescadores', the fishermen's quarter. It is here that every working day the auction of the fishermen's catch is held. Traditionally the catch is auctioned to the crowd by the fishermen's wives. All varieties of fish will be found on sale here, but for the locals sardines and whiting are of greatest interest.

This is a very ancient community with customs similar to those found in Galicia and in Brittany, suggesting a remote common ancestry. Marriages are normally within the community itself and a powerful patriarchal tradition passes on authority within each family from father to son from generation to generation. The youngest son normally inherits the fishing boat as he is considered the most likely to be of an age to look after his father in his old age. It is a strangely incongruous community to find, with its stacked 'huts' of seaweed drying in the sun, among the casinos and luxury hotels. Yet for all the obvious fragility of the community's economy these mounds of seaweed seem somehow more enduring and permanent than the anonymous high rise buildings around them.

Anyone who spends even a little time in the Minho cannot help but appreciate the beauty of the gold and silver jewelry that adorns the local women particularly on festive occasions. The Gomes workshop on the Rua de Junqueira provides a great opportunity to watch the goldsmiths and silversmiths at work. Povoa de Varzim's great *festas*, when the finest work of the smiths is likely to be on view, is the Feast of the Assumption on the 15 August. A procession of fishermen carry statues of the saints down to the sea.

A few kilometres to the south and contrasting markedly with the atmosphere of Povoa de Varzim is the delightful old town of **Vila do Conde**. The town's great attraction which is perhaps unique in the Iberian Peninsula is that of the building of wooden ships entirely by traditional methods largely using hand tools. The shipyard is easy to find as it is at the edge of the River Ave, just a few minute's walk from the town centre. Seven or eight ships are usually being made here at any one time and the wooden skeletons sit by the water's edge on wooden scaffolding. Twenty to thirty men and their apprentices are normally at work in the yard and as there is no fencing between the road and the yard one can view the craftsmen at close quarters. There has been a recent revival in the fishing trade so that more vessels are required and there are plans to move the shipyard to the other side of the Ave. It is unlikely to provide such a pleasant, almost domestic, setting as it does now with the ships so close to the picturesque streets of the old town.

The shipyard at Vila do Conde

Just beyond the shipyard at the end of the harbour, with a platform that gives an attractive view overlooking the River Ave, is the sixteenth-century chapel of Our Lady of Help. It was founded in 1603 by Gaspar Manuel, one of the Knights of the Order of Christ and one of the captains to open up the sea routes to the Far East.

The town has another interesting cottage industry, that of lace making. Begun in the seventeenth century the original designs were based on the sea and the lives of the fisherfolk. Its reputation in this area was ensured by the establishment of a lace making school, the Escola de Rendas, in 1909 on the Rua de Lidador. The school welcomes visitors and the dexterity of the weavers is remarkable. Vila do Conde is also a traditional centre for the production of chocolate.

The largest craft fair in Portugal is held in Vila do Conde in the last week in July and the first week in August. A large part of the town is given over to craftworkers from all over the country demonstrating their particular skill. Ceramics, jewelry, leather goods, pottery, linen goods — the list of craftwork on sale is almost endless.

One other local product ought to be mentioned as a means of introducing the massive, monumental Convent of Santa Clara, whose white walls on the hill above the town dominate the whole estuary, and that is sweetcakes. The convent like many others in the

The fishermen's quarter at Vila do Conde

The Convent of Santa Clara, Vila do Conde

country specialised in the Middle Ages in the development of novel recipes and that tradition is maintained in the town to this day, with cakes such as the *papos de anjo*, or 'crop of the angel', and the *doce de travessa* or 'sweet of the wicked one', still being produced.

The Convent of Santa Clara was founded in 1318 by Dom Afonso Sanches, the illegitimate son of the king, Dom Dinis, and his wife, Dona Teresa Martins. The main building, now used as a rehabilitation centre, dates from the eighteenth century, and the last nun died here in 1893. The nearby aqueduct was originally designed to bring water to the convent from Terroso, near Povoa de Varzim, and was built between 1704 and 1714. The fountain in the centre of the eighteenth-century cloister was intended to be the terminal for the aqueduct.

The conventual church is the only part of the convent to have retained the original style. The single naved Gothic building is very attractive and has a carved wooden ceiling. The chapel of the Conception on the left-hand side of the church contains the tombs of the two founders and two of their children who died in their infancy. The carvings on Dom Afonso's tomb show events from the life of Christ, and St Clare defending the church at Assisi from attack by the Moors. On Dona Teresa Martin's tomb are shown Christ's Passion and St

Francis recieving his wounds. On the children's tombs are shown, to the left, the doctors of the church and, to the right, the Four Evangelists respectively.

The finest monument in Vila do Conde is, however, the parish church in the heart of the town. It is a very handsome construction built between 1496 and 1512 in the Manueline style. Its main doorway and tympanum are particularly attractive as they were the work of the same master craftsmen from Biscay who worked on the cathedral at Braga and the Convent of Christ at Tomar. The tympanum shows John the Baptist and the symbols of the Four Evangelists. The tower to the left of the façade dates from the end of the seventeenth century. There are two baptismal fonts dating from the sixteenth century, a statue of St John in Anca stone and several gilt retables.

Opposite the church stands a pillory showing justice brandishing a sword. This was formerly the place of judicial execution in the town. Originally Renaissance, the pillory was remodelled in the eighteenth century.

Before leaving Vila do Conde it is well worth visiting the Church of the Misericórdia, built in 1559, the interior being decorated with seventeenth-century tiles, and next to it the even older Casa do Despacho, which has a fine Manueline window.

Vila do Conde has many secular and religious festivals throughout the year. The finest of them, however, which should be seen if at all possible is the feast of St John, that takes place on 23-24 June. Folk music and dancing go on throughout the festival. The highlight, however, is the ancient traditional candlelit procession of the town's lacemakers and then the rest of the town's population across the town and down to the sea.

Vila do Conde also has a fine sandy beach, often made more interesting by the presence of lines of newly caught fish being hung out to dry in the sun before salting. There is some good accommodation particularly in the conveniently situated Estalagem do Brasão on the Avenida Conde Alberto Graca. The weekly market day is Friday.

A kilometre south of here, along the E1 N13, is **Azurara** which has along its seafront a fine fortified church, built in 1517, with extensive Manueline decoration which was almost certainly the work of some of the Biscayan artists that worked in Vila do Conde. The large scale of the church is a reminder that the duke referred to in the name of Vila do Conde was the powerful Duke of Bragança and that the church would have been built on his orders. The arms of the house of Bragança can be seen on the bell tower. The interior of the church has fine hexagonal Gothic pillars with Manueline decoration and some fascinating paintings which are almost Expressionist in the force of their conception of Hell.

On the exterior of the building is a tiny, but beautiful statue of Our Lady with the crucified Christ across her knees. The pained expression on her face is quite remarkable and seems untouched by the salty weathering effected on the rest of the Manueline knots and coils. In the square before the Parish church is a Manueline pillory and crucifix, with an armillary sphere, the symbol of Manuel I, and Our Lady on the reverse of the crucifix.

Further Information

— The Costa Verde —

Tourist Information Offices

Barcelos
Rua Duque de Bragança
☎ 053 82882

Braga
Avenida da Liberdade
☎ 053 22550

Esposende/Ofir
Rua Primero de Dezembro
☎ 053 961354

Guimarães
Avenida Resistência ao Fascismo
☎ 053 412450

Povoa de Varzim
Av Mouzinho de Albuquerque
☎ 052 624609

Vila do Conde
Rua 25 de Abril
☎ 052 631472

Places of Interest

Barcelos
Regional Ceramic Museum
Rua Conago Joaquim Gaiolas
Open: winter 10am-5pm, summer 10am-7pm. Closed Mondays

Archaeolgical Museum
Town Hall
Open: October to March 10am-5pm: April to September 10am-7pm.

Braga
Museum of Religious Art
Largo de Santiago
Open: 10am-12.30pm, 3-6pm. Closed Mondays.

Casa dos Biscainhos Musem
Rua Biscainhos
Open: 10am-12.15pm, 2-5.15pm. Closed Mondays and holidays.

Cathedral Museum
Open: summer 8.30am-12.30pm,
1.30-6.30pm; winter 8.30am-
12.30pm, 1.30-5.30pm.

Railway Museum
Braga Railway Station
Open: 9am-12 noon, 2-6pm. Closed
Wednesday, Friday and holidays.

Caldas de Taipas
Spa
Open: June to October.

Caldas de Vizela
Spa
Open May to mid-November.

Guimarães
*Archaeological Museum of Martins
    Sarmento*
Rua de Paio Galvão
Open: 10am-12.30pm, 2-5pm.
Closed Mondays and holidays.

Alberto Sampaio Regional Museum
Rua Alfredo Guimarães
Open: 10am-12.30pm, 2-5pm.
Closed Mondays and holidays

Palace of the Braganças
Open June to September 10am-
1pm, 2.30-5pm. Closed Tuesdays

Markets

Barcelos — Thursday

Braga — Tuesday

Vila do Conde
Craft Fair — end of July to early
August

Festivals

Barcelos
Festas das Cruzes
Beginning of May

Braga
Holy Week and Easter
Festas de São João
23-24 June

Guimarães
Romaria de São Torcato
Early July

São Gaulter
5-8 August

3 • Porto

Portugal's second city and the capital of the North, Porto (as it is known to most Portuguese or Oporto as it is known officially) gave to the nation its name and its greatest hero, Henry the Navigator. It is a rapidly expanding city of half a million people and is one of the main benefactors of the improvements in Portugal's transport systems which have been financed by the EEC. It has an international airport at Pedras Rubras, with car hire facilities immediately available, just a couple of kilometres (1 mile) from the city centre. An internal flight from Lisbon takes forty minutes. It has two main railway stations, and is now linked by motorway to Lisbon on the A1, to within 14km (9 miles) of Braga on the A3 and to the east to Amarante and Vila Real on the A4 and N15. The port itself is the point of departure for some 75 per cent of Portugal's exports, these mainly being textiles, footwear, and forestry products.

The city's main attraction is undoubtedly the port wine lodges of **Vila Nova de Gaia**, and any visitor to Porto will certainly want to visit them. The visitor is advised that driving in the centre of Porto is extremely hazardous. The city fortunately has an excellent bus service and most of the sights are in any case in such close proximity to each other that it is reasonably straightforward, and often a pleasure, to walk.

The port wine, stored in huge casks, has traditionally been kept in Vila Nova de Gaia on the south side of the river as here it recieves less sunlight and hence the steady temperature that is required for wine to mature is easier to maintain. The lodges, especially those that are at the river's edge, receive a steady stream of visitors.

A lodge that is less often visited than those on the waterfront and, indeed, the only lodge that is still wholly owned by a Portuguese family is the Noval lodge to be found half a kilometre or so away from the river in the Rua Candido dos Reis. Owned by the Da Silva

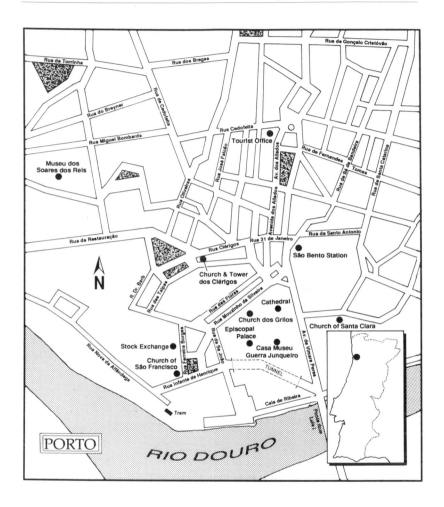

family, it was founded in 1715. From the reception one is taken across the road to the lodge to walk among the huge barrels, each of which holds 500 litres (110 gallons) or more.

A number of the high prowed boats, the *barco rabelos*, that were used to transport the young wine down to Gaia before the taming of the river by dams, are moored near the lodges. Their square sails announce the lodge that owns them.

The vines are harvested in the area around Pinhão in September and October; the best of the crop is still trod by foot and these will go on to make the finest of the ports, the vintage and the tawny. The crucial determinant in the particular flavour of Port is its 'musting'

The Casa Museu de Teixeira Lopes at Vila Nova de Gaia

with brandy. Approximately one litre of brandy is added to every five litres of wine. The different years, whose quality is judged by the Port Wine Institute in Regua, are then blended in the huge barrels all around. The wine that is held to be exceptionally good is nominated a vintage and is bottled separately after two or three years in dark glass bottles, again, in order to try to keep its temperature constant. This, like the blended wine in the casks, can be left for many years to mature. After the tour various dry and sweet ports are available to be sampled, and, of course a great variety of ports are available for purchase.

While in Gaia it is worth walking to the top of the Rua dos Candidos dos Reis to visit the former residence of the Portugal's most famous sculptor, Teixeira Lopes. The house, designed by the sculptor's brother, is now a museum. The sculptor lived here from just after the turn of the century until his death in 1942. It has been left essentially as it was when Lopes lived here. There are many aspects of his work displayed all over the house, busts of literary figures, such as Camoes, and Luis de Souza, a low relief sculpture of the Napoleonic invasion, and large scale studies of a peasant woman, entitled *Flower*, and of a grieving mother and child. The house itself is delightful, with an attractive courtyard full of sculptures of birds and animals. Perhaps the most remarkable rooms, however are the workshop in which the man himself worked and, best of all, the library with its beautiful carved ceiling and small stage on which the sculptor's friends in the acting profession would come to amuse themselves and their host. Several busts of actors and actresses can be seen around the house.

Before venturing over to Porto the finest view available of Portugal's second city is from the former convent of Nossa Senhora da Serra do Pilar, next to the upper tier entrance to the Dom Luis Bridge. The city skyline is dominated by the baroque towers of the Clerigos and the cathedral. It is also an appropriate spot to recall the origin of the country's name. The Romans were the first to call the settlement on the north bank *Portus* meaning the port, and that on the south bank, now Vila Nova de Gaia, *Cale*. The areas surrounding the lower Douro later became known as the county, or Dukedom of Portucale, and it was from this stronghold, among others, that Christian monarchs gradually extended their control, eventually expelling the Moors from their last foothold in Portugal, the Algarve, in 1249. The church of the former convent is worth visiting. It was built in an octagonal shape in the sixteenth century, and has an attractive circular Renaissance cloister, built with Ionic columns.

Porto is a bustling, vibrant city, whose hinterland produces 60 per cent of the nation's gross national product. The wine industry is still pre-eminent, but there are also textile, chemical and furniture making industries here. A large fishing fleet also exists to the north and south of the Douro estuary and the catch is processed and canned here too. In the old Portuguese phrase: Braga prays, Coimbra studies, Lisbon shows off and Porto works. Yet it remains a very traditional, historical town with a densely populated, slightly ramshackle working class quarter at its centre that has a charm all of its own.

Driving in the centre of Porto is not really to be recommended as the smaller streets are a maze of narrow alleys and the main avenues are usually a log-jam of traffic. The main sights are in any case within easy walking distance of each other. The effective centre, and the easiest place to catch a bus or tram to is the main railway station, São Bento.

If you can avoid the lottery ticket and magazine sellers it is worth walking into the station forecourt to see the extensive figurative ceramic tiles that cover the walls of the São Bento station. They were

Gardens near the Praça da Liberdade and the town hall in Porto

painted in 1930 by Jorge Colaco, who specialised in a narrative style of ceramic. The tiles here show important scenes in the history of Porto, such as the siege of the North African town of Ceuta, by João of Avis in 1415, which as we shall see later had a profound effect on the culinary habits of the people of Porto. Look out for the shoe shine 'boys' who work around the station; a sight rarely seen in European cities these days.

There are rather more low-key sights of particular interest in the town than major attractions and the greatest part of one's enjoyment of the city is in appreciating the particular atmosphere of its *quartiers*. For that reason the 'major' sights will be described quite briefly in the interest of a comprehensive overview of the more unusual sights and activities.

South of the station, towards the river, along the Avenida de Vimara Peres, is the **cathedral**. Originally a twelfth century fortress-style building it was extensively remodelled in the seventeenth and eighteenth centuries. Of the original building there remains a fine Romanesque rose window. The lavish baroque interior is not as impressive as some of the smaller churches in the city. The finest of the chapels is the Chapel of the Holy Sacrament, off the north transept. Through the south transept there is a fourteenth-century cloister, decorated with eighteenth-century tiles. Just to the left of the main entrance in the baptistery is a bronze relief statue of the Baptism of Christ by St John by Teixeira Lopes. The bishop's palace next to the cathedral is now used for city council offices.

On the Rua de Dom Hugo, rounding the cathedral towards the river is the **Museum of Guerra Junqueiro**. Junqueiro was an eighteenth-century poet who collected art treasures, including furniture, ceramics, and tapestries.

West of the São Bento station, crossing the bottom of the Avenida dos Aliados, is the church and tower of the **Clerigos**. Built in the eighteenth century by the finest baroque architect working in Portugal at the time, the Italian Nicolo Nasoni, it was the first to be built to an oval plan. The bell tower, 76m (250ft) high with 225 steps, has a fine view over the city, Gaia, and the countryside.

The best known of the museums in Porto is the **Museu do Soares dos Reis**. This former royal palace to be found to the west of the city centre behind the hospital was Portugal's first national museum and is now named after the finest Portuguese sculptor of the last century. His most famous work, with obvious significance for the Portuguese, is *O Desterro*, the Exile, which is housed in the museum. As well as some of his best known works there is a fine collection of French, Italian, and Flemish paintings. Also noteworthy is a fine collection of early gold and silver jewellery. This type of filligree craftsmanship is still a strong tradition in the city.

To the west and the east end of the waterfront, the Cais de Ribeira, are a series of attractions that are less well known. To the west on the Rua Infante de Henrique stands the remarkable church of **São Francisco**. No longer a functioning church it contains a decorated wooden rococo interior of extraordinary exuberance. The gilt wood ceiling almost appears molten, dripping in its religious fervour. This fervour reaches its apogee in the complex configuration of figures known as 'the Tree of Jesse' on the north side wall. Carved around 1718, it shows the twelve kings of Judah, standing upon the branches of a tree that emerges from the recumbent body of Jesse. It is one of the most fascinating churches in Portugal.

Next door to the church is the museum of St Francis. The collection is largely made up of items salvaged from the monastery that once occupied the site. Bizarrely, however, an ossuary is to be found in the cellars containing the mortal remains of thousands of Porto's former residents.

Just around the corner in the Praça de Infanta Dom Enrique is the Palacio de Bolsa, or **Stock Exchange**. The guide proudly announces that it was visited by President Kennedy among others. The attractive central courtyard was in the eighteenth century the floor of the Stock Exchange itself. It has an impressive roof in glass and iron. The emblems and coats of arms represent the different countries with which the merchants of Porto traded. There is also the so-called Moorish Hall, decorated with gold and with chandeliers in an attempt to emulate the magnificence of the Alhambra at Granada in southern Spain.

Returning to the church of São Francisco, at its foot on the Caias de Ribeira is the starting point for an enjoyable journey by tram along the mouth of the Douro estuary to Matosinhos. The ancient iron and wood tram is splendidly rickety and provides a good way to see the fishing communities and their small houses that still line the quay. The tram also provides a good point from which to view the last of the three bridges that croses the Douro between Gaia and Porto, the new road bridge, the Ponte de Arrabeda. Designed by Edgar Cardoso in the 1960s, Portugal's most famous living architect, it

Praça do Infanta Dom Henrique, Porto

crosses the river in a single span of nearly 270m (885ft).

As the estuary widens and at its edges becomes shallower whelk and mussel pickers can be seen out among the rocks. The entrance to the river itself is marked by the São Miguel lighthouse, originally built in 1527, and the Fort of São João da Foz set in the Passeio Alegre gardens. A Benedictine monastery had originally occupied the site from the thirteenth century, but the Queen Regent, Dona Catarina, insisted on the construction of a fort in 1560. People still live within the walls of the fort.

The tram swings around along the Atlantic coast proper and follows the Avenida de Brazil, a long palm tree-lined promenade. It has many cafes and attractive gardens and it is a good place to have lunch, overlooking the beaches of Molhe and Gondarem. The easiest place to stop is at the **Fort of São Francisco Xavier**, also known as the Queijo, or Cheese Fort. The mid-seventeenth-century battlements, watchtower, drawbridge, and weapons are all well preserved. In the foundations of the fort there is said to be a boulder sacred to the Celts six centuries before Christ and on which the Druids made sacrifices.

The area beyond here is the town of **Matosinhos**, which was once a fishing port but is now largely given over to industry. Local tourist leaflets may recommend the beaches at Matosinhos but the beaches further north are probably cleaner and certainly quieter. The baroque church of Bom Jesus in Matosinhos has a façade by the celebrated Italian architect Nicolo Nasoni.

To the north-west of the city along the Rua de Cedofeita, isolated from the other main attractions, but worth taking the time to see, is the **Church of Cedofeita**. In marked contrast to the baroque exuberance of most of Porto's main building it is a comparatively simple Romanesque structure built in the twelfth century. The site is reckoned to have been previously been occupied by one of the first churches in Portugal built by the Suevi King Theodomir in the sixth century. The name *cedo feita* means 'built quickly'.

Turning now to the opposite end of the Caias de Ribeira, at the foot of the Ponte de Luis is another route through some of the less appreciated sights of the city. The Cais de Ribeira itself is a charming place, with market stalls, pleasant bars and beautifully situated and reasonably inexpensive restaurants amongst the arcades.

Walking along the *cais* or quay, towards the Dom Luis bridge one may well notice a large plaque set into the quayside wall commemorating the city's victims of the Peninsula War against Napoleon at the beginning of the nineteenth century. The city defenders retreated before the advance of the French troops and sought to evade capture by crossing the River Douro on an improvised pontoon bridge of boats. Unfortunately many were drowned.

Below the bridge itself are the **Escadas de Condecal**. The Escadas, or steps, rise steeply between houses that seem to be defying gravity, so precipitously perched are they on the side of the gorge. The houses are dilapidated, yet they are lively and full of character. Women talk on their doorsteps, children play and the washing billows, strung out between windows across the street. Some reconstruction work is being done in these streets but the city authorities hope that they will not transform the traditional character of the area.

At the top of the Escadas there is a police station, and rounding this to the right is the gateway to the church of Santa Clara. Standing in the courtyard just within the gateway, it is possible to appreciate that all of these buildings, including the police station, were up to 1940 all part of the **Convent of Santa Clara**. The convent was founded in 1426. Now the buildings are used as private residences, a health centre, as well as a police station.

The convent church itself remains as does the old baroque gate-

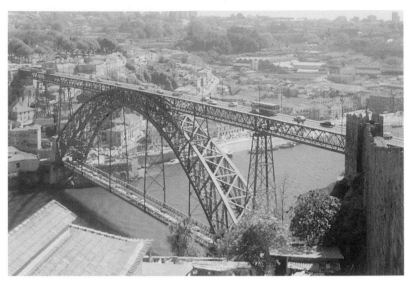

The double-decker Dom Luís I bridge over the River Douro

way to the convent, built in 1697. The statue above the doorway is of Our Lady of the Immaculate Conception. The statues above the entrance to the church are those of St Francis and St Clare. The church has an extraordinary gilt baroque interior and is beautifully proportioned. It clearly illustrates the degree to which the baroque was the appropriate architectural style for a country that suddenly found itself immensely wealthy from its overseas colonies. The richly ornate and exuberant woodcarvings of angels, cherubs and animals are gilt from ceiling to floor. It is one of the finest examples of the baroque in Portugal and more off-the-beaten-track today than when Sachaverell Sitwell visited it and described it as 'the apogee of the Baroque'.

Two distinctive features of the church are also to be seen at the rear of the nave. To the right is a veiled, almost naked statue of Christ, encased in glass. It is prone and life size and, if spotted unawares, its likeness to life can be quite unsettling. To the left is a small door leading into a room preserved from the original convent. Its plain stone walls and polished wooden floors are in stark contrast to the opulence of the church interior.

Returning to the courtyard and passing beyond the church, to the right is to be found a large stone flagged platform which abuts to the left the old city wall. This was built in the reign of King Fernando between 1336 and 1376 and gives a commanding view of the city. The crennellated city wall originally extended over a kilometre ($^1/_2$ mile) but it was gradually demolished as the city expanded.

There are steps off the platform leading onto the city wall itself. A little way along it there is a tremendous view west to the **Bridge of Dom Luís I**, and east to the railway bridge of Dona Maria Pia. The Bridge of Dom Luís with its distinctive tiers linking the upper and lower quarters of Gaia and Porto is the city's most distinctive and elegant structure. It was built of iron to a design of Seyrig, a pupil of Eiffel, and was opened in 1886. What is not generally well known is that the Maria Pia railway bridge slightly further up river was actually the work of the master himself. This bridge was completed in 1877, and set the style for the latter work.

All of Porto's delights, however, are not either ecclesiastical or architectural. There are three cafés here that have a particular grace and style that should not be missed. The Café Brasiliera, beyond the São Bento station has a delightful art nouveau interior, with a restaurant and a snack bar — great meeting place for the locals, it is always bustling. The Café Majestic in the shopping area of the Rua de Senhora de Bandeira is quieter and a remarkable remnant of Edwardian elegance. Fading leather backed banquettes line the room and an older clientele than the business people of the Brasiliera take their time over coffee in the late afternoon. Best of all, however, is the Café Imperial, splendidly art deco, with a remarkable stained glass interior, to be found on the Avenida dos Aliados. Here is the place one is most likely to spot the Euro-chic professionals and entrepeneurs who it is hoped will lead Portugal into the twenty-first century on a sound economic basis. Do not be afraid though to let the waiters know clearly that you wish to pay and leave. They seem to have every expectation that the visitor will be there all day.

Porto is also a university city and the streets leading off the Avenida dos Aliados opposite the Café Imperial contain some of the finest general and specialist bookshops in Portugal. Among these is one specialising in English language publications. Avenida dos Aliados is also home to the city's very helpful tourist office. The city has a great range of hotels and accommodation, including a campsite on its outskirts, about which the tourist office can give detailed information. Here too detailed information can be found on river cruises, city tours by bus, and sports facilities including Porto's golf

The Café Imperial on the Avenida dos Aliados, Porto

course, over a hundred years old and the second oldest on the Continent of Europe. The city has modern shopping malls and cinemas, normally showing English language films with Portuguese sub-titles.

Most of Porto's night life is centred around the Cais de Ribeira. Taking a drink on the river front the view across the Douro to the lights of Gaia, with the names of the various port wine lodges prominent on the hillside is one of the best night sights in the country. The lodge names such as Sandeman, Croft and Taylors, give occasion to consider the old alliance between the city and Britain, which began when two young shippers from the English city of Liverpool, accidentally discovered around 1678 that putting brandy in barrels of red Douro wine in order to preserve the wine on the long journey to England actually produced a delicious fortified wine in itself. The Treaty of Metheun that followed in 1703 formalised trading links between the two countries: Portugal sending Port wine and the British mainly textiles. During the Peninsular War the Duke of Wellington came to the aid of Porto, using disused wine barges to cross the river and attack Napoleon's troops encamped in the city in 1809. Though the greatest consumers of Port are now the French, a considerable ex-patriate British community continues to live in the city and

The long horned Minho cattle are still used to pull carts in the Douro Valley

A typical remote village in the Trás-os-Montes

The town hall in the Praça de Camões, Chaves, Trás-os-Montes

View of the town of Montalegre from its castle, Trás-os-Montes

maintains the traditional English club.

In the restaurants along the front the one obligatory dish is *tripas a modo do Porto*. Though tripe may not be immediately appealing the dish has an interesting history and is, preconceptions put aside, fairly delicious. When Prince Henry the Navigator was preparing a fleet in the city's shipyards for his father, João I, for Portugal's, first colonial adventure in North Africa in 1415, the local people became so enthusiastic about the venture that they slaughtered all their cattle to supply the vessels, only leaving themselves tripe to eat. The subsequent victory of the fleet at Ceuta, pictured in the tiles of São Bento station, set Portugal on its long history of colonial exploration and ultimately brought great wealth to Porto.

Should the hustle and bustle of the *cais* get too much the workers' cafés, a kind of rough and ready equivalent of Amsterdam's 'Brown cafés', are to be found in the Ribeira district, a few steps away across the Praça de Ribeira. Here the food, mostly locally caught fish is served up fresh and simply cooked and the local wines are ridiculously cheap and drawn straight from the barrel. Normally one or other of the *cais* bars will have musical entertainment, even *fado* singing and there are discos in the city, though they tend to be expensive.

Porto has celebrations and *festas* throughout the year, but one of the most characteristic is the Feast of São Goncalo and São Cristovao at the beginning of January. A statue of São Goncalo said to have been found in the Douro centuries ago is carried through the streets in procession. The Douro boatmen carry other religious figures all accompanied by drums, music, port and the eating of cakes. As at Amarante on the River Tâmega, a tributary of the Douro, the cakes are phallic shaped as São Goncalo is the patron saint of women seeking a husband. The Feast of St John's Eve, the night of the 23- 24 June is, if anything an even more bizarre festival when it is customary, among the dancing and drinking, for people to hit each other with leeks!

One of the best nights out throughout the summer though is definitely to be had at the Crystal Palace and its gardens, near to the Museu Soares dos Reis, on the Rua de D. Manuel II. The huge funfair that is set up in the gardens combines the usual gravity- and death-defying rides with small shooting galleries and food stalls. There is also a small boating lake. The atmosphere is happy and it is quite usual to see three generations — grandparents, wives, mothers and children — walking around the bright lights late into the night with sons, husbands and fathers who work throughout the rest of the year in France, Germany, or Brazil.

Further Information

— Porto —

Tourist Information Offices

Porto
Avenida dos Aliados
☎ 02 312740

Praça Dom João I
☎ 02 317514

Places of Interest

Porto
Guerra Junqueiro Museum
Rua de Dom Hugo
Open: 11:30am-12:30pm, 2.306pm
Tuesday to Saturday.

Museum of Sacred Art
Cathedral Square
Open: 2-4pm Tuesday to Friday.

Palacio de Bolsa
(Stock Exchange)
Praça Infante Dom Henrique
Open: 10am-5pm. Closed weekends.

Soares dos Reis National Museum
Palacio dos Carrancas
Rua Dom Manuel II
Open: 10:am-12 noon, 2.305pm.
Closed Mondays and holidays.

_Solar do Vinho do Porto and Romantic
    Museum_
Quinta da Maceirinha
Rua de Entre Quineros
Museum open: 10am-5pm. Closed
Sundays, Mondays and holidays.

Oporto Golf Course
Espinho
☎ 52 684201

River Cruises
Praça de Ribeira
Muro dos Bacalheiros
☎ 02 383235

Vila Nova de Gaia
Casa Museu Teixeira Lopes
Rua Teixeira Lopes
Open: 9.30am-12.30pm, 2-5.30pm
(except Mondays).

Port wine lodges near the river are open for tours until 6pm.

Markets
Vandoma Fair (antiques)
Next to cathedral every day.

Espinho — Monday

Festivals

Porto
São João
23-24 June

São Bartolomeu
August

Vila Nova de Gaia
São Goncalo and São Cristovao
Early January

4 • The Douro Valley

The River Douro, which rises hundreds of miles from Portugal in the heart of Spain, cuts a deep dramatic gorge through the north of the country. It is one of the most spectacular, and least known, of all European rivers. This tour follows the river from the coast as far as the Upper Douro towns of Pinhão and Peso da Régua and the baked terraced banks that are the cradle for the Port wine grapes that are unique in the world.

The Lower Douro extends inland as far as the Serra de Marão mountains, taking in the baroque town of Lamego, peaceful spas and tranquil villages. Diversions from the river normally follow the course of the Douro's main tributaries, the Paiva, Arda, Sousa, and especially the Tâmega, on whose upper reaches is the beautiful town of Amarante. Near to the Douro too are fine views and walks in the mountains of Montemuro and Marão.

In the past the rainy climate caused by the presence of the mountains and the number of tributaries would mean that the Golden River (*d'ouro* means 'of gold') would cascade down its lower reaches and the brave helmsmen in their *barcos rabelos* would have to risk life and limb to bring the young wine down to the dark, musty vaults of Vila Nova de Gaia. After heavy rains the Douro is still liable to flooding and has not yet been fully tamed.

The N106 out of Porto follows closely the north bank of the River Douro, like the railway line, which is, incidentally, one of the most spectacular in Europe, and for which only the British could have been responsible. It bends and twists with the river, giving at various points in both directions spectacular views. To the east lies the interior of the country and to the west the port and the sea.

At 3-4km (2-3 miles) out of Porto the gorge is at its widest point and there are long sandy beaches. These are used by the residents of the city for swimming and bathing. Fifteen kilometres (10 miles)

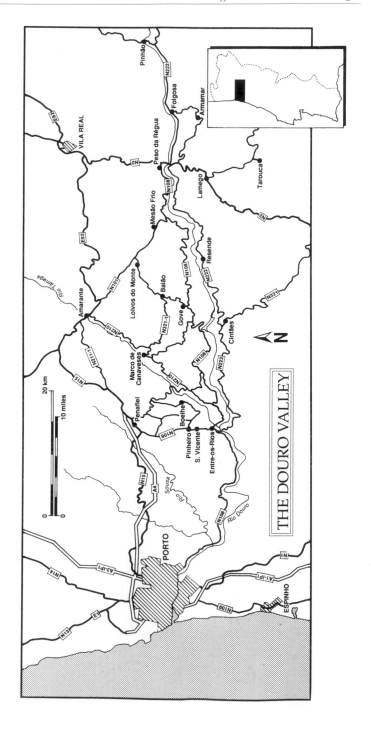

further on the fertile and densely cultivated valley of the River Sousa, a tributary of the Douro joins the main river. Just beyond here is the Barragem de Crestuma the first of the huge dams that have partially tamed the once turbulent and rapidly moving river. In line with Portugal's preparations for the Single European Market all of these dams are being adapted for a lock system that will make the Douro navigable all the way into Spain. The considerable deposits of coal and iron ore in Trás-os-Montes will then more easily be exploited.

The hills on either side of the gorge rise to 400-600m (1,300-2,000ft) and they can be ventured into profitably for the first time at Entre Os Rios where the river Tâmega joins the Douro, then following the N106 to **São Vicente**. In the centre of this pleasant town is the remains of the walled foundations of the original Roman baths dating from the first century AD. It is preserved in the middle of a neatly ordered garden with huge palm trees testifying to the mildness of the climate in this area.

Proceeding north through São Vicente and Pinheiro 6km (4 miles) along the N106 to the left-hand side is the turning to the village of **Paço de Sousa** on the N106-3. The village has a pleasant picnic spot near to the River Sousa, and in its parish church is the tomb of Egaz Moniz, an important Portuguese historical figure. In the very early days of the Portuguese kingdom the young Afonso Henriques had usurped the authority of his grandfather, the King of Leon, by declaring himself king of Portugal in 1127. It was Egaz Moniz who negotiated a treaty with Leon whereby Afonso could concentrate on defending his southern flank against the Moors. Moniz is regarded as personifying the virtue of loyalty because when the King of Leon considered that Afonso had broken the treaty and was about to attack Portugal, Moniz went to Leon and, while arguing his master's case, offered to take on himself any punishment that might be due. Duly impressed Leon relented and allowed Moniz to return home. The panels around the tomb depict these episodes from his life,

Returning to Pinheiro along the N106 and taking the N312 through **Paracelsos** and **Boelhe** high above the River Tâmega, the traditional lifestyle and attitudes of these still largely agricultural communities becomes clear. The roadside is dotted with small religious statues and crosses, as well as the large stone sinks of the communal washhouses. In front of the barns and farmhouses are large, flat stone surfaces. On these platforms the farmer traditionally uses his animals to tread his wheat or grain, thereby saving on the

Working in the fields in the Douro Valley

expense of a mechanical grinder. Maize is stored in *espiguieros*.These are large, rather coffin-like stone structures, usually raised a half metre ($1^1/_2$ft) off the earth by boulders or stones placed beneath each corner. Many of them are fifty, sixty or even as much as a hundred years old.

Beyond Boelhe at Luzim, the N312 reaches an altitude of 556m (1,800ft) and provides spectacular views back over the Douro and Tâmega valleys. The village of **Luzim** has an attractive church typical of the area. Although the exterior is plain, the altar and side chapel contain highly decorous gilded, timbered altar pieces. In the side chapel is a foundation stone dating back to 1662. Note too the stone gateway dated 1842 on the right-hand side of the road north out of Luzim.

Descending towards the Tâmega along the scenic N320 and crossing the river to join the delightful N210 that follows the course of the river, the visitor has a number of options on reaching the small town of **Marco de Canaveses**. On Mondays and Thursdays the town hosts an enjoyable, lively market fair. A tourist village, with accommodation, disco, swimming pool and other sports facilities, the Torre de Nevoes, is located in the pine woods near to the town. For those interested in walking, however, Baião, 15km (10 miles) to the east along the N 321-1 provides an entry point into the Serra de Marão.

This mountain range rises to 995m (3,200ft) yet it is certainly not remote and a gentle walk to Soalhães (4km, $2^1/_2$ miles) or a longer one to Loivos de Monte (10km, 6 miles) are worth tackling in order to see the lives of the shepherds first hand. Accommodation is sparse here so it may be worth checking in Marco de Canaveses on the availability of accommodation in the villages of the Serra de Marão. Less energetically, the river route, with several fine places to stroll and picnic or even fish for trout in the river continues to wind its way to Amarante.

Continuing from Marco de Canaveses on the N 210 or from Loivos do Monte on the N101 either road leads to the delightful town of **Amarante**, originally of Roman origin. The descent into the town, built steeply around the River Tâmega passes through narrow streets of elegant houses with verandas and balconies. At the heart of the town the old bridge over the Tâmega is a national monument.

The São Gonçalo bridge has been a main crossing place for centuries. There are references to a bridge here as along ago as 220 AD when, according to legend, São Gonçalo on his return from journeys in Africa and Italy set about building one. That bridge lasted up to 1763. The even earlier Roman bridge, of which there is now not a trace was built in the time of the Emperor Trajan. São Gonçalo's bridge was a good source of revenue for the local feudal lords, the Counts of Redondo, to whom a toll was paid until a flood in the eighteenth century carried the bridge away. The present structure is an elegant baroque work in granite. The central arch spans a remarkable distance and at the entrances are pyramidal columns. A marble plaque on one of these obelisks records the succesful defence of the bridge in 1809 during the Peninsular War of a combination of General Silveira's Portuguese troops and local people against a detachment of Napoleon's French troops.

Amarante's most prominent monument overlooking the bridge is the Church and Monastery of São Gonçalo. It was begun in 1540, but only completed in the seventeenth century. The majestic side doorway is decorated with three tiers in Renaissance style. In the centre of the first tier in a central niche is a statue of São Gonçalo. The loggia to the left of the doorway is decorated with statues of the kings, João III, Sebastiao, Henrique, and Filipe I. Presiding over the bridge from the walls of the convent is a little carved granite figure,

The bridge over the River Tâmega and the Convento de São Gonçalo, Amarante

Nossa Senhora de Ponte, Our Lady of the Bridge, a Romanesque statue dating from the fourteenth century.

While in Amarante, if one does not fancy the delights of a swim along the river beach or the hiring of a rowing boat, it is as well to know that the town is famous in Portugal for its cakes and sweets. The café balconies are a delightful place to watch the life on the river go by. With inspired names like, *brisas de Tamega* or 'breezes of the Tâmega', *papos de anjo* or 'crops of angels' and *foguetes* or 'rockets', the sweets are made out of almonds, sugar and eggs.

There is a local ancient custom for unmarried young men to present one of these sweetmeats, normally baked in a phallic shape, to unmarried young women on the feast of São Gonçalo, that is the first Saturday in June. This is believed to be a survival of a pre-Christian fertility rite. In the church of the monastery the saint's tomb is said to ensure a quick marriage to anyone who touches it. Above the tomb is inscribed a reproach to the single man:

Why do you not wed the young brides? What harm have they done you?

The religious festival is, of course, as everywhere in the north accompanied by noisy fireworks to frighten off evil spirits, traditional craft displays, folk singing and dancing, and a fun fair. Gonçalo, himself, incidentally, was a thirteenth-century hermit. One wonders what he would have made of it all.

The town's only museum lies behind the church of São Gonçalo on the first floor of what was formerly the monastery. The Albano Sardoeira Museum of Modern Art is very attractively laid out and contains interesting works by Portuguese painters and sculptors. The finest pieces are perhaps by the cubist painter, Amadeo de Souza Cardoso.

There is ample accommodation to be found in the town centre, and there are two fine campsites on either bank a little further upriver.

Much of the fine embroidery displayed at local fairs is produced by women in the surrounding villages. Many of them can be seen working on the steps of their homes in the early summer evenings, and this is much the best time to get a bargain. The very scenic area to the north west of Amarante along the N211-1 is worth visiting for this reason. In many of the villages, such as Travanca, Freixo de Baixo, and Mancelos there are also fine examples of Romanesque churches and monasteries dating from the tenth and twelfth centuries.

From Amarante there is a beautifully scenic route of 34km (20 miles) over the Serra de Marão, following the N101 to Peso da Régua, where the River Corgo joins the Douro, the traditional heart of the Port wine industry. Reaching the Douro at Mesão Frio, the port wine region begins just to the south of here at the village of Barqueiros from where high above the river there is a spectacular view. It begins here because the port wine grapes will only grow in the soils of the underlying schist rock, not on the granite that is found to the west of there.

Mesão Frio is an agreeable and very old town that is worth pausing at just before the N101 joins the Tâmega. It contains a beautiful eighteenth-century house, the Casa de Rede, with baroque decoration and a fine garden that overlooks the river.

Peso da Régua is an attractive town strung out along the north bank of the River Douro which is here at least 100m (330ft) wide beneath gently sloping green hills. The name of the town derives from the Roman settlement of the area and the presence here of a *Villa Regula*.

The town's fortunes have, since the eighteenth century, always been intimately linked with those of the Port wine trade. It was with the establishment of the 'Royal Company of the Producers of Wine in the Upper Douro' in the eighteenth century on the orders of the Marquess of Pombal that the town really came of age. In 1756 Pombal established a demarcated wine growing region around the Upper Douro, in an attempt to break the control of the British shippers who had established themselves in Porto. This was, in fact, the first demarcated region in the world for wine production. The region extended along the Douro and its tributaries from Barqueiros to Barca de Alva, and was marked by 335 granite marking posts which were inscribed with the word *feitoria*, meaning 'factory'. A few of these can still be seen around the countryside.

The descendants of the Royal Company who defend the interests of the growers are the Syndicated Federation of the Wine Growers of the Douro Region, more generally known as the Casa Do Douro. The demarcated zone has, of course, considerably expanded since the eighteenth century and now extends from Barquieros to Barca de Alva on the frontier with Spain. Their headquarters can be visited in the centre of Régua. This and the port wine cellars of the Ramos Pinto company and those of the Casa do Douro itself, to be found just to the east of the railway station, near the river, which can also be visited, are the main attractions in the town. The cellars provide pleasant informative tours surrounded by gigantic wine barrels each containing over 500 gallons of wine. There is, of course an opportunity to sample and to buy some of the wines at the end of the tour.

The Casa De Douro headquarters was built in 1943. It is effectively the administrative centre of the whole industry. It keeps up to date records on about 96,000 wine growing estates in the demarcated region. Here is recorded the location of each property, the qualities of its soil, its degree of exposure to the sun, the number and age of the vinestock. Every year the institute stipulates the amount of the unfortified wine, called must, that each grower is allowed to convert into Port. It then issues certificates to authenticate the produce and controls the price of the wine by buying up unsold wine at the end of the year at a price announced prior to the harvest.

It also houses, perhaps, the most attractive modern stained glass window in Portugal. Covering an approximate area of 50 sq m (540 sq ft), and forming a tryptych, it was completed in 1945 by the celebrated Portuguese painter, Lino Antonio. In the central panel

Flocks of sheep are often seen alongside the road in rural Portugal

there are three figures. The central one represents the Casa do Douro itself and is shown displaying a parchment declaring the establishment of the institute by governmental decree in 1932. The figure to the left, with a hoe at his feet, represents agriculture and the figure to the right, with a staff in his hand, represents commerce. Their handshake obviously symbolises their co-operation. In the top left of the panel is pictured the chapel dedicated to Santa Marta, the Queen of the Douro. Along the top of the central panel are important dates in the history of the trade, beginning with 1678, with the first recorded export of the wine by the Customs in Oporto, and ending in 1926 with the creation of the *entreposto*, the warehouses of Vila Nova de Gaia, to store port wines for export. The left panel dedicated to agriculture shows figures engaged in toil in the typical landscape of the Douro. The right panel, dedicated to commerce, shows the city of Oporto and the distinctive *barco rabelos* that brought the wine barrels down the once turbulent River Douro.

The road along the Douro from Peso da Régua to the final destination of this tour of the Douro at Pinhão, takes the visitor through some of the best Port wine growing areas in the region. The N202 follows the steep valley sides of the Douro and the tremendous effort that has been required to terrace the land and plant the vines is obvious. In the traditional Portuguese expression it is a wine that 'eats stone and drinks sun'.

The demarcated region of the Douro accounts for about 14 per cent of the whole country's wine production in an area of about 250,000 hectares (1,000 sq miles). The large and well known producers of Port wine own substantial portions of this land, but there are still about 34,400 smallholders, whose average holding is only 1.2 hectares ($^1/_2$ acre). The terrain is so difficult that at times the rocks are broken up using explosives. The clay soil contains potassium and in combination with the long dry summers produces full bodied, deep coloured wines, low in acid and high in alcohol. The region is divided into three regions by its two main rivers into the Lower Corgo, the Upper Corgo and the Upper Douro.

Over the years the wine has been variously known as 'Cima Douro', 'Riba Douro', the 'wine of Lamego', that town being the centre of the industry up until the seventeenth century, and the 'Vinho de Embarque'. Port has one of the most elaborate of processes of classification of any of the world's wines. The red ports do not all have the same colour and are divided into ruby, red, tawny red, tawny, and pale tawny. The white ports are divided into pale white, straw white and amber white. Its sweetness is also divided into extra dry, dry, medium dry, sweet and very sweet, also known as *lagrima*.

These different flavours and colours are produced firstly by the ageing process. As it ages the wine grows paler becoming first ruby, then tawny in colour. They are also produced by the relative amounts of the fourteen different types of white grapes and the fifteen different types of red grapes that go to make up the wine. The wine must have an alcoholic content of no less than 19 cent and no more than 22 per cent. Dry white and extra dry white wines cannot, however, have less than $16^1/_2$ per cent. Vintage port is set aside in the year of a particularly good harvest, and spends two years in the cask before being bottled and left to age. The rest of the port is left to age in the casks.

It should not be forgotten, however, that 60 per cent of the wine production in this region is actually that of white and red table wines. The red is usually labelled as *Douro* or *Vinho de Ramo*. Some of the wines from the following areas, normally produced by local co-operatives and therefore very inexpensive, are worth trying: Mesão Frio, Meda, Vila Real, Cumieira, Pegarinhos, Lamego, Armamar, and Murca.

Undoubtedly the best time to be in the region is during the *vindima*, or harvesting period between mid-September and mid-October. Tours from Porto are organised for visitors. Almost all other work in the rural villages ceases while everyone contributes to bringing in the grapes before the arrival of a potentially disastrous early frost. The spectacle of the harvest lies in the hostility of the terrain that will not permit any mechanisation. Large wicker baskets on the backs of the grapepickers is still the only way of bringing the harvest off the steep hillsides. The finest of the grapes are still trod with bare feet in some of the small villages around the town of Pinhão.

Lying between the folds of the hills about 25km (15 miles) to the east of Peso da Régua along the N222, **Pinhão** is today the main centre for the despatching of Port wine to the warehouses of Vila Nova de Gaia. Pinhão became the natural point for this, being more centrally situated in the demarcated region than Peso da Régua, with the arrival of the railway in 1880.

The vital connection between the railway and the town is, indeed, recognised in the town's main tourist attraction that is part of the railway station itself. This is a remarkable twenty-four panel depiction of the life and culture that surrounds the growing of the Port wine vines in polychrome tiles or *azulejos*. The tiles were commisioned by the Parish Council and the Port Wine Institute of Oporto in 1940.

Accommodation is fairly easy to find in Peso da Régua but less so in Pinhão. However, 12km (7 miles) to the north of here on the N322.2 is the village of Alijo where there is a comfortable *pousada*, the 'Barrao de Forrester'. In the region around the nearby village of Favaios, an unusual muscatel wine is produced, derived from the *muscatel galego* grape.

Returning from Pinhão along the Douro towards Peso da Régua, it is worth turning into the hills at the village of Folgosa to visit the village of **Armamar**, 9km ($5^1/_2$ miles) away. The main church in this quiet relaxing vilage is a fine example of the Romanesque style of architecture. Restored in 1956, it is thought to have been built in the thirteenth century. According to local tradition it was built with the stones of a nearby abandoned castle.

In the area of São Domingos de Fontelo, which was formerly the site of a small monastery, near to Armamar, it is worth looking out for a simple hermitage, with a Gothic and Romanesque doorway. It was used as a place of pilgrimage in the fifteenth century by the king,

Dom Juan II, on two occasions. That it should have been used as a place of retreat and contemplation is no surprise as the views of the surrounding area, including a long stretch of the Douro, and in the far distance the town of Vila Real, are very beautiful.

Continuing along the N313 high above the Douro the views over the river remain quite spectacular until the road joins the N2 south of Peso da Régua. From here it is a mere 12km ($7^1/_2$ miles) to the elegant baroque town of Lamego.

Lamego has an ancient and proud place in the history of Portugal. With its wide streets and baroque mansions Lamego nestles between two hills, on one of which sits the pilgrimage church of Nossa Senhora de los Remédios, and on the other a twelfth-century castle. It could make a strong claim to be the prettiest town in the North of Portugal.

Lamego's place in the history books is assured as it was here that the first ever parliament, or *cortes*, of Portuguese nobles, clergy and town officials met in 1143 to recognise Afonso Henriques as the first King of Portugal and to pass the Law of Succession whereby no foreigner could accede to the throne. It is said this parliament took place in the beautiful church of Almacave, to be found on the summit of the Rua de Almacave just outside the old town walls and the castle. The church may also originally have been a mosque. The aristocracy of the seventeenth and eighteenth century, the Carvalhos, Fonsecas, and many others built the fine houses that can still be seen gracing the main streets of the town.

Although the town is of great antiquity, only the belfry tower remains of the original twelfth-century Romanesque cathedral, which has occupied the same site for nearly a thousand years. The attractive main façade is Gothic as is the crown of the belfry and was built in the sixteenth century.The interior was renovated in the eighteenth century. The highlight of a visit to the cathedral is undoubtedly, the elegant and airy sixteenth-century cloister. The chapel of St Nicholas in the cloister has some magnificent tiles, possibly by Policarpo de Oliveira Bernandes, one of the great innovators in the art form who worked in the first half of the eighteenth century. There is also a shrine to St John behind an iron grille.

Lying just to the left and behind the Largo de Se, or Cathedral Place, is the Largo de Camoes, on which is to be found, housed in what was formerly the palace of the Bishops of Lamego, the regional museum. Built in the eighteenth century it houses thirty-four rooms, with a particular emphasis on painting and religious art. The finest works are, perhaps, the five remaining painted panels that formerly adorned the cathedral altar, and were commissioned in 1506 by the Bishop of Lamego from the celebrated painter Vasco Fernandes, known as Grão Vasco. The finest of these and most definitely attributable to the master himself is *The Visitation*. The others are more likely to have been the work of members of his school. There are also six Brussels tapestries from the first third of the sixteenth century, entitled *Music*, *The Temple of Latona*, *Laius consults the Oracle*, *Oedipus in Corinth*, *Oedipus in Tebas*, and *Oedipus with Queen Jocasta*. They are works of remarkable detail.

The ground floor is made up for the most part of early religious art from the Romanesque period to the baroque, the most interesting of which are some fourteenth-century statues of the pregnant Virgin. The upper floor is more varied with later seventeenth-century religious works, such as richly decorated gold and silver chalices. There is also a collection showing the development of the tile as a decorative art form from the sixteenth to the eighteenth century. This includes some fine Mozarabic tiles taken from the cathedral at Coimbra, and a set of panels depicting exotic birds and a hunting scene taken from Visconde de Valmor near Lisbon. A Chinese room including porcelain and painting on silk is also worth visiting.

Finally and rather curiously there is a series of baroque chapels, one on the ground floor and two on the upper floor which were taken and preserved from destruction in the Convent of Chagas, when it was pulled down to make room for a school to be built on its site. It is a very well cared for museum and is a pleasant place to spend an hour's browsing.

Returning to the Largo de Camoes the narrow streets through the old quarter of town opposite lead up to the ruins of the twelfth century castle that once commanded the whole of the surrounding area. It was a site occupied in turn by Romans, Moors and Christians. Half way up the hill on the Rua de Castelhino there is a thirteenth-century cistern, the town's ancient water source. It is very unusual in being located above ground. Built of great granite blocks, the marks of the stonemason can still clearly be seen. It can be difficult to gain access to the cistern so ask in the tourist office, just outside the old town walls, at the foot of the hill, for their advice.

Lamego's most famous monument, however, is the pilgrimage church of Nossa Senhora de los Remédios. From the cathedral it lies

Houses clinging to the banks of the River Barosa near Balsemão

directly to the west along the Avenida Dr A. De Sousa, and then along a delightful, broad, leafy avenue, laid out with four ornamental pools that represent the four seasons. The avenue is lined with cafés and is an excellent place from which to watch the busy life of the town.

Like Bom Jesus at Braga, Nossa Senhora de los Remédios is approached by a great eighteenth-century stone staircase. It is traditional for the faithful and contrite to atone for their sins by climbing the staircase on their knees. The most likely time to see this spectacle is during the great annual pilgrimage on 7-8 September. This is also a time of great celebration, with dances, concerts and a fun fair. The 700 steps of the staircase are divided into several different levels and on each of these have been placed small chapels and statues. The finest of these is the final one, the 'Largo dos Reis', or Courtyard of the Kings, with its granite columns, statues of the Prophets and star-topped granite obelisk. The baroque façade of the eighteenth-century church itself, with its strong curves, tall twin bell towers and twin clock faces is very appealing.

Lamego is famous in Portugal not only for Nossa Senhora de los Remédios, but also for its gastronomy. The most surprising aspect of this is to be found just behind Nossa Senhora de los Remédios, on the

The rugged landscape of the Serra de Estrela near Torre, the highest point; Dão Lafoes

The Manuline portal to the Coimbra University Chapel, Dão Lafoes

The traditional stone built village of Piódão, Dão Lafoes

Castro Daire road in the caves storing the locally produced wine, Raposeira. Founded in 1898 the caves store the sparkling, light, white wine that is the closest thing to champagne to be found in the country. There is a free tour and free tasting of the three varieties produced.

Other gastronomic specialities of the town include the sweet-meats, or *bolas de carne* which were first produced by the nuns of the local convent of Chagas. Like Chaves in Trás-Os-Montes, Lamego is also famous for its ham. It is normally smoked, when it is known as *presunto*, and can be seen around the town hanging in any supermarket or butchers.

Lamego has a variety of accommodation. Behind Nossa Senhora de los Remédios is to be found a state run *estalagem*. In the elegant town centre there are a number of the more expensive hotels, *residencias*, or some cheaper *dormidas*. There is also a swimming pool, just to the left at the top of the Avenida Dr A De Sousa, and, as you might expect there are a number of fine restaurants, in particular for good value and excellent food the restaurant next to the bus station behind the museum merits consideration.

The local campsite, too, is worth a visit, even if one is not camping. It is 4km ($2^1/_2$ miles) out of town sitting atop the Serra das Meadas, from where the view is quite impressive. At the summit is a huge and rather oppressive statue of a bishop, who donated it to the town himself. On the second Sunday in June these heights are the site of a *festa*.

Taking a different route out of Lamego to the south from behind the cathedral brings the visitor to what may well be the oldest church in Portugal, the Capela de Balsemão. From the back of the cathedral proceed to the right in the direction of Guarda for about 500m (550yd) to the Capela de Desterro or Chapel of the Exile, perhaps pausing to admire the seventeenth-century tiles within. The road oppostite then leads to the left and descends into the old part of the town. This overcrowded area of narrow streets huddled around an old bridge above a small river is known as the Bairro do Fonte. It presents a quite different image from the Lamego of baroque mansions of the Upper Town.

Beyond the bridge there is a narrow road descending to the left that follows the picturesque bends of the River Barosa. After a kilometro or so ($^1/_2$ mile) one reaches the end of the road and a dusty small square before the unprepossesing granite façade of the Chapel

The Capela de Balsemão, possibly the oldest church in Portugal

of Balsemão. The seventh-century chapel is one of the few remaining reminders of the Suevi, the 'barbarian' people who occupied the mountainous north of the country in the wake of the fall of the Roman Empire.

The distinctiveness of the Suevi's settled agricultural culture in contrast to the nomadic, herding lifesyle of the Visigoths who settled the rest of the Peninsula is in many ways the root of the independence and identity of the Portuguese as a nation. Reminders of them are very difficult to find however and the curls carved onto the archway above the choir, within the dark interior of the church, are precious for that reason. In the centre of the church is the tomb of the aristocrat, Dom Afonso of Porto. The ornate carving on the capitals are from the fourteenth century.

A final point of call before leaving this area, further down the River Barosa off the N226 in the direction of Guarda is the ancient convent of St John of Tarouca. Just a few kilometres (2 miles) south of the village of **Mondim de Beira** the monastery is as remarkable in its setting as it is in its history. Set in a wide, pretty valley with the River Barosa swiftly flowing below the convent walls, it is a beautiful spot. A simple medieval bridge straddles the river.

The convent was the first of the Cistercian order to be constructed in Portugal. The foundation stone was reputedly laid by the first King of Portugal, Dom Afonso Henriques in 1124, while returning north to his castle at Guimarães after a great victory against the Moors at Transcoso to the south. There is an old story that the site of the convent was chosen by a soldier turned monk, Brother João Cirita, who was the recipient of a miraculous vision of the site. The monastery exercised spiritual jurisdiction over a great deal of the surrounding area and at one time had over fifty monks.

The originally Romanesque chapel can still evoke something of the spiritual and cultural atmosphere of the former glory. Though the church was extensively remodelled in the seventeenth century, it was consecrated in 1169. The church has three naves, the centre one being twice the height of the other two. The third altar is graced by the beautiful *St Peter in Majesty* painting of the famous artist Gaspar Vaz who died about 1568. The Gothic influence in his work can also be seen in his paintings of the *Virgin in Majesty* and of St Michael that are also to be found in the church.

A fourteenth-century polychrome granite statue of the Virgin and Child is to be seen in the passageway between the chapels and the sacristy. It is particularly exceptional among Romaneque statues with a height of 2m ($6^1/_2$ft). The sacristy contains fine tiles as does the chancel where they depict the life of St Bernard, and the walls of the north transept which show scenes from the life of John the Baptist including the Baptism of Christ.

The church's spectacular organ was built by the Portuguese sculptor, Lius Pereira da Costa, in 1729. The tomb of the Count of Barcelos, an illegitimate son of Dom Dinis, with attractive carvings of hunting scenes is to be found in a side aisle. The count, who died in 1354 is regarded as one of the finest writers of the Middle Ages in Portugal, his most famous work being the *General Chronicle of 1344*.

Returning to Mondim de Beira and the N226 a tour of the lower Douro is completed by following this road until it joins the N222 and the southern bank of the river. There still remain a number of villages that are worth visiting. There is a spectacular view over the gorge at Miradoura da Boa Vista 6km ($3^1/_2$ miles) after the road has rejoined the river.

A further few kilometres (2 miles) towards Porto there is a turning inland to the village of **São Martinho de Mouros**. It is around this village that a curious black pottery is made. The ancient method of production involves firing the clay in a hole in the ground allowing

The lower Douro valley near Entre-os-Rios

the smoke to penetrate the clay over a period of days until the typical black colour is achieved. The village has a fine example of a Romanesque church.

Resende and **Cinfães**, just off the N222, have fine churches and are good places to pause before driving the final few kilometres (2 miles) to **Entre Os Rios**. Here amid grand scenery the N222 crosses the gorge and offers a final opportunity to appreciate one of the most exciting and spectacular river valleys in Europe.

Further Information

— The Douro Valley —

Tourist Information Offices

Amarante
Rua Candido dos Reis
☎ 055 422980

Lamego
Avenida Viscondes Guedes
Teixeira
☎ 054 62005

Peso da Régua
Largo da Estacao
☎ 054 22846

Places of Interest

Amarante
Alberto Sardoeira Museum Library
Convento de São Gonçalo
Open:10am-12.30pm, 2-5pm.
Closed holidays

Peso da Régua
Casa do Douro
Rua dos Camilos
☎ 054 23811

Markets

Amarante — first Saturday and
17th of each month

Marco de Canaveses — Monday
and Thursday

Lamego — Wednesday

Espinho — Monday

Festivals

Amarante
Festa de São Goncalo
Early June

Penafiel
Corpo de Deus
18 June

Peso da Régua
São Pedro
29 June

Nossa Senhora de Socorro
5 August

Lamego
Nossa Senhora dos Remédios
Late August to mid-September.

5 • Trás-os-Montes

Trás-os-Montes — the land 'beyond the mountains' — is the least known and appreciated of Portugal's regions, and for good reason. Separated from the province of Minho by the Marão and Gerês mountain ranges, its high, exposed, rocky plateaux could, in the past, only be crossed with difficulty in the severe cold of winter or in the arid heat of the summer. These plateaux, in the north of the province are known locally as the *Terra Fria* or 'cold lands'. Even the *Terra Quente* or 'warm lands' of the river valleys of the Douro, Corgo, and Tua, that cut deep into the province of Trás-os-Montes did not provide any easy means of communication. The rivers were fast moving and proved a treacherous means of transportation. This led amongst other things to the development of the *barco rabelo*, the steep sided small boats that were used to transport port wine barrels from the vineyards of the warm lands of the Upper Douro. On the plateaux, in the rain shadow of the Gerês and Marão mountains, the temperature plunges below freezing for long periods in winter, while the harsh granite can reflect back temperatures well over 100 °F (38 °C) throughout the summer.

Trás-os-Montes though is beginning to be tamed. The rivers have had their power harnessed for the development of hydro-electric power, which has left them as placid as a lake for much of the time and new roads such as the N103 and the N15 link the interior as far as the ancient medieval town of Bragança, 50km (31 miles) from the Spanish border, with the densely populated province of Minho.

The traditional products of Trás-os-Montes and its accompanying way of life still persist. The cold lands produce rye, chestnuts, and on the steeply terraced edges of the plateaux, olives, figs and almond trees are cultivated and bees are kept. As well as the grapes for Port wine the valleys produce fruit trees, maize and vegetables. Traditional forms of collective farming, begun when the area was re-

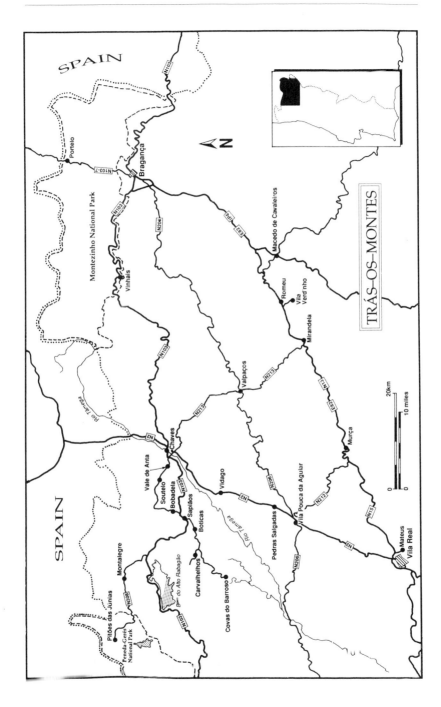

Trás-os-Montes — the land beyond the mountains

settled in the twelfth and thirteenth centuries on the orders of the Dukes of the emergent Portuguese nation, are still practised in the remote villages. The area was inhabited long before this period, however, by prehistoric tribes who have left their mark in this region more than in any other in Portugal.

The tour described in this chapter consists of more or less a circular route through a region two and a half times the size of the Minho with only half the population, and begins and ends in the pleasant town of Vila Real, the 'gateway to Trás-os-Montes'. It takes in what is perhaps the most beautiful private palace in Portugal at Mateus, the medieval towns of Mirandela and Bragança, the old Roman town of Chaves, the famous spa towns of Pedras Salgadas and Vidago, the fascinating 'medieval' village of Pitões de Júnias, and the National Parks of Alvão, Montezinho and Peneda-Gerês.

As will become evident to even the casual visitor Trás-os-Montes can be, particularly in the summer, a hot, harsh terrain in which to travel. Nonetheless it has an austere beauty and a tranquil timelessness about both its towns and villages which greatly rewards the visitor and makes it, perhaps, the most unique and unforgettable of the landscapes of the Portuguese regions.

Vila Real is justifiably known as the 'gateway to Trás-os-

Montes'. Just less than 100km (60 miles) from Porto along the new A4 motorway and the N15, and about the same distance from Viseu along the N2 from the south, it has a magnificent setting between two mountain ranges, the Serra de Marão and the Serra de Alvão. It is a thriving, lively town and the main industrial centre of the North-East of the country. The old part of the town, however, has preserved much of its character and is grouped around the Avenida Carvalho Araujo. This is a wide boulevard with attractive tree-lined gardens and along with the sixteenth- and eighteenth-century nobleman's town houses, gives to the town some grace and style.

The finest of these granite houses on the Avenida Carvalho Araujo is the former palace of the Dukes of Vila Real which now houses the town's very helpful tourist office. The façade has four plain but nonetheless attractive Manueline windows.

Descending the *avenida* leads to the Square of the Pelourinho, or pillory. Directly across the square on the far side of the *avenida* is the church of the former monastery of St Domingo, also known as the cathedral. The church was built in the Gothic period, though this antiquity is belied by the modern stained glass windows. It is unimpressive in scale but is worth visiting for the Romanesque carvings on the column capitals of the nave.

Further down the avenue on the right hand-side at number 19 is another nobleman's house whose present façade was designed in the sixteenth century in Italian Renaissance style. The house was the birthplace of the navigator, Diogo Cão. Setting sail from the school of exploration set up in Sagres by Prince Henry the Navigator, Cão was the first European to reach the mouth of the Congo river in West Africa in 1482. It is now used as a café.

Behind the town hall at the end of the *avenida* there is a pleasant, shady walk by the fourteenth-century chapel of São Bras and the old town walls. The view down into the gorge of the River Corgo and its tributary the Cabril leaves the visitor again, as elsewhere in the country to marvel at the ingenuity of the Portuguese who build their houses on such steep slopes.

A leisurely walk in the streets off the main avenue around the Largo de Pelourinho also brings its reward with an opportunity to admire the many sixteenth- and eighteenth-century mansions that are to be found there. The coats of arms of the families who built them can often be seen carved in granite in low relief above the doorways.

Like Porto and Braga, Vila Real has some stylish bars and cafés,

The gardens and rear façade of the Palace of Mateus

the best of which is probably the Excelsior, on the Rua Serpa Pinto with its fine cakes, marble tops, pool tables and old men checking their lottery tickets.

In such a large city there is, of course a good range of accommodation and restaurants particularly around the Rua Teixeira de Sousa and near the cathedral and there is a campsite with a swimming pool and tennis courts near the river off the Avenida 1 de Maio to the north-west of the city. Vila Real also has a modern shopping centre.

The villages in the surrounding countryside produce a very fine and unusual black graphite pottery. This can be bought in the town, particularly during the festival of St Peter on the 29 June, but it is worth asking directions in the tourist office on how to reach some of the villages, such as Bizalhaes and Granja that lie a few kilometres (2 miles) to the west of the city, where it may still be possible to see the pots being made.

One of the best known sights in Northern Portugal, but paradoxically not nearly so often visited, lies just 4km (2 miles) to the east of Vila Real on the road to Sabroso. The façade of the Palace of **Mateus** is well known throughout the world as an illustration of it adorns the label of every bottle of the famous delicate rosé wine that comes from here and is one of Portugal's best known exported wines. The palace itself is regarded by some as the finest baroque building in the country.

Built in the first half of the eighteenth century by the Italian architect Nicolo Nasoni, whose Torre de los Clerigos stands in the centre of Porto, its setting is certainly one of the most charming in Portugal. Set among vine-terraced hills from which the famous wine is produced, the palace is approached along a curving tree-lined avenue which ends in a fine view of the ornate façade. Before it and bearing its reflection is a large artificial pool. The twin wings of the palace extend towards the pool while the central section with its elegant balustraded stairway lies at the far end of a cobbled court-yard. The house is still occupied and these wings form the working quarters of the farm and estate.

Some scholars consider the pinnacles and allegorical figures above the pediment to be on too grand a scale for a relatively small building but it is nonetheless a memorable façade. The pink stone statue of a woman in the pool is by the modern Lisbon artist, João Cudiliero, whose work is extensively displayed in the Cultural Centre in Almansil in the Eastern Algarve. To the left of the main building, but unfortunately not open to visitors is an elegant baroque chapel also designed by Nicolo Nasoni.

There is a guided tour of the interior of the palace when the intricately carved and vaulted chestnut ceilings of the main hall and the main salon can be admired. There is also some fine Indo-Portuguese ebony furniture and a few other individual items of merit, such as a sixteenth-century ivory crucifix. The most interesting of the rooms, though, is that which contains the personal correspondence of the palace's owners, the Counts of Vila Real. Letters can be seen from the old royal family of Portugal, from former governors of Brazil, and even from George Canning who was Prime Minister of Britain in 1827. There is also kept in the glass cases here a very early edition of the Portugese Odyssey, *The Lusiads*, by the sixteenth-century writer, Luis de Camões, and ordered by one of the first of the Counts of Vila Real.

It must be admitted however, that as the count and his family are still in residence, the tour is quite limited. Perhaps the best way to appreciate and enjoy the interior is to look out for advertisements around the palace entrance or in the tourist office in the town for the classical music concerts that make use of the fine acoustics of the palace's main salons throughout the summer.

Before leaving the Palace of Mateus it is worth walking through the courtyard to the rear of the building to admire the dwarf box hedges of the garden that have been cut into formal patterns. An avenue of cedars, their branches grown so thickly as to almost completely block out the light from the path beneath leads to a lower garden. All around are the vines on which the wealth and the pre-eminence of the family has always depended as well as orchards of pears, apples, and figs.

Five kilometres (3 miles) beyond the Palace of Mateus along the N322 is the ancient Roman site of *Panoias*, which has a number of sacrificial slabs, thought to have been dedicated to Hellenic deities. The village of **Sabroso**,10km (6 miles) beyond here, is famous as the birthplace of Fernão de Magalhães, usually called Magellan, though it is now perhaps better known for its wine. Although he is remembered as the first man to circumnavigate the globe, he was, in fact, killed in the Phillipines, and it was his crew who completed the epic three-year journey which was begun in 1519.

Returning to the most likely route into Trás-os-Montes, the N15 road rises steadily, with fine views to either side and the Serra de Vilarelho ahead. From the village of Codaval it is possible to take a scenic route north along the N212 to Vila Pouca de Aguia and Chaves. These towns will be described later in the tour. From Codaval too there is a pleasant twisting and turning descent through pine woods to the small town of Murca.

Like Vinhais to the north **Murca** occupies an advantageous position between Vila Real to the west and Mirandela to the east. Originally a Roman settlement, it is now the market town for much of the surrounding countryside. The town square is normally lively and bustling, with some farmers and tinkers still bringing their wares in on packhorses and mules.

In its centre is a remarkable prehistoric stone boar, known as a *porco*. At least two thousand years old it is reckoned to have formed part of an Iron Age fertility cult, or to have been used to ward off evil spirits from the fields. It is similar to the one to be found in the old town of Bragança, but it is if anything better preserved.

Next to the *porco* is the parish church, with a fine neo-Classical interior, unusual in an area renowned for its baroque churches. There are no less than five side altars. Should the church be closed ask in the clothes shop opposite for the key. To the right of the church is

The prehistoric porco *in the main square at Murca*

Farmers near Murca still come to town on horses

another pleasantly shady square with a fine Manueline pillory.

Returning to the town square on the far side is the wooden kiosk of the local wine making co-operative, the Adega Cooperative de

Murca. The wine is very good and unbelievably cheap. The winery itself is a kilometre or so out of town and a visit is possible on request at the kiosk.

The road from Murca to the town of Mirandela, the N15, is flanked by olive trees and beehives on the steep slopes that are typical of Trás-os-Montes. There are also lemon trees and new plantings of the fast growing recent import, the eucalyptus tree. This imported tree is the cause of heated political debate in this region and throughout the country. The grey leaved eucalyptus is popular with the timber industry because it grows quickly. Environmentalists however point out that its thirsty roots take up rainfall so effectively that other plants and shrubs struggle to survive, with the result that the more attractive native pines are being rapidly displaced.

Drivers should beware of the donkeys and mules that are still used to transport produce here and are often met struggling gamely up the hills. The views from the road are often breathtaking and the silence is almost palpable.

Mirandela is a lively, bustling provincial market town, set on the wide sandy banks of the River Tua. The main features of the town are the bridges that span the 200m (650ft) wide river. The old bridge, built by the Romans, was extensively renovated in the fifteenth century and its seventeen arches are all still intact. It is not unusual in the summer when the water level is low to see white sheets laid out in the sands to dry by the local women having washed them in the Tua.

Dominating the town is the former Tavora Palace. Built in the seventeenth century, it has a distinctive whitewashed baroque façade. It is now used as the town hall. The Tavoras were Mirandela's most powerful family in the first three hundred years after the birth of the new Portuguese state in the fourteenth century. Their fortune stemmed from Pero Lourenço de Tavora's having fought alongside the young João of Avis at his crucial defeat of the Castilians at the battle of Aljubarrota in 1385. Unfortunately the Tavoras devotion to the first ruling dynasty also extended to accompanying the martyr King Sebastião on his ill-fated attack on the Moors of Morocco in 1587. The family's fortunes irrevocably declined from this time.

Mirandela also has an unexpected and interesting Museum of Modern Art in the town centre, dedicated largely to the work of local artist, Armindo Teixera Lopes, and named after him. His work mostly comprises landscapes of the surrounding area and of Lisbon.

The other permanent exhibition is a selection of works by other modern Portuguese painters.

Just to the south of the town there is a convenient campsite along the N213 next to the River Tua. There is a river beach and canoes can be hired at the site office regardless of whether one is camping or not.

Mirandela has several plain but wholesome restaurants near to the river and the Rua Dom Afonso III. The local specialities are garlic sausage and steak cooked in the traditional manner over a wood fire. There are also some fine local wines. As regards accommodation there are a couple of reasonable *pensions*.

The best time to be in Mirandela is during the exceptionally long festival of Nossa Senhora de Amparos, from 25 July until 15 August. The town is thronged with visitors and the medieval bridge and the baroque curves of the town hall are lit up with bright lights. More or less the whole population of the town strolls back and forth across the river, enjoying a ride or two on the fun fair that pitches on the far side of the river. Just to the left of the bridge near to the tourist office a brass band is often set up and an impromptu dance begins. The small stalls around the town sell craft work, traditional sweets and *farturas* or Portuguese doughnuts.

There are two ancient monuments in the Mirandela district, the dolmen, or burial chamber, at Caravelas, reached to the south via the N315 off the N15 and the recently discovered menhir, or fertility symbol at Bouca, 24km (15 miles) to the north along the N315. For precise directions to locate the monuments which are usually away from main roads it is best to ask at the tourist office on the Rua Dom Afonso III in Mirandela.

North of Mirandela the N15 passes through an impressive but harsh landscape of granite and schist. About 10km (6 miles) out of Mirandela there is a turning off to the right to the village of **Vila Verdinho** and a little further along the main road itself the village of **Romeu**. These villages have been designated by the national government to be particularly representative of the traditional architecture, lifestyle and environment of Trás-os-Montes, and as a result have recently been renovated.

In Romeu there is a park, a small zoo and a rather unusual museum, called the 'Loja das Curiosidades'. It is made up of the personal collection of a local philanthropist Manuel Mcneres, and consists largely of early versions of modern machines, such as typewriters and sewing machines. There is also a small vintage car museum.

Ten kilometres (6 miles) beyond Romeu is the turning to **Macedo de Cavaleiros** along the N216. The derivation of the town's name is more interesting than the town itself. Legend has it that two local nobles set about the Moors with clubs during the reconquest. On hearing of this the king ordered the town to be renamed 'Knight's Club'. Should you be interested in hunting the Estalagem do Cacedor or Hunter's Lodge, is a good place to stay with lots of antique furniture among the prize trophies. Much of the hunting these days, in fact, consists of the shooting of small game birds such as partridge.

South of Macedo along the N216 lies some very fine scenery, and some of the best areas for shooting in Portugal, until the town of **Mogadouro** is reached. The twelfh-century castle of Mogadouro was once of strategic importance in the struggle to resist the incursions of Leon and Castile. It was later given to the Tavora family of Mirandela. Although now in ruins its walls still give a fine view over the surrounding countryside. Though remote, an air of lethargy seems to seep over the town in the summer's heat, but it does have reasonable restaurants and hotels.

Returning to Macedo de Cavaleiros and the N102, the route north on to the N15 heads towards the medieval town of Bragança. To the east of the main road the Azibe dam can soon be seen. Descending to the lakeside village of **Santa Combinha** it is possible to hire a boat, swim, windsurf or fish in the lake.

The remainder of the journey to Bragança is in the harsh shadow of the Serra de Noguiera and the sight of the old town, with its still impressive castle, in the distance comes as a welcome relief.

Before describing the town itself another popular approach to the town which is often used by visitors coming into Portugal from Spain is briefly described.

Coming into Portugal from Spain through the border crossing of Portelo the N130-1 to Bragança takes the traveller through some of the highest points of the National Park of Montezinho, well over 1,000m (3,300ft) above sea level. The views across the countryside and, in particular, down the valley of the River Sabor are very grand. Nonetheless as one drives south the folds of the granite hill tops all around are harsh and barren. The lower slopes of red clay are covered in summer with fields of golden wheat.

In the valley bottoms, where there is usually a tributary of the

River scenery in the Trás-os-Montes

Sabor or the river itself, the land is intensely cultivated in ways that have not greatly changed since the Suevi brought the heavy plough-share to Portugal over 1,500 years ago. The steep slopes and poor soil of Trás-os-Montes, as is the case in much of the North, is unsuitable to new highly mechanised farming methods, so the land is farmed in strips and in rotation, planting in particular maize and potatoes. At the fields' edge twisted trees and branches are used to grow vines. The poorness of the soil is masked here, as elsewhere in the country, by the physical industry of the Portuguese.

Even the high slopes are utilised as they are often terraced and have wooden beehives placed on them. The harsh surface of the granite reflects back the heat of the sun, making hot conditions which are ideal for bees. The honey of these areas is a local delicacy and can be bought throughout the region in the villages and sometimes even at the roadside. The lower slopes are dotted with horse chestnuts, honeysuckle, and schumack trees. The houses in the rather dusty roadside villages are decorated with hyacinth, chrysanthemum and sweet pea. There are also fields of huge sunflowers and of canes and trellisses for hops.

At **França** there is an equestrian centre, the Centro Hipico de França. It is signposted from the road to the left down a dirt track, and past a traditional watermill which is in the process of being restored. If the staff are out on a ride ask in the tourist office in Bragança for the times of rides. Hacking in the hills for riders of all levels of experience can be arranged.

Six kilometres (4 miles) below França on the left-hand side of the N103-1 there is a delightful, leafy bathing place. The River Sabor has been dammed here and the resulting pool, deep but without any dangerous currents, is very popular with the locals. In the rocky stream beyond the dam one can usually see local women washing their family's clothes against the rocks. A kilometre or so ($^1/_2$ mile) beyond here is a rudimentary but beautifully situated campsite.

Bragança is both an ancient walled town, built to defend the young Portuguese state against the incursions of its powerful Castilian neighbour, and a rapidly expanding modern provincial town, keen to exploit its advantageous position between the industrial centre of Porto and the large cities of the Central Iberian Plain. At an altitude of 660m (2,160ft) in the Serra de Noguera, it is a fine base from which to explore Trás-os-Montes. There is a *pousada*, named after St Bartolomeu, excellent hotels and restaurants as well as nightclubs. Regular *festas* are held behind the cathedral in the town centre and these are often visited by families of dark-eyed gypsies who come in from Spain to sell their goods at the Bragança market.

The town has been settled since before Christ but its distinguishing feature is the medieval town enclosed on top of a hill with a circle of medieval walls which is still complete. In 1464 King Don Afonso granted a royal charter to the town granting it the status of a duchy. This stonghold became the base for the Bragança noble family whose power in the Middle Ages so came to rival the ruling family, the House of Avis that in 1481 the new king, João II, thought it necessary to humble those his father had exalted and had the third duke Fernando summarily tried and executed in Elvas in 1483. In João's defence it should be admitted that the duke was indeed plotting against the king. Before the fifteenth century was out, however, the duke had moved his residence and court to the Alentejan town of Vila Vicosa. (See Chapter 8, The Alto Alentejo.)

The view from the walls is spectacular, overlooking the new town, the Park of Montesinho, and in the distance, the old enemy, Spain. The most remarkable feature of the old town is that it remains so complete and a living community. Families and their livestock still live in the small, pretty houses in the narrow streets and they are

Castle keep, the Domus Municipalis and the church of Santa Maria, Bragança

very evocative of the stronghold's long history.

In the heart of the town is the church of Santa Maria, originally constructed in the sixteenth century. It is a pleasant church, whose doorway is flanked by two twisted columns carved with vines. It also has an eighteenth-century barrel-vaulted painted ceiling depicting the Assumption, though this is not as appealing as the one in the church of São Bento, just below the castle walls. It also has a long haired and semi-naked statue of Mary Magdalene, which if one is accustomed to the rather passionless restraint of North European devotion can be slightly shocking.

The tall castle keep opposite the church, built in 1187, and restored in 1928, is now an interesting military museum. It is well kept, and is made up for the most part, rather predictably, of sixteenth-century broadswords and chain mail, and eighteenth- and nineteenth-century cavalry officers' swords, lances and helmets. The most fascinating section of the museum, however, is that on the ground floor, devoted to the Portuguese colonies of Mozambique and Angola. There are African tribal masks, canes and votary offerings. The captured and, apparently, tyrranical African leader, Gungunhana is pictured on the wall and the trousers and shirt given him to wear by the Portuguese are displayed, evidently to illustrate

Interior of the Domus Municipalis, the twelfth-century town council building

what a giant of a man he was. The sense that he was big game, an impressive trophy, for his captors, like a lion or tiger, is hard to avoid.

By far the most remarkable building in the old town, however, is the Domus Municipalis, or town council building, almost hidden behind the church of St Maria. It was built in the twelfth century in a plain Romanesque style and, most unusually, is in a pentagonal shape. Ask or mime to one of the old women nearby if there is a key and they will be delighted to fetch one for you. The internal arches and their decorative bosses have suffered less from the attrition of the weather than those externally. The beauty of the carving of human and animal faces is plain to see. Your guide will point out the ancient cistern that can be seen through a small grill in the floor and above the doorway can be seen fishes carved into the stone, early symbols of a Christian community. It is one of only a very small number of Romanesque civil buildings that survive and its simplicity and harmonious proportions, symbolic of an early striving for democratic decision making, are very pleasing. In this context the only jarring note is sounded by a plaque commemorating a visit by Marcelo Caetano, Salazar's succesor as dictator of Portugal.

In the shadow of the castle keep is an even earlier monument to human civilisation. A tall decorated column, known as a *pelourinho,*

The prehistoric porco and pillory, Bragança

has been placed on the back of a prehistoric stone, roughtly hewn in the shape of a boar or pig, and known locally as a *porco*. It was, apparently, created in the Iron Age by the pre-Christian community as a symbol of fertility and health. This is a little difficult to appreciate today when the area around is used as a car park. The pride of place in the main square of the village of Murca given to its *porco* is in great contrast. However, the old town of Bragança, off-the-beaten-track as it certainly is, must be seen as one of the most complete medieval monuments in Portugal.

There are two churches outside of the old walls that are worth visiting. The cathedral in the centre of the new town is deceptively small and disappointing, though the baroque calvary that lies before it in the square is worth seeing. The aforementioned church of São Bento lies along the road to the right on leaving the old town by the main gate. Originally constructed in 1590, it has a plain Renaissance exterior, but a quite remarkable eighteenth-century, barrel-vaulted painted ceiling. It depicts at its centre Father, Son, and Holy Ghost, and to each side of them, Mary and St Peter. Its colours are exceptionally clear and the neo-Classical illusion of depth created by the depiction of windows and columns that seem to extend up from the walls of the church can work as a very effective *trompe l'oiel*. There is also opposite the entrance a portrait of the Virgin Mary, pierced by six swords. These represent the sufferings she underwent in her son's persecution and death. This literal depiction of suffering, which to the outsider appears rather gruesome, is very typical of these northern communities in which the statues and religious paintings reflect the arduous unyielding physical labour on the land which the people have endured for centuries.

This recognition of suffering does not become morbid, or as it might in Spain, mystical, however, as can be clearly seen in the Church of São Vicente, to be found on the square of the same name, descending from the gateway of the old town along the Rua Costa Grande. Here the initial gloom of the church is belied by the exuberance of the coiled, gilded altar piece. Essentially secular images of grapes, birds and cherubs decorate the columns in a celebration of Nature's plenitude. The popularity, among the people, of these baroque churches to be found all over the North is in the clear recognition of suffering and an essentially cheerful faith in a beneficent Nature and God.

This church, in particular, has a place in the most famous and romantic of episodes in Portuguese history as the place where in 1345 the young prince, Dom Pedro, claimed to have defied his father, the King Afonso IV, by marrying his Castilian lover, Ines de Castro. The king opposed the liaison as two of Ines' brothers had been implicated in a plot against the powerful Castilian King, Pedro the Cruel. To appease Pedro and avoid any precipitant attack on the fledgling Portuguese kingdom Afonso had his men track Ines down to Coimbra, where she was put to death in what is now known as 'The Garden of Tears'. In a gruesome footnote to the story after his father's death Dom Pedro had Ines' decayed remains exhumed, dressed and enthroned in the Monastery of Santa Cruz in Coimbra. All the courtiers were then 'requested' to kiss her hand.

To the right of the church down the Rua Abilio Beca is the former bishop's palace, which now houses the Museum of Abade de Bacal.

The old town within the walls of Bragança castle

The interior of São Vicente, Bragança

The abbot of the small parish of Bacal, near to Bragança, was a remarkable man. Francisco Manuel Alves was born in Bragança in 1865, remote from any centres of enlightened or 'radical' thinking.

Yet he had views that would not be out of place in the liberal wing of many of today's Christian churches, calling on the Church to defend the poor and insisting on religious tolerance as a properly Christian virtue. This was obviously not an easy thing to do in the days of the Inquisition.

In many ways however Alves was being true to the traditions of his native city. From the time when an illegitimate son of João I and his mistress, the daughter of a Jewish merchant, was granted the Dukedom of Bragança in 1442 it has been a place of refuge and retreat in particular for the Jews who fled there from persecution in Spain throughout the Middle Ages. One of the abbot's best known works was indeed about the Jews who had come to settle in Bragança.

The highlights of the museum are the remarkably colourful and feminine male costumes of the *pauliteiros*, or stick dancers who still perform at festivals in the village of Miranda do Douro, 84km (52 miles) south-east of Bragança on the N218. The third Sunday in August, the feast of Sta Barbara is the best time to see the dancers in Miranda. The origins of the dance are thought to lie in older sword fighting rituals. The town also has its own dialect, Mirandes, though this is rapidly dying out.

The Museum of The Abbot of Bacal also contains some fine Indo-Portuguese ivory carvings and some landscapes and portraits by the Portuguese painter, Alberto Souza, that perfectly capture the tranquil, yet colourful spirit of Trás-os-Montes. In the collection there are also some medieval tapestries and illuminated manuscripts of note.

Braganca's market, in the new town next to the cathedral, like all those in the North, is well worth a visit; all varieties of fruit and vegetables are plentiful and cheap here. The local smoked goat's cheese, a speciality of the region, should certainly be tried. Braganca's other speciality which might be tried at a restaurant are *alheiras*, sausages made of veal and bread.

Next to the market is the site of local *festas*, the garden of Antonio Jose Almeida, a pleasantly sheltered spot to sit and relax. The two big summer festivals are the Festas da Nossa Senhora das Gracas and the Festas de São Bartolomeu in August, when the square is full of dancers.

Bragança has long made a virtue of being off-the-beaten-track, and is still full of surprises, among them the bright red postboxes and telephone boxes, which although brought from Britain seem perfectly appropriate in this setting.

Bragança is an excellent place from which to begin an exploration of the 30,000 hectares (117 sq miles) of the **National Park of Montezinho**. The national park headquarters, which has leaflets and routes for both the serious and the occasional rambler, is located on the Rua Alexandre Herculano. The park guides claim that hare, quail, rabbits, and foxes are to be found in the park. Though the guides claim that there are also wild boars and wolves, these species are probably pretty close to extinction if they remain at all.

The N103 to Vinhais and then to Chaves passes through some of the delightful scenery of the park and gives to the motorist a good sense of how the normally harsh, barren landscape is softened by micro-climates of grassy valley bottoms and hillsides covered in woods of oak and horse chestnut.

Excursions off this road to the villages of **Paco**, **Soiera**, or **Vilar de Ossos** will give an idea of the traditional way of life in these settlements of rough stone houses and wooden balconies. Of necessity the villagers have for centuries been largely self sufficient. Their animals are traditionally kept in the ground floor of the house to provide heat for the family quarters on the floor above in the winter, and with the cattle in the fields, cooling ventilation in the heat of the summer. The families produce their own bread and wine, cheeses and hams.

After 20km (12 miles) the road reaches the small agricultural town of **Vinhais**. Founded by King Sancho in the thirteenth century, it is a bustling town with spring water being drunk from a small fountain on the main street and with several lively bars and cafés. Little remains of the original castle but some people do still live within its walls. The main monument in the town is the baroque convent of São Francisco, which has a fine painted ceiling. Although accommodation is sparse in the town there is a *pension* on the Rua Nova.

Continuing on the N103 to Chaves the views are still uniformly magnificent. Over 65km (40 miles) the road rises and falls over the river valleys of the Rabacal and the Calvo. The flatlands between the valleys are burnt ochre in the summer sun. The Tâmega valley, wide and green, is a welcome sight.

Chaves, in many ways the north-western gateway to Trás-os-Montes is a pleasant and ancient town set in the wide fertile plain of the River Tâmega. It is a spa town and the name is a corruption of the original Roman name of the town, *Aquae Fluviae*, meaning 'hot

Farmers and their donkeys on the road to Chaves

waters'. Though the Portuguese word for keys is *chaves* this is not the derivation of the town's name.

The Romans are well remembered in the town as two of the columns of their original bridge, built by the Emperor Trajan, over the Tâmega still stand. They are stout cylindrical columns with details of the honours bestowed by the emperor on local governors or generals clearly legible on them. They were also milestones indicating distances to the important settlements of Astorga in Spanish Leon and Braga. Unfortunately the bridge is so narrow in relation to the needs of the modern town that there is always a bottleneck of traffic at either end. In the summer the river is usually so low that horses and donkeys are let out on the river bed to graze.

When the town was recaptured from the Moors in 1160 it was fortified in order to assure command of the Tâmega valley in the face of the Spanish stronghold of Verin, a mere 27km (17 miles) further up the valley. The castle keep, an imposing battlemented tower, and a section of the outer wall are all that remain of the medieval castle built by King Dinis, as one of the residences of the first Duke of Bragança. Surrounded by a pretty and impeccably kept garden, with colourful flower borders, the keep is now used to house a military museum. The first two floors are rather predictably filled with an-

The castle keep at Chaves

*The bridge with its
Roman milestones
over the River
Tâmega at Chaves*

*The Manueline
pillory at Chaves*

cient guns and armour, but the upper floors provide an interesting insight into the Portuguese experience of World War I and her colonial wars in Angola and elsewhere. The view of the Alto Tâmega from the battlements is superb. On very hot summer days it is not unusual to see a column of smoke rising in the distance. Forest fires, normally caused through the carelessness of visitors when the heat has made the undergrowth as dry as tinder, are a common occurrence.

In the foreground next to the river the modern and convenient municipal swimming pool, which has an outdoor grassy sunbathing area can be seen. The thermal spa itself is also located directly in front of the keep.

Chaves' military history can also be appreciated in the elaborate fortifications of the fort of São Francisco that stands off the Rua de Santo Antonio on the hill near to the railway and bus stations. Chaves was indeed the site of a recidivist Royalist attack launched from Spain, two years after Portugal had become a republic in 1912.

The municipal museum, the Museu de Região Flaviense, is to be found behind the old keep in the lovely Praça de Camões. A large stone coat of arms of the Duke of Bragança sits imposingly above the doorway. The museum details the history of the area through archaeology and ethnography. There are remains of the Roman occupation, such as coins and pottery, and prehistoric stone relics among which is a human figure probably made about 2,000BC.

The baroque Church of the Misericórdia, also in the Praça de Camões, is also worth visiting for its fine and extensive tiles depicting scenes from the Bible and the life of Christ. The pillory that stands in the square is Manueline while the parish church of Santa Maria Maior is, at least partly, Romanesque.

The evening provides the best time to walk around the city, perhaps after having enjoyed a meal at one of the riverside restaurants near to the Ponte Trajano. The manor houses with their attractive verandas around the Praça de Camões and along the Rua Direita provide the perfect atmosphere to round off an evening with a coffee on one of the terraces of the nearby cafés.

The warm springs that originally led to a settlement here are to be found near the river below the keep and city walls. The water can be sampled here. It is alkaline and warm at 73 F (23°C) and above. Ever popular with the Portuguese, the waters are still used to treat rheumatism and digestive disorders. This seems very appropriate as the town is also well known throughout Portugal for its gastronomy. Its most famous dish is *presunto,* a delicate pink smoked ham. It also produces a good red wine and *bolos de carne* or meat cakes. Chaves provides a reasonable range and variety of accommodation and some fine, though not exclusive restaurants around the town centre. There is also a centrally located campsite right next to the Bridge Trajano.

An enjoyable excursion from Chaves is about 2km (1 mile) to the west to **Vale de Anta**, with its prehistoric cave drawings and the huge prehistoric rock of Aboboleira. Having reached the village of Vale de Anta the locals will on request direct the visitor to the rock that is situated down narrow lanes on a stony stretch of heathland. It is a huge granite outcrop with carved elementary human figures and images of axes and axe heads. The carvings probably date from 2,600BC.

The village of **Soutelo**, just a few kilometres (2 miles) further along the road from Chaves, is famous for the weaving of blankets and shawls and is a good place to seek out a bargain, particularly in the early evenings when the local women sit and work together on their front steps.

The traveller from Chaves is faced with a number of options in travelling on from the town. The N2 leads south to the spa town of Vidago. It is also worth taking a diversion, however, out of the Trás-os-Montes region to the remote town of Montalegre to the north, and the remarkable, still essentially medieval, village of Pitões de Júnias.

Both these areas, strictly speaking, lie within the Peneda-Gerês National Park, but Chaves is the nearest town from which they are readily accessible. The N103 initially follows the richly fertile and attractive Tamega valley. Diverging from the course of the river the road passes through dense and shady pine forests.

At the village of Sapiaos, 19km (12 miles) from Chaves, connoisseurs of wine may consider taking the road to **Boticas**, 4km (2 miles) away where the 'Vinho dos Mortos', the wine of the dead, is produced. It is so called because after bottling the wine is kept out of the heat and light by its being buried in the earth and left there for six months. The custom of burying the wine began during the Peninsular War at the beginning of the nineteenth century. In order to prevent Napoleon's French troops from taking their stores of wine the locals hid it underground when they could think of nowhere else. When they recovered the bottles some months later they found the

The castle keep at Montalegre

flavour enhanced and so took up the practice as routine. The Restaurant Santa Cruz, overlooking the River Tâmega is one of the finest in the area.

Five kilometres (3 miles) further along the N311 is the spa town of **Carvalhelos**, worth visiting for its attractive gardens and the nearby *castro*, or hilltop fort, one of the most fascinating Iron Age settlements in the area. Its extensive ditches and defensive pointed stones suggest it was the object of repeated attacks. Carvalhelhos also has a comfortable *estalagem* which is a good base from which to hike and explore the remote villages of the Serra de Barroso, such as Alturas de Barroso and Vilharino Seco.

Returning to the main N103 the road rises into the mountains of the Serra do Barroso. At Gralhos the road to Montalegre, the N308, begins. It travels across a high plateau, generally over 900m (3,000ft) above sea level. It is a harsh landscape of moorland, heather and gorse.

Montalegre, itself, is a busy agricultural market town, serving the remote villages of the Upper Cavado valley. At its heart is a recently restored medieval castle, built in the fourteenth ventury. It is, in its way, a minor classic of medieval military architecture. The small circular bailey has tremendously thick walls and along its

The countryside near Pitões das Júnias

upper platform, narrow long bow slits. In the central courtyard there is a very deep well with a small staircase cut into its sides. The keep has been made safe to climb and has yet to be made into the almost obligatory military museum. The floors have been left with just their original stone benches. The view across the plateau from the top of the keep gives a clear idea of how austerely beautiful, and how off-the-beaten-track, Montalegre is.

From Montalegre it is a mere 9km (5 miles) to the border of the Peneda-Gerês National Park along the N308. The park was founded in 1971 and covers over 28,000 hectares (110 sq miles), making it the largest nature reserve in Portugal. Although very little known abroad, it is an area much appreciated and visited by the Portuguese themselves. It is an area of densely wooded hills, tumbling streams, huge reservoirs and deep gorges. Wild horses, stags and eagles have all made their homes in the park. There are still wolves, too, some kept in special reserves, others wild, though rarely sighted. It is, as one might expect, excellent walking country, and though there are small park offices dotted around the park, the best place to obtain informaton on walking routes is at the head office in Braga, in the Rua de São Geraldo.

At the park border the road runs alongside the Alto Cavado

The simple stone buildings of Pitões das Júnias

reservoir. Hydro-electric power is produced here as at many other places in the park and it contributes substantially to the energy needs of the national economy.

A kilometre ($^1/_2$ mile) beyond the dam at Covalhães lies the road to one of the most interesting villages in the country, **Pitões das Júnias**. Though there is some new building being done in the area around it the village itself has not greatly changed in at least a hundred years. The cottages with their thatched roofs are solidly built out of roughly hewn granite blocks. The lower level of the cottages is used to house oxen, hens and ducks. The families live in the upper floor with their rickety wooden balconies. The design of the houses is well suited to the extremes of weather in this region. In the winter the livestock's body heat helps to warm the house while their absence toiling in the fields or at pasture in the summer keeps the house cool in the heat. The ground floor is also used for storing winter feed for the animals and cereals and potatoes for the families.

The villagers are very open and friendly as they see very few visitors, but it is impossible to sentimentalise their lives as the lack of proper gutters and an underground water system often makes the narrow lanes muddy and dirty. The skins of recently slaughtered goats can usually be seen hanging outside some of the houses. It is a

A deserted monastery near Pitões

fascinating place in which to stroll and it is worth looking out for a beautifully made sundial that has been carved into the side walls of one of the houses.

As one leaves the village there is a turning to the right indicating the *cascadas*, or waterfalls. There is a small carpark just a minute's drive along this path and from this highpoint there is a fine view across this northern section of the park. There is then a path to follow to the magnificent falls of a tributary of the Cavado. Following the river back up the valley away from the falls is rather difficult initially as there is no clear path. However it is well worth it as there are a sequence of delightful, secluded, peaceful and crystal clear natural pools in which to swim and relax.

At the top of the hill there is also a signpost to the *mosteiro*. This, now abandoned, ancient monastery that sits picturequely at the riverside is again worth visiting. Much of the decoration of the doorway and windows is Celtic in inspiration.

All in all Pitões is a fine point at which to end this diversion out of Trás-os-Montes into the National Park of Peneda-Gerês.

South from Chaves towards our starting point of Vila Real, is the new N2 road that follows the Tâmega valley to the spa town of **Vidago**. If the visitor has spent any length of time in Portugal he or

The spa at Vidago

she cannot have failed to have noticed the bottled mineral water that bears the town's name. Vidago is, indeed, probably the most productive of all the country's spas. It is apparently good for the treatment of digestive complaints, containing as it does sodium bicarbonate and, according to its publicity leaflets, radioactive elements.

Before visiting the wide leafy oak lined avenue on either side of which are the hotels and health resorts that make up Vidago, it is worth pausing at the parish church that lies at the head of the valley. This church has a quite beautifully carved Romanesque doorway and a Gothic rose window. The interior, in contrast to the anticipated gilt is predominantly pale blue.

Along the main avenue itself local lace sellers hang their wares between trees. The spa was opened in 1870, and the hotels that sit beneath the trees are mostly Edwardian. The largest and most impressive of these is the huge Palace Hotel with its tremendously grand fenestrated façade. Built in 1910 it houses perhaps the finest grand horseshoe staircase in the North of Portugal and an elegant dining room. It also boasts a swimming pool and, surprisingly perhaps, a state-of-the-art disco. The hotel restaurant is recommended by the local people.

In the grounds of the Palace Hotel is the spa itself, housed in a

The interior of Vidago spa

colourful art-nouveau pavilion. Inside in the marble well sunk 3m (10ft) into the ground, two white uniformed nurses dispense the faintly effervescent water. The water is supposed to be beneficial in relation to allergies and, somehow not surprisingly, like other spas in Portugal, good for digestive complaints. The stained glass of the windows and the marble is decorated in an extraordinary mixture of Classical and Moorish styles. The tiles depict personifications of figures such as glory and fame.

There is a cheerful insouciance about the place despite its ostensible purpose which reflects the optimism of the Edwardian era. In the grounds of the hotel there are tennis courts which are open to the public. There is also a nine-hole golf course on the outskirts of the town, boat trips on the lake near the spa and horses for hire. There is a river beach nearby on the banks of the Tâmega.

South of Vidago on the N2 the scenery is, once again, spectacular as the road rises over the hills of the Serra de Padrela. The town of **Pedras Salgadas** is 12km (7 miles) along this road. Like Vidago, this too is a well known spa town, with attractive gardens and some good hotels. It, again, has swimming pools in the woods, tennis, mini-golf and is a centre for equestrian events and has a general feeling of the *belle epoque*. The waters containing sodium and iron reputedly help

The Palace Hotel, Vidago

with diabetes and cholesterol.

At **Vila Pouca de Aguiar**, set in the green and fertile Aguiar valley, there are interesting places to visit lying in several directions, though the town itself is probably the best place to seek out the local handicrafts of pottery, and weaving in wool and linen.

To the north-east is the turning back into the heart of Trás-os-Montes, on the N206. The road travels through an impressive landscape of round, rolling hills, the harsh granite glinting in the sun often scored by rivers and streams flanked with olive trees. These rivers are particularly suitable for trout fishing. The villages of Algeriz and Argemil are tranquil, traditional communities.

The best place to explore is, perhaps, **Valpaços**, though it is 50km (31 miles) from Vila Pouca de Aguiar along the N206. Valpaços is a very pretty village found between the two picturesque valleys of the River Rabacal and the River Torto. It is a good area from which to fish or to hunt for partridge. It also has an interesting parish church, and some restaurants in which to sample some of the unusual traditional dishes of Trás-os-Montes. These include some of the locally caught and oven-roasted trout, mountain-bean stew and *alheiras*, locally made sausages. The wines from the local co-operative cellars are excellent and cheap, and can, perhaps, be followed up with *cereja de saco*, a local brew made from cherries. The town of Tresminas, off the N206, has a Gothic parish church.

To the south east is the scenic N212 that leads into the Serra de Vilarelho. Old gold mines lie to the right of the road, easily recognisable by the artificial lakes that have been left by the excavations. Thirteen kilometres (9 miles) from Vila Pouca de Aguiar, near to the village of **Alfarela de Jales** lies the remains of the Roman camp of *Cidadelha*.

Heading more or less directly south to the town of Vila Real where these explorations of the 'forgotten' province of Trás-os-Montes began, there is yet one more brief diversion off the main N2. which is worth considering. The N313 through the villages of Adufe and Borbela leads into the **National Park of the Alvão**. It is extremely picturesque and very much off-the-beaten-track even for the Portuguese themselves. There are fine waterfalls at Fisgas de Ermelo and Galegos de Serra. The tiny villages in the park seem to huddle together in the face of the elements. It is also worth looking out for the traditional straw roofed and conical huts that are shelter for shepherds in inclement weather.

Further Information

— Trás-os-Montes —

Tourist Information Offices

Bragança
Avenida 25 Abril
☎ 073 22271

Chaves
Rua de Santo António
☎ 07621029

Vidago
Largo Miguel de Carvalho
☎ 076 97470

Vila Real
Avenida Carvalho Araujo
☎ 059 22819

Places of Interest

Bragança
Museu do Abade de Bacal
(Regional Museum)
Rua Conselheiro Abilio Beça
Open: 10am-12noon, 2-5pm (except
Mondays and holidays).

Chaves
Regional and Military Museum
Camara Municipal de Chaves
Open: 10am-12 noon, 12.30-6pm
(except Mondays).

Spa
1 June to 31 October.

Pedras Salgadas and Vidagão Spas
1 June to 10 October.

Mirandela
Museum of Modern Art
Open: 12.30:6pm Monday to
Friday.

Romeu
Loja das Curiosidades
Open: 9am-7pm.

Vila Real
Mateus Palace
Mateus village
Sabroso road.
Open: guided tours 9am-1pm, 2-
6pm.

Markets

Chaves
Feira dos Santos
31 October and 1 November.

Festivals

Vila Real
Santo Antonio
3 June

São Pedro
29 June.

Bragança
Nossa Senhora das Gracas and São
Bartolomeu
August 14-22.

Mirandela Nossa Senhora de
Amparo
Late July to early August.

São Sebastião
Mid September.

Vinhais
Nossa Senhora da Assuncão
15 August.

6 • Dão Lafoes

The Dão Lafoes region of Portugal stretching in the west to the Serra de Estrela, to the south to the Roman settlement of *Conimbriga*, to the west to the Forest of Buçaco and to the north to the university town of Viseu, is one of the most varied and fascinating areas of the country. More than any other area, too, apart from Trás-os-Montes, it is essentially unexplored.

The best spot from which to begin an exploration of the area is, perhaps, the extensive Roman archaeological site at *Conimbriga*, just below Coimbra. This is an easy place to reach as it is the point at which the A1 from the north ends and where the N1(E1)E80 from Lisbon and the south joins it.

Conimbriga is the largest Roman settlement yet discovered in Portugal, although much of it has still to be excavated. A Celtic town almost certainly stood on the site long before the Romans settled here in the early years of the first century. *Conimbriga* became an important town as it lay on the road between *Olissipo* in the south, the present day Lisbon, and *Augusta Braccara*, now known as Braga. As the excavations have shown the town enjoyed considerable prosperity over several hundrd years, but was nonetheless eventually sacked by the 'barbarian' Suevi as they advanced across the Peninsula in 468. The huge wall which divides the site, apparently hastily constructed since it left some of the finest residences outside of its defences, was probably built around the third century when the inhabitants were in fear of an imminent attack.

Approaching the site from the entrance the visitor is walking along the original road from *Olissipo* to *Augusta Braccara*. To the left of the arch through the defensive wall lie a series of houses, and to the right the complex of rooms known as the Casa dos Repuxos, or House of the Fountains. This is a beautiful example of a Roman villa, dating from the third century. The mosaic floors are clearly visible as

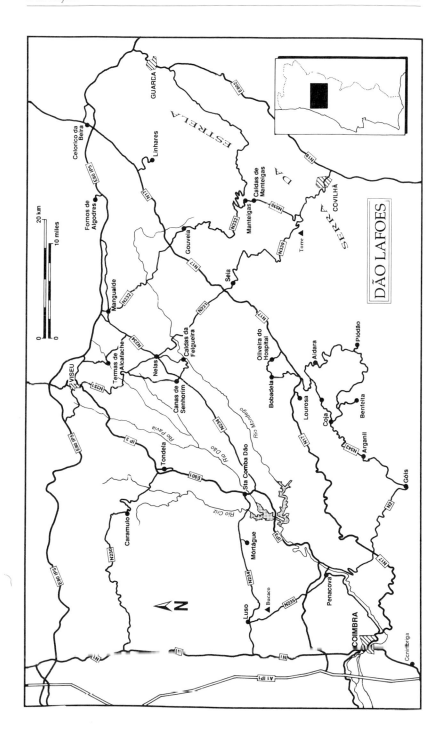

DÃO LAFOES

are the bases of some of the original columns and it is possible to make out the plan of the rooms. The large space at the centre with its small garden was the *peristylum* or central courtyard. In one corner of it can be seen an extraordinarily vivid mosaic, depicting Perseus, the sea god, offering Medusa's head to a creature from the deep. Almost bordering this mosaic was the *atrium*, or entrance hall and at the opposite end of the courtyard, the *triclinium*, originally used as a living room and dining room. The enclosed spaces surrounding these central rooms were originally other living rooms, bedrooms, and kitchens. The room to the left of here has a beautiful mosaic depicting four horses pulling a chariot, some hunting scenes and the four seasons.

Running almost alongside the old Roman road is the tank in which rain water was collected. To the right of it is a lovely mosaic of figures engaged in a deer hunt, and to the left, there is a complex partly geometric composition showing Silenus on an ass. Originally a figure from Greek mythology he was a satyr attendant upon the God of wine, Dionysus. Finally between it and the courtyard is a sitting room with a mosaic of a centaur, holding a standard and surrounded by dolphins, sting rays and wading birds.

Though the houses to the left contain some fine mosaics, especially the House of the Skeletons, so called because after the defensive wall was built this area was used as a cemetery, the other main villa to be described in detail, the House of Cantaber, lies just through the arch and to the left. Unusually, a little is known of the occupants of this house as the Roman chronicler, Idacio of Chaves wrote in 465 that the Suevi had made captives of Cantaber's wife and children. A colonnade originally stood just before the entrance hall. A stone in the paving at the entrance to the courtyard has been sculpted in a rose tracery, exposing the drain below. Following the path through the house the rooms that run along the town wall were all part of the owner's private baths and one of these, surrounded by columns, has a single column that still retains its original decorative red stucco. The rooms at the far end of the house are the *frigidarium*, or cold baths, the *tepidarium*, or warm baths and the *caldarium*, or hot baths. Some of the original lead pipes can still be seen.

In contrast across the path from these final rooms lies the remains of a sixth-century Christian church and a medieval burial area. Some medieval skeletons are exhibited in glass cases nearby.

Much remains to be fully excavated on the site including the

Part of the Roman site of Conimbriga

The central dividing wall at Conimbriga

forum, the amphitheatre, the public baths and private villas. It is a fascinating place to visit and is only likely to change in becoming more so.

The houses made up a civil settlement and in the accompanying museum tools and examples of the work of the ironmongers, carpenters, jewellers, and glass makers who once worked here, have been collected together. All aspects of the life of this provincial roman town are covered so finds such as coins, bronze jewelry and, rather more surprisingly, small badges symbolising commitment to the Roman phallic cult are all on display. As part of the modern complex of which the museum is a part there is also a pleasant café.

Approaching **Coimbra** from Conimbriga along the N1(E1)E80 from the south it is worth remaining on the south side of the River Mondego to visit a couple of the less well known sights in this old university town.

Sitting high above the river and the town the New Convent of Santa Clara affords a great view. The church is dedicated to the Queen Saint Isabel, wife of Dom Dinis, and patron saint of Coimbra, whose goodness was legendary in the kingdom. Her seventeenth-century silver tomb on the high altar of the church is impressive, and was paid for by public subscription among the people of the town. At the other end of the church, behind the iron grill screen, is the saint's original fourteenth-century tomb in Anca stone. As was the custom of the time the noblewoman's effigy is dressed in the habit of a nun, in this case of the Order of the Poor Clares. Part of the complex of buildings has now been leased to the army and houses a small military museum. The vast cloister paid for by João V is also worth seeing.

The Old Convent of Santa Clara, which can be seen from the courtyard in front of the New Convent, off the main road to the Ponte Santa Clara, the Avenida João das Regras, was the original resting place of the Queen Saint and is a marvellously atmospheric and evocative place. This elegant Gothic structure is slowly sinking into the Mondego sands. However it can still be visited and as the visitor admires the fish that swim among the sunken arches the ghostly atmosphere can be savoured. Much of this atmosphere derives from the legend of Ines de Castro.

This convent was also the original resting place of this fourteenth-century Castilian noblewoman whose affair with the young Don Pedro, heir to the Portuguese throne brought their respective countries to the brink of war. The setting for her tomb can still clearly be seen, beautifully carved and with the Castilian coat of arms at its head. Although entirely innocent of treachery herself Ines was

The Old Convent of Santa Clara, Coimbra, slowly sinking into the sands of the River Mondego

hounded by the king of Portugal, Afonso, because her brothers had
been discovered in a plot against Pedro the Cruel of Castile. By
killing Ines, his son's lover, the king could show his good faith and
avoid Pedro's wrath. Ines was finally caught and murdered in the
Garden of Tears in 1355, just half a kilometre and an easy walk
further up the river, along the Avenida Ines de Castro. After her
death Pedro claimed to have secretly married Ines in the church of
São Vicente in the remote north eastern city of Bragança. When he
became king Pedro had Ines' body exhumed, dressed and set upon
a throne across the river in the Mosteiro de Santa Cruz. His courtiers
were then required to pay her homage. The significance of this tragic
figure lies, perhaps, in her symbolising the thousands of innocent
lives that were to be lost in the struggles between Portugal and Spain
over the ensuing centuries.

Before leaving the south side of the town it may be a pleasant
contrast to visit the model village, encompassing all historical and
regional architectural styles in the country in 'Portugal Dos
Pequininos', which is located almost right next to the Old Convent.

Though the main sights of Coimbra lie on the hill above the river
on the north side, on the main street, the Rua de Sofia is to be found
another of the country's great historical buildings, the aforementioned Monastery of Santa Cruz.

The building was originally constructed by São Teotonio in the
twelfth century. When this was destroyed the present edifice was
worked upon in the sixteenth century by the Coimbra school of
sculptors, Nicholas Chanterene, Jean de Rouen and Diogo and João
Castilho. They both worked on the complex Renaissance portico of
the exterior, though the fineness of their work is being lost through
the effects of weathering and the city's fumes.

Inside the church on either side of the high altar are situated the
tombs of the country's first kings, the redoubtable Afonso
Henriques, and his successor, Sancho I. Along with the Renaissance
pulpit they form some of the finest works of the Coimbra school of
sculpure. The ceiling is Manueline and in the gallery are some beautifully carved wooden stalls dating from the sixteenth century. The
chairs are surmounted by wooden friezes of armillary spheres, the
symbol of Manuel I, and ships and castles, symbols of the expansion-
ism of the kingdom in its Golden Age.

The sacristy, which contains four sixteenth-century paintings,
leads into the Cloister of Silence, designd by Marcos Pires in 1524,

Coimbra and the River Mondego from the Old University

showing the Manueline style at its most elegant and uncomplicated. The bas relief scenes around its walls show Christ's life and passion.

Coimbra is most famous, of course, as the home of Portugal's first university which originated around 1290 with the teachings of the monks of the Santa Cruz monastery. Ancient traditions are maintained by the students, who live in democratic groups known as *repúblicas* determined by the region of the country from which they come. The romantic Coimbra *fado* songs, traditionally composed by students may be heard during term time in the small bars off the Rua da Sofia, near the Santa Cruz monastery, and in the bars around the old cathedral.

The main sixteenth-century university buildings are on the hill overlooking the town, arranged around a large and impressive courtyard, overlooked by a baroque clock tower, nicknamed 'the Goat'. At the centre of it is a statue of João III. The double stairway to the right of and below the tower leads to the administrative heart of the university and the Sala dos Capelos, where students matriculate and receive their degrees, which can be visited. The Manueline-style ceiling has fine decorative gilt work and the walls are hung with pictures of former kings. From the catwalk on the exterior of the building there is a fine view of the town. Returning to the courtyard

The courtyard of Coimbra University

immediately noticeable to the left is the twisted Manueline coils of the doorway to the university chapel. Designed by Marco Pires, its interior is decorated with tiles and an unusual frescoed ceiling.

The most famous of the university buildings is the library that lies further down the same side of the courtyard. Like the Cloister of Silence at the New Convent of Santa Clara, it was presented to the university by João V in the early eighteenth century. The sequence of three rooms contain what must be some of the richest decoration of a secular building to be found anywhere. The shelves are inlaid with jacaranda and rosewood and decorated with marble and gold leaf in a rapture of baroque exuberance. The portrait at the far end of the room is of the library's founder, João V.

Leaving the courtyard by the arched exit that lies diagonally opposite the library, and turning to the left past the rather nonde-script New Cathedral brings the visitor to Coimbra's finest museum housed in what was formerly the Archbishop's palace, the Museum of Machado Castro. The Renaissance porch gives on to a delightful courtyard and on the far side there is a loggia designed by the seventeenth-century Italian architect, Filippo Terzi, which gives a great view over the Old Cathedral and the town below. The museum feels modern and spacious despite the age of the building. The

A family working in the fields near Linares

Young women make carpets in the villages near Nelas

The Temple of Diana, Évora

The restored interior of the fin-de-siecle *salon, Cadaval Palace, Évora*

ground floor is devoted to Coimbra's extensive sculptural heritage. Among the medieval works is a delightful statue of a knight on horseback with his mace slung over his shoulder. Other fifteenth- and sixteenth-century sculptures have works from the Coimbra school by Nicholas Chantarene and Jean de Rouen. The upper floor contains some rooms that are interesting in themselves, for example, the fifteenth-century 'Macao Salon' and the 'Arab Salon', with its Mudejar ceiling. Its exhibits are a great mixture of religious painting, Portuguese pottery, French furniture from the period of Louis XV and oriental art.

Halfway down the hill sits the last of Coimbra's great historical monuments, the Old Cathedral. This is probably the most important Romanesque building in Portugal and constructed between 1140 and 1175, it is certainly one of the oldest. Realistically, however, it is not one of the most attractive, the natural tendency to dullness in the Romanesque style being here further accentuated by the original need to build a place of worship that could resist armed attack. In the Middle Ages Coimbra was often the front line between Christian and Moor. The façade is therefore very reminiscent of a fortress. The design was again the responsibility of French craftsmen, predecessors of the more well known Rouen and Chanterene. The north door, added to the building in 1530, and one of the first to show the influence of the Renaisssance, has been attributed to Jean de Rouen, but as it is weathering very badly this may never be known for certain.

Inside the cathedral the presence in the Chapel of St Peter of some rare tiles from Sevilla should be noted, as should the exuberance of the high altar with its complex succession of figures. At the base of this gothic work are the four Evangelists supporting the Resurrection and the Nativity. Above that is a depiction of the Assumption of the Virgin. The cloister is an interesting example of early Gothic, built in the thirteenth century.

In the eastern section of the city near to the Praça de Dom Dinis there is an enjoyable contrast to the historical sights that dominate Coimbra. The Botanical Garden has a great variety of exotic and rare species of plants. Its pleasant leafy avenues were laid out on the orders of the effective dictator of Portugal of the time, the Marquis of Pombal, in the eighteenth century. Next to the garden is the six- teenth-century São Sebastião aqueduct, built to take water to the upper parts of the town.

Coimbra has an extensive range of hotels and restaurants, though the cheapest hotels near the central railway station, and incidentally the 'red light' district, should be avoided. The central railway station also has a well known car hire agency office. There is also a campsite and youth hostel in the town. The A1 motorway from just beyond the north-west edge of the city is a fast route to Oporto, the main city of the north of the country.

From Coimbra a good route to gain a flavour of the landscape that dominates the Dão Lafoes is the N110, along the River Mondego to Penacova. The road winds its way along the north bank of the river through pine woods and at the water's edge are tiny fields of maize and orange groves. Intermittently there are strips of sandy beaches and these are good spots for a swim. When the banks rise more steeply there are olive groves, and above them ridges of granite. About 10km (6 miles) or so out of Coimbra is the tiny village of **Foz de Caneiro**. This place is solely remarkable for the extremely precipitant slopes on which the houses have been built. They rise in tiers above the river.

Penacova, a larger town set high above the river, is an excellent place to stop for a meal or for the night. It has some excellent restaurants, one of which, the Restaurante Panoramica, as its name implies has one of the most attractive views in the Dão Lafoes. This same view can also be enjoyed from the balcony that forms one side of the town's main square. The River Mondego majestically winds its way to the town of Coimbra far below. The church at Penacova, too, is worth visiting; built in 1627, it has two unusual neo-Classical side altars.

Across the river from Penacova is a campsite and also the picking up point for an enterprising venture by the University Canoeing Club. From here the visitor can hire a canoe for an exciting trip back to Coimbra. The organisers, at the same time take all of their customers' luggage to the meeting point in the city. Among the local crafts are the curious delicately and elaborately carved cocktail sticks that are on sale in the local shops. There are a couple of comfortable and respectable *pensions* in the village.

An accessible trip in the vicinity of Penacova is to the ancient Benedictine convent of Lorvão. The road from the village is unnumbered but is clearly signposted. The convent was founded in the ninth century, though most of the buildings date from the eighteenth century. Much of the complex is now used as a psychiatric institu-

A herd of mountain goats in the Serra de Estrela

tion, but the church which reputedly contains the skull of a Moorish king can still be visited.

From Penacova there is a delightful scenic route north west to the Buçaco forest along the N235, but that area will be described in detail in a later part of this chapter. To the north-east along the N2 the route is at first along the valley of the River Mondego and then the road rises steeply towards the impressive hydroelectric dams at Oliveira and Aguiera.

South from here the N112 winds its way through pine forests and quiet villages like Arrifana and Vila Nova de Poaires until it reaches the wide, beautiful and fertile River Ceira at **Vila Nova de Ceira**. Following the N342-3 from Vila Nova into the foothills of the Serra da Lousa gives a fine panoramic view of the surrounding area. Returning to the N2, $5^1/_2$km (3 miles) beyond Vila Nova is the small town of **Góis**. Set picturesquely on the river, it is a pleasant tranquil town. The bridge bears the crest of Don Manuel I, and is claimed locally to have been built in the Manueline period, but it has obviously been rebuilt several times. There is not a great deal to do in the town except to walk the narrow cobbled streets, sit in the cafés and enjoy the excellent cakes that are made in the area.

Arganil, a quietly stylish local town, lies just a few kilometres (2

Most of the population in the Serra de Açor still work on the land

miles) north of Góis along the N342. The centre has several surprisingly modern paved walkways in its shopping area. The traditional Portugal is still here though. There are low relief tableaux of the stations of the cross dotted around the town centre. The parish church is also remarkable for the fifty painted panels of the Saints to be seen on its ceiling.

The town hall is partially occupied by a small archaeological museum containing prehistoric arrow heads, flints,and necklaces taken from sites at Seixo da Beira, near Oliveira do Hospital, and San Pedro Dias near Poiares. There are also some Roman exhibits, candle holders, shards of pottery and coins taken from old Roman settlements in the area.

There is a locally renowned sanctuary to visit at Nossa Senhora de Mont Alto, just a few kilometres (2 miles) to the south-west, which can the more easily be found by picking up one of the local maps at the town hall. A succesion of churches line the route before the last and best of them, the Capelo de Senhor de Ladeira, which has been a local place of pilgrimage for many years. The greatest feast day when the whole of Arganil visits the place is on 15 August. In front of the gates of the sanctuary is one of the strangest statues in the region, one of Christ as a child dressed in the clothes of the Napo-

Typical slate houses in the Serra de Açor

leonic era. The view from the Mount to the Serra de Lousa in the west and the Serra de Estrela in the east is very impressive.

The most ancient church in the region, however, is to be found on the road to Sarzedo, the N342.4, just a kilometre ($^1/_2$ mile) out of town to the north-west. This chapel of São Pedro is an austere thirteenth-century church, unusual in so far as it is not, like most provincial churches of this period, Romanesque, but is rather of Gothic design. The church walls are constructed out of roughly hewn stones, but the three-naved building still has a simple grandeur.

Travelling further along this road there is a fine campsite along the River Alva, which has boats and canoes for hire and is an excellent spot from which to explore the beauty of the surrounding woods on foot.

Travelling north from Arganil, along the N342, the landscape is that of moorland. The hills are rolling and covered with heather and gorse and golden bracken. The occasional houses are surrounded by maize fields. Twelve kilometres (7 miles) along the road is **Coja**, an attractive town set on both sides of the River Alva. It has a good campsite, and, again, if tranquility and rural beauty is desired, is a good spot from which to explore the surrounding countryside.

The particular nature of the landscape is due to the presence of

A farmer in the Serra de Açor

the brown slate-like rock, schist. This means that much of the high ground in the area is only suitable for keeping goats. Following the N344 south towards Benfeita and Piódão, around the hairpin bends of harsh schist, the landscape is full of striking contrasts. In the valleys below there are lush green pastures around little streams providing pasture for cattle and the growing of maize, next to the brown-orange hues of houses built of schist. There is a strong sense here of a centuries-old way of life left undisturbed.

The village of **Benfeita** is a very old, pretty village, its main street lined with vine trellisses. It is built close to the stream at the valley bottom, and exploring off the main street there are a maze of narrow schist surfaced alleys. The hard impermeable sides of the hillsides around mean that rain water rushes straight off and brings a constant danger of flooding to the village. At the foot of many of the doors can be seen sandbags or planks of wood. The villagers are very friendly and will enthusiastically point you on to the protected parkland of the Serra de Acor, and, in particular to the beautiful waterfall of Fraga de Pena.

The **Serra de Açor** is located just a few kilometres (2 miles) to the south via a road that is unmarked on most maps and which, though occasionally quite rough, is passable. Though the hills here have

*The waterfalls of
Fraga de Pena*

suffered quite badly from forest fires in recent years the parkland is still a remarkably remote, tranquil and beautiful area.

The waterfalls of **Fraga de Pena** are certainly worth any trouble taken to reach them. They are located on the right-hand side of the road and are clearly marked. Though there are some picnic tables set up near the lowest of the falls the place is usually deserted even in mid-summer. Steps have been built to help visitors climb up the side of the falls and at each succesive fall there is an old watermill, with its machinery still intact inside, and a beautifully clear rock pool. Hollowed out tree trunks, too, can be seen that were once used to channel the stream to the mills. The falls are particularly attractive because of the way in which the schist, which is here intermingled with marble, is worn by the water into flat, sheer surfaces. This gives a curiously beautiful effect, especially at the highest of the falls, some

*The terraced hillside
at Piódão*

25-30m (80-100ft) tall, which rather resembles a Cubist painting. It is
worth climbing to the top for the rather surprising sight of a fertile
field of maize and peach trees at the head of the falls. The highest rock
pool is an ideal place for a swim as it is quite deep.

The tiny village of **Padroeiro** lies between the falls and the Mata
Nature Reserve. It is an essentially unremarkable village except for
the presence here of the workshop of a maker of traditional wooden
spoons. The villagers will readily point the way and his tiny, clut-
tered workshop, full of wood shavings and spoons stacked ready for
sale, is worth seeing. With encouragement he will demonstrate his
skill, producing an attractive implement from a rough hewn piece of
pine wood in a matter of minutes, using only two knives. For a tiny
investment the spoon can of course then be purchased. The craftsman's shavings are used by the villagers for barbecuing sardines.

The narrow streets of the village of Piódão

The road to Piódão now goes through the Mata Nature Reserve. Opposite the reserve's headquarters, just 200m into the park, there is a path on the left-hand side down to a typical traditional schist house, set among attractive horse chestnut and oak trees. This is a good area to explore on foot.

Travelling on by car, however, the road becomes steep and at times quite rutted. Nonethless the views from the tops of what are effectively the foothills of the Serra de Estrela are quite magnificent. The town ahead that can be seen from the first summit is Monte Frio, and, as its name suggests, the wind is quite cold up here. Eagles nest on these exposed hillsides and can often be seen hanging on the air currents high in the valleys.

If anything, however, the views become even more spectacular as the road rises to the final ridge before Piódão and a rapid descent to what must be one of the most unusual, and certainly the most off-the-beaten-track, villages in Portugal. **Piódão** has been designated by the Portuguese government as a village in which the traditional construction of the houses in schist will be maintained. Indeed, when houses of more modern construction become due for repair they are replaced by schist buildings. Not only the houses, however, but also the roads and steps, the guttering and the drains are all made from the traditional material. The quite beautiful effect is that of a village that has grown out of the layers of rock of the hillside.

It is an extraordinary place to explore with hens running loose in the narrow streets and the sounds of other livestock in the rooms beneath the houses. All cars are parked in the area in front of the parish church as the streets of the village are too narrow to accommmodate them. There is a simple bar and the locals are friendly. The one incongruous note is sounded by the curious parish church which seems to be of recent construction and emphasises the curious connection between the indigenous architectural style, known as the Manueline, and the type of fairy castle made famous by Walt Disney. Accommodation may be available on request in the bar but it is likely to be very rudimentary.

Travelling north from Piódão to Aldcia das Dez the landscape is outstandingly pictureque and remote. Many of the slopes are terraced for the cultivation of vines, or are covered with pine forests. The local wine is excellent. Just ask for the wine of the region in the shops. There is a fine campsite and a *pensão* and restaurant, just beyond Penalva de Alva at the Ponte de Tres Entradas or Bridge of

A stonemason at work by the side of the road near Lourosa

the Three Entrances. The campsite, like many others in the Dão Lafoes, is set at the river's edge and is a good place from which to swim or hire a boat.

Just a few kilometres to the north is the main N17 road from Coimbra to Guarda. Along this particular stretch of the road are a large number of craftsmen and their workshops. For example, stonemasons stand at the roadside chipping away at great slabs of rock to make beautiful granite and marble hearths. Each one will take about two weeks of constant work. Unfortunately, the lack of protection for the stonemason's ears has left many of them very hard of hearing. There are also along the way a carpenter and a coppersmith's workshop.

Just off this road too at **Bobadela**, there is a small museum with an interesting collection of eighteenth- and nineteenth-century clothes, and in front of the parish church a well-preserved Roman arch, set next to a Manueline pillory. Near the village there are the remains of a Roman theatre.

Should the general atmosphere of this region have charmed the visitor then there are many other small towns and villages off the main road to explore, each with something of interest. The small town of **Oliveira do Hospital** on the N230 has a beautiful chapel, the

The ancient church at Lourosa

Capela dos Ferreiros, with a celebrated statue of a horseman shoul-dering his mace. Oliveira has at least one good hotel and at Povoa das Quartas a little further along the N17 to the north there is the Pousada de Santa Barbara.

Returning to the main road and heading just a few kilometres south the village of **Lourosa** lies just off the main road, and in it is to be found one of the finest and least known of the monuments heavily influenced by the Moors in Portugal. The parish church of Lourosa, situated in a leafy little square where villagers gather to talk in the evenings, was built in the Mozarabic style perhaps as far back as 950AD. Its horseshoe arches are all original and give to the interior an unmistakably Moorish sense of simplicity and harmony. It is small in scale, but in its way is as perfect as any other monument to the Moors in the Iberian Peninsula.

The building was subsequently used by the Christian church prior to the Reformation. Just to the left of the side entrance is a stone slab about knee height. This was the original confession seat on which the priest would sit to hear the sins of the penitent kneeling before him. To the right of the main entrance, too, is another re-minder of the early church. The stone slab on the floor with a slight well in it was the first baptismal stone, at a time when many christians were adult converts who would be baptised standing up.

The church, as a whole, is in such fine condition because of the extensive restoration works that were carried out in the 1940s. The bell tower that was once part of the front doorway was removed and rebuilt in its present place just behind the church. The baroque pulpit and altar were also removed in order to gain a sense of the simple elegance of the original construction. The visitor will almost certainly be shown around this precious architectural gem by a charming local housewife whose mimed explanations of the various parts of the church add to one's sense of a rather special discovery.

The N17 in effect forms the south and eastern boundary of the Dão Lafoes region. It is bordered at this point by the highest mountain range in Portugal, the Serra da Estrela. Fortunately for the visitor there is, indeed, easy access to the highest point of the range, Torre, and some its finest scenery.

The N336 through the rather disappointing, ugly industrial town of **Seia** takes one on a delightful scenic route rising reasonably gently to 1,993m (6,537ft) at Torre. Seia has a government-run hotel, an *estalagem* with an excellent restaurant, and there are several *pensions* and restaurants along the way. The tourist office in Seia also has information about manor houses in the national park itself which, if they can be afforded, provide the best way to enjoy a couple of days walking in beautiful mountain scenery. The views are uniformly delightful and a good place to stop on the journey to Torre is at the first hydroelectric dam at the Escura Lake.

The local strong mountain cheeses made from goat's milk, famous throughout the country, are available here. Seia, like Gouveia and other towns in the region has cheese fairs in February and March. The herds of goats in the area may be as many as two hundred in number, and may be herded by the extraordinary mountain dog that is unique to these mountains. It is a large brindled dog rather like an athletic St Bernard and exudes a sense of authority in its powerful stride and sharp bark. It is said to have been cross bred with wolves. The shepherds check on the herds every morning and evening but otherwise the dog is left with the responsibility of keeping the herd together and protecting it. Each of the herds has a 'lead' goat which is easily identified by the bell around its neck.

The pine woods of the lower slopes have now given way to gorse, bracken and exposed peaks. It is likely that some of the peaks around will be covered with clouds. Unfortunately the highest point,

*Souvenir stalls on
the summit of Torre
selling leather and
goat skins*

Torre, has been spoilt by excessive commercialisation that leaves the
visitor struggling to appreciate the view through the souvenir stalls
of goat skins and leather coats. However the disappointment is
compensated for by the peace and tranquility of the dammed lake,
the Lagoa do Viriato, just a few kilometres further along the road to
Covilhã which is a pleasant place to swim, to sunbathe or to walk.

Undoubtedly the highlight of this detour into the mountains is
a trip down the N338 along the Zêzere glacial valley. This is again just
off the Torre to Covilhã road. It is a classic glacial valley and very
lovely with scree and rocks on the western side and pine trees on the
eastern. The flat valley bottom is green and cultivated with thatched
cottages and stone corrals for the animals. At the far end of the valley
just before it reaches the pleasant spa town of Caldas de Manteigas,
are some cottages which can be approached and inspected. Should

The Zêzere glacial valley

you be visiting the area in the winter look out for the sign to the right to the Poço do Inferno, the 'Well of Hell', a mountain waterfall that freezes over as the temperature falls.

Manteigas itself has several good hotels. Just outside of Manteigas, 8km (5 miles) along the Gouveia road is the Pousada de São Lourenço. Along the route watch out for the many strangely shaped rocks on the exposed hillsides in particular about mid-way to Gouveia, an upright outcrop called the Cabeca do Velho, a name which translates as 'the head of the old man'.

Gouveia, like Seia, is an industrial district and contains little to detain the visitor. The scrubland on the plain around it, too, is rather unattractive. The tourist office can, however, give detailed directions to the nearby ancient *castro* of Alfatima. The name, legend has it, came from a Moorish princess who took refuge there during Christian attacks upon the Moor's stronghold. A stone tablet was found at the site which apparently records a visit by Julius Caesar in 38BC. The tablet is now in the Santa Maria church in Manteigas. Gouveia also has an attractive modern art gallery and some reasonable accommodation.

Returning north to the main N17 soon brings the traveller to the turning to the fortress town of Linhares. The valley leading to

Donkeys are still used for carrying agricultural products in the Dão Lafoes

Linhares is green and rolling with deciduous woods of oak, and elm and with vines, maize and potatoes being grown here. Traditional methods of farming are still used; for instance a number of family groups work together in the fields to harvest quickly a crop belonging to just one family that might otherwise be lost. A visit in the late summer might well coincide with oxen being used to plough up and harvest the potato crop.

Linhares itself is a very ancient town that has obviously seen in the past much greater wealth than it currently enjoys. A donkey carrying a farmer is almost as likely to be seen in the streets than a car. Nonetheless many of the houses in the narrow streets are large with attractive balconies or grills and several have delightful Manueline decoration around their windows, such as in the Largo de Misericórdia. The town pillory, too, is decorated with an armillary sphere, the symbol of Dom Manuel.

The defensive wall of the town stands on the exposed rocks at the western edge of the town. The walls give splendid views over the surrounding area, and roughly hewn as they are from huge rocks themselves they seem almost to have grown out of the granite terrain. Just within the walls is the parish church, set in a pretty little square. Houses around the square are dated as early as 1709. The

The gateway into the main courtyard of Évora University

Painted tiles or azulejos in the courtyard of Évora University

Monsaraz from the castle keep, Alto Alentejo

A Manueline window and a stable entrance in the town of Linhares

church was extensively rebuilt in 1743, but some of the original Romanesque carvings can be seen in the figures and crosses carved above the side door. The interior of the church is attractively decorated and, rather surprisingly for a place genuinely off-the-beaten-track, the church contains three wall paintings by Portugal's finest classical painter, the Grão Vasco. Linhares is, overall, a curiously timeless town which seems quietly content that its days of importance and wealth have gone.

The main N17 road passes through the fortress town of **Celorico da Beira**, which has several good hotels. Should sixteenth- and seventeenth-century castles be to your liking then another one can be reached 17km (11 miles) north of Celorico da Beira along the N102 at **Trancoso**.

The N16 to the beautiful town of Viseu, however, can be picked up before reaching Celorico da Beira. About 11km (7miles) along the N16 is the turning to the village of Fornos de Algodres, and beyond it, the tiny village of Algodres itself.

Along the road north from the N16 the landscape is very attractively wooded with pines. In **Algodres** is the church of Santa Maria Maior, whose age, beauty and decoration would suggest that the village was once a much more important place than it is now. The church, formerly the principal one of the district, is named after the statue of Our Lady above the altar, and it is one of only four or five churches in Portugal that are allowed to exhibit this type of statue. The church was first mentioned in the reign of Dom Sancho I. The principal beauty of the place, however, are the Hispano-Arab tiles (probably seventeenth century)that decorate the two side altars. This is one of very few places were these beautiful geometric tiles can still be seen in their original position, on the side altars, where they are protected from dust and sunlight by curtains. The tiles were, indeed, only discovered in 1988, as they had been hidden by, and therefore protected by, painted wooden screens.

In the vestry the visitor will be surprised to see a series of portraits of the Twelve Apostles and two angels. They are dusty and in need of careful restoration yet they are still very attractive and, judging by the lack of perspective, medieval. The background of stars on the central panel would suggest a link to Santiago de Compostela. Perhaps the former importance of the church lay in its lying on the pilgrim's route to the supposed burial place of St James at Santaigo in northern Spain.

A quiet village near Linhares

Women making lace tablecloths at Carvalho near Nelas

The views over the valley of the River Mondego as the road drops to Fornos de Algodres are very attractive. In the village itself there is a disco and several restaurants.

The new, fast IP5 road from Guarda to Viseu can be picked up 14 km (9 miles) from Viseu. Before exploring that lovely city, however, it is worth taking a road south from Mangualde into the main wine growing portion of the region.

Shortly after passing through Mangualde, on the N234, there is a right-hand turning to the pleasant spa town of **Termas de Alcafache**, built on the banks of the River Dão. South of Mangualde is the prehistoric dolmen, known as the Anta da Cunha Baixa. The N234 continues south to the small town of Nelas noted for its carpet making.

Like many other towns in the region Termas de Alcafache is essentially a health resort. The large grey building on the far side of the river in the centre of the town is the spa itself which can be visited. It is comprised of a large number of baths, showers and rooms in which patients are hosed down with the therapeutic waters. If a visit inside does not appeal it is still possible to appreciate the natural spring as the water that emerges at the riverside in front of the spa is natural spring water. What is surprising is at just what a high tem-

Painted tiles on the bottling plant for Dão wine at Nelas

perature the water emerges from the earth. There is swimming on both sides of the picturesque bridge from small beaches.

South of the spa and before the town of Santar is the tiny village of **Carvalho**. This village is noted in the region for the quality of its handicrafts. In the early evening in particular, groups of young women sit together on the steps of their houses weaving carpets, made with wool embroidered onto canvas. Older women, too, sit together engaged in the tremendously delicate work of making lace tablecloths and antimacassars.

Returning to the main N241 south from Viseu and travelling towards **Nelas** brings the pleasure of visiting a centre for the bottling and distribution of Dão wines. The Vinicola de Nelas, $^1/_2$ km ($^1/_4$ mile) outside of the town, is an exporter of Dão wines all over Europe, turning out over a thousand bottles per day. Each vintage is graded by the Dão Wine Institue in Viseu. There is a tour of the bottling plant by one of the plant officials, though his English is liable to be very limited, and an opportunity to buy some excellent wine at a very attractive price.

Travelling north from the Termas de Alcafache very quickly brings the traveller to the second great historical city of the region after Coimbra, **Viseu**. It is an ancient settlement with at its northern end the remains of the foundations of a Roman fort. This was probably built by Brutus Callaecus, in the second century, during his victorious march northwards to the Douro and beyond after the defeat of the Lusitanians, and the death of their remarkable leader, Viriatus.

Ironically enough the area has popuarly been known as the 'Cava de Viriato', in the erroneous belief that the barbarian leader laid the foundations. His statue, the figure set in a suitably martial pose, stands nearby. Responsible for holding the Romans at bay in the Iberian Peninsula for over ten years he was only finally defeated when the Romans bribed his own lieutenants to murder him. As Viriatus fought most of his battles in what is now modern Spain, the sculptor was appropriately a Spaniard, Mariano Benliure. The large square before the statue provides a good place from which to get one's bearings.

The old town of Viseu stands before you on the hill. To the right is the Romanesque cathedral and next to it the white baroque towers of the Church of the Misericórdia. It is reached by passing over the rather dirty and unappealing River Pavia, a tributary of the Mondego.

Viseu contains a very fine old quarter. The cobbled cathedral square provides one of the most appealingly proportioned public spaces in the country, and the maze of medieval streets that lie behind it are a delight to wander in and explore. The cathedral was originally built in the twelfth century when the royal couple, Dom Afonso and Dona Teresa had made the town their home. It was only after the town had been sacked by the Castilians that João I, in the fourteenth century, insisted on the building of a defensive wall around the old town. The main remnant of this can be seen in the Porto do Soar gate built in 1472 by Afonso V which forms the entrance to the old town from the Rua de Serpa Pinto.

The present façade of the cathedral dates from the seventeenth century. At its centre is the twelfth-century patron saint of Viseu, São

*The statue of Dom
Duarte with the
cathedral behind,
Viseu*

Teotonio, Portugal's first saint. The interior is a hybrid of diferent
styles while its atmosphere is almost broodingly spiritual. The vault
is Manueline, dating from the sixteenth century while the twisted
columns are Gothic. The shafts of light that fall from the stained glass
windows in the towers above the nave emphasise the moorish influence, while the way in which the twin pulpits emerge, twisting from
their supporting pillars suggests the easy transition from the Gothic
to the baroque in Portugal.

The keystones of the vault are decorated with the arms of various
bishops and the symbols of kings, such as the pelican of João II. The
baroque altarpiece is impressive but it unfortunately replaced, on the
orders of the bishop, João of Melo in 1674, what must have been the
even more remarkable fourteen-panel life of Christ painted by the
school of the Grão Vasco. This series can now be seen in the nearby

Grão Vasco Museum. Above the high altar is a beautiful thirteenth-century Virgin in Anca stone, probably produced in Coimbra. The stalls of the choir, decorated with Manueline motifs, are very attractive as is the lectern made from wood imported from Brazil.

The highlight of the cathedral is probably, however, the Renaissance cloister, with its Ionic columns, one of the most elegant in Portugal. Its lower level is lined with eighteenth-century tiles, statues and a series of small chapels with votive candles on metal stands before each one. The finest of these chapels, that of Our Lady of Mercy, contains a beautiful sixteenth-century low relief of Christ's descent from the Cross, again believed to have been produced by the Coimbra school. The monumental doorway that leads from the cloister back into the cathedral is in a transitional style between the Romanesque and the Gothic. It is one of the earliest examples of Portuguese art influenced by the Renaissance.

Above the cloister, in what was the chapterhouse, a small museum of sacred art has been installed. Its finest exhibits are a twelfth-century Gospel and Byzantine cross, and two-thirteenth century Limoges enamel coffers.

Fascinating as Viseu's cathedral is with its hybrid of styles, the artistic pride of place in the town defintely goes to the Grão Vasco Museum, which, with its well organised and maintained presentation of the golden period of Portuguese paintings, sits next to the cathedral.

The museum occupies what was once the bishop's palace, built in the sixteenth century and then known as the 'Paco dos Tres Escaloes'. The Viseu School, as Vasco Fernandes — usually known as the 'Grão Vasco' or Great Vasco — Gaspar Vaz and their pupils came to be known, worked in the town between 1505 and 1550. They, like the Portuguese Primitives before them, were heavily influenced by Flemish art and in particular by Van Eyck. They developed their own unique style, however, with an increased realism in their use of colour and in their depiction of backgrounds. Another feature of their work as can be seen in the size of many of their canvases was a realism in the depiction of the height and size of human figures.

Though Gaspar Vaz's finest works are to be found in the church of São João in Tarouca, two mature works are to be seen in the museum, the *The Last Supper* and *Christ in the House of Martha*. Vasco Fernandes' principal works are to be found in the museum and it was he above all who introduced a new note of realism and drama into

The Church of the Misericórdia, Largo de Se, Viseu

his compositions. The second floor is devoted to the school's work. The Grão Vasco's two masterpieces are *Calvary* and *St Peter on his Throne*. The latter was undertaken to rival Gaspar Vaz's composition on the same theme that now hangs in Tarouca. The former fourteen-panelled cathedral altarpiece is also to be seen here and its variable quality suggests that it was the work of a number of painters from the school.

The ground floor of the museum contains a range of sculpture from the thirteenth to the eighteenth century. The finest pieces are a fourteenth-century *Throne of Grace* and a thirteenth-century Virgin with the body of Christ. On the first floor are some Spanish paintings dating from the Spanish government of Portugal in the sixteenth century and a selection of work by modern Portuguese painters.

The final, and very distinctive building on the Largo de Se is the eighteenth-century Church of the Misericórdia. The elegant baroque façade, facing the cathedral, however, rather belies the austere neo-Classical interior whose only concession to exuberant decoration is the organ. Ask in the local tourist office about any classical music concerts that occasionally take place on the steps of the Misericórdia in the summer.

Before leaving the old quarter the narrow surrounding streets with their sixteenth- and seventeenth-century houses should be visited. One of the original gateways through the old city walls, the Porta do Soar, lies just below the Misericórdia on the Rua de Serpa Pinto on the descent into the modern town centre. The ancient keep on the Rua Dom Duarte has a strikingly decorated Manueline window.

The modern heart of the town lies at the foot of the Rua Formosa around the Praça de República, known locally as the Rossio. This spacious tree-lined square has a statue of the Infante Dom Henrique, better known to the outside world as Henry the Navigator, the First Duke of Viseu. At one end of the Rossio, too, are some fine modern tiles showing the life of the people in the surrounding countryside, by the contemporary painter, Joaquim Lopes.

At the junction of Rua Formosa and the Rua do Commercio is to be found Viseu's market which is open every weekday morning. It is a colourful lively place with the locals noisily bartering and great armfuls of cabbages or potatoes being weighed out on ancient mechanical scales.

Viseu's great, and mainly agricultural fair, dedicated to São Mateus is in September. On 24 June in the village of Vila de Moinhos on the River Pavia just outside Viseu there is an annual procession in traditional dress in honour of John the Baptist. A whole range of hotels, and *pensions* are available in Viseu.

Travelling south from Viseu along the N2/E801 is a very pleasant drive in the shadow of the Serra de Caramulo. The villages are quiet and very rarely see visitors. Nonetheless they still have a charm of their own and often contain curious monuments to intrigue the visitor. A good example is to be found in the tiny village of **Fial**. In the square next to the church are laid three large slabs of stone, one set crosswise over the other two. This rudimentary seat is believed to have been the point from which justice was distributed by an elementary tribunal among the Lusitanians prior to the Roman Conquest. Taking a diversion into the countryside to the north-west, near the village of Paranhos is a fine example of a rudimentary prehistoric stone structure known as an *anta*.

This area to the south of Viseu has been a wine growing region for centuries with some of the vineyards having been established as long ago as the thirteenth century. The Dão wine grows best near to the rivers Pavia, Criz, the Dão itself, and the Mondego where the soil is principally granite and schist. Though the region officially demarcated for the growing of Dão grapes in 1908 covers around 1,600 hectares (6 sq miles) in the triangle between Coimbra, Guarda, and Viseu only about 10 per cent of the land is currently being cultivated because of the harshness of the mountainous landscape. On the land that is planted harvesting grapes can still be difficult and as the slopes are unsuitable for modern machinery the grapes are still carried to the vats on the harvesters' heads.

Red wine is produced in far larger quantities than white. The finest of the red grapes are the Alvarelho, Bastardo, Tinta Pinheira and Tourigo. They produce full bodied wines with a strong flavour and a good level of alcohol. Their texture should be distinctly smooth due to their high glycerine content. Dão wines are often labelled Grão Vasco after Viseu's most famous son with small reproductions of his better known paintings on the labels. The white wines produced in the region are dry. The finest of the white grapes is the Arinto which may have been a transplant from the German Riesling.

Just beyond the turning to Caramulo and the mountains is the town of **Tondela**. Well provided with hotels and shops it is a good base in the region and has an attractive centre, the finest features of which are the seventeenth-century Solar dos Teles, a nobleman's house, and next to it, built out of the walls of the grounds, the Fountain of the Mermaids. In the square a little further up the hill is the baroque façade of the church of Santa Mariana, and in the square before it the seventeenth-century fountain of Sirena. The clear air in this area, local reputation has it, is good for rheumatism and respiratory ailments. There is tennis and fishing on the River Dinha nearby, and a river beach at Nandufe just outside the town. Ask in Tondela for detailed directions.

South of here lies **Santa Comba Dão** and many of the finest vineyards of the Dão wine growing region. Santa Comba Dão is named after the head of the Benedictine convent that once existed in the village. The abbess was beatified after she and several of her sisters were martyred by Al Mansur, the Moorish king of Cordoba in 982. In this century it is best known as the birth place of the dictator, Antonio Salazar. It is a likeable little town with an interesting old quarter around the Rossio, with ancient houses built of great slabs of stone, thought to have been built around the fifteenth century.

Travelling west from Tondela leads, along the winding N230, into the Serra de Caramulo. As the road rises the views become ever more spectacular. The remarkable village and museum of **Caramulo** lies off-the-beaten-track on a twisting road across the Sierra de Caramulinho, on the N230 between Águeda and Tondela. It is 19km (12 miles) from Tondela to Caramulo and the road rises steeply to the north-west through woods of pine, eucalyptus and chestnut. On the inside of the steep hairpin bends small streams tumble down the rocks. Over some of these streams small stone huts have been built by farmers to ensure the stream is channelled to irrigate evenly the fields of maize and olive groves below. Water is precious in Portugal, and many disputes still arise over water rights between farmers. Such disputes are behind a fair proportion of the murders in the country. As the road rises the whole of the Dão Lafoes region is displayed below, all the way to the mountains of the Serra de Estrela in the far distance.

The spa village of Caramulo, with its parks and gardens, is as quiet and tranquil a place as anyone could possibly wish for. It has only one *pensão* and restaurant, the São Cristovao, but this is excellent, and serves local delicacies such as veal and roast mountain goat. The village sits quietly beneath Caramulinho, the highest point of the Serra de Caramulo at an altitude of 1,275m (4,182ft). This is a half-hour walk from the village and gives a breathtaking, panoramic view. The Lapa range lies to the north-east, the Estrela range to the south-east, the Lousa and Buçaco ranges to the south, the coastal plain lies to the west and to the north are the Serras de Gratheira and do Montemura.

It is then a little surprising to find in a village so far off-the-beaten-track, one of the country's finest and most interesting museums. On the road to Aveiro just 100m from the village centre is the Museum of Caramulo. The museum, with its entrance tucked between its neo-Classical pillars, is a welcoming place. It is slightly more expensive than is usual in Portuguese museums, but to compensate it is better organised and maintained. The second floor contains exhibits of all the plastic arts. They range from Romanesque statues, Roman crucifixes in bronze, Persian and Chinese pottery, Tournai tapestries to Indo-Portuguese inlaid jacaranda furniture. There is also an eclectic but fascinating collection of modern paintings, including work by Picasso, Leger and Chagall. There is even a painting by the British artist, Graham Sutherland, which is accompanied by a letter from its donor, Queen Elizabeth II, testifying to the painting's authenticity.

The cloister beneath the gallery, too, has an interesting history.

The founder of the museum was Abel de Lacerda, a wealthy philanthropist. When the museum was founded in 1953 he had the cloister constructed by moving it, stone by stone, from its original site in the Convent of Nossa Senhora de Fraga at Sátão. Unfortunately he did not live to see the museum fully completed. He can be seen pictured with Picasso in a photograph next to the artist's still life *Natureza Morta*.

The remaining section of the bottom floor and an adjoining building together form, in striking contrast to the upper tier, a vintage car and motorcycle museum. There are over fifty vehicles collected by the founder's brother, João Lacerda. They range from an Oldsmobile of 1902, and a Model T Ford, to a Rolls Royce Silver Ghost and two Cadillacs, all in immaculate condition.

The effect of this combination of examples of fine art and icons of popular mass culture is to create a sense of fun and proportion. This is far off the European high culture rounds, but it is still a fine museum.

Returning to Tondela and the N2 E801, the road south leads to Santa Comba Dão and two final places to visit before a return back to Coimbra. They are Luso and the Buçaco forest. The road into the Serra de Buçaco to reach them provides some very enjoyable views back over the Dão Lafoes region.

The spa town of **Luso**, though it may be crowded with Portuguese visitors at the weekends, is generally a stylish and relaxing place to visit or to stay in as a base from which to explore the nearby forest. It is just a few kilometres along the N234 and just 7km (4 miles) from the N1, the main route between Lisbon and Oporto. Most Portuguese, who are great lovers of spas, visit the town in the hope that the radioactive waters that emerge from St John's spring will be particularly effective in the treatment of kidney problems. Next to the tourist information office is to be found a delightful art nouveau tea room. As you would expect there are pleasant walks in the woods around the town and the nearby lake. The presence of local holiday makers has also led to the establishment of discos and cinemas. There is a good range of hotels and restaurants available in the town.

The **Forest of Buçaco** though very well known in Portugal is certainly off-the-beaten-track for most foreign visitors, yet it is one of the most interesting forests in Europe from the point of view of both natural and social history. In the thousand or so acres of the forest are to be found a tremendous variey of species of trees, many of which were introduced into the forest from abroad and some of which have ceased to be found in their native countries.

The first inhabitants are believed to have been sixth-century Benedictine monks from the monastery at Lorvão, who built a hermitage among the trees for solitary contemplation. Ecclesiastical care of the forest was maintained through to the eleventh century by the church authorities at Coimbra. The present organisation of the forest, however, really began with the establishment of a Carmelite monastery on the site of the present Palace Hotel in 1628. This was, of course during the period of overseas expansion by the Portuguese and the monks were the recipients of many varieties of exotic trees, the most famous of which, perhaps, are the huge Mexican cypresses. The fame of the collection, which also included laurels, maples and Austrian oaks, was such that a papal bull was issued by the Pope in 1643 that threatened anyone who harmed the trees of Buçaco with excommunication.

The Carmelite monastery is still standing though it is somewhat dwarfed at the summit of the hill by the Palace Hotel. Several of the monks cell are lined with cork and it was in one of these that the Duke of Wellington spent the night before one of his most famous victories over Napoleon's forces who were commanded by the French general Massena. A twisted old olive tree nearby on the drive is said to be where he tethered his horse for the night of 26 September 1810. Seeking to attack what his advisers had told him was Wellington's impregnable position at Buçaco, Massena watched 4,500 of his troops fall in a vain assault. The campaign is well documented in the small military museum to be found along the path to the rear of the hotel through the Queen's Gate.

The monumental Palace Hotel itself was built as a hunting lodge for the last but one of the Portuguese monarchs, Dom Carlos. It was designed by Luigi Manini, an Italian scene painter at the Lisbon Opera House in a rather bizarre pastiche of the Manueline style and was constructed between 1888 and 1907. After the declaration of the Republic and the ousting of the Braganças two years later the lodge became a hotel. All visitors are welcome to the hotel and are free to wander and admire the tiles in the great hall that depict Wellington's great victory, and those in the arcades that show scenes from the great Portuguese epic, *The Lusiads* by Camões. The gallery of double arches were modelled on the cloisters in the Hieronymite Monastery in Lisbon.

Between the Battle of Buçaco and the establishment of the hotel, however, other events had taken place that greatly affected the fate of the forest. The principal among these was the decree of 1834 that banned all religious orders from Portugal, including the Carmelites who had so dedicated themselves to the guarding of the forest. Fortunately it then became the responsibility of the Government's Water and Forest Department who not only protected its native trees but also maintained the Carmelite's tradition of introducing new varieties. These include Himalayan pines, Japanese camphor trees and monkey puzzle trees to name but a few. There are several marked paths through the woods that take in some of the ten hermitages that were used by the monks and, most beautiful of all, the Cold Fountain whose waters rise in a cave within the mountain and cascade down 144 steps into a lovely pool lined with magnolias and hydrangeas. Nearby is the delightful Fern Valley Lake.

The highest point in the forest is the Cruz Alta or High Cross, which can be reached either by car past the military museum and the obelisk, another memorial to the Battle of Buçaco, or by foot along a sevententh-century 'Way of the Cross' which passes a sequence of small baroque chapels. In either case the remarkable view over the Serra de Caramulo to the right, and to the left the mass of Coimbra with the Mondego valley and the heights of the Serra de Estrela in the distance provides an exceptionally beautiful vista.

Further Information

— Dao Lafoes —

Tourist Information Offices

Arganil
Praça Simoes Dias
☎ 035 22856

Caramulo
Estrada Principal
☎ 032 86437

Coimbra
Largo da Portagem
☎ 039 25576/23886

Combarinho Natural Park
Praça Con Morais de Carvalho
Vouzela
☎ 032 77517

Gouveia
Avenida 1 de Mão
☎ 038 42185

Luso-Buçaco
Rua Antonio Granja
Luso
☎ 031 93133.

Nelas
Praca Dr Veiga Simão
☎ 032 94308

Oliveira do Hospital
Edificio da Camara
☎ 032 52522

Seia
Largo do Mercado
☎ 038 22846

Viseu
Avenida Calouste Gulbenkian
☎ 032 27994

Places of Interest

Buçaco
Palace Hotel
Mata do Buçaco Mealhada
☎ 031 93101/2

Coimbra
Conimbriga
Open: Roman ruins everyday 9am-
12.30pm, 2-6pm (winter) and 12
noon-8pm (summer).
Museum closed on Mondays.

Portugal dos Pequininos
Rossio Santa Clara
Open: Summer 9am-5pm

Military Museum
Buçaco Forest
Open: 9am-7pm (except Mondays
and holidays)

Museu Machado Castro
Rua de Borges Carneiro
Open: 10am-1pm, 2.30-5pm (except
Mondays and holidays).

University buildings
Open: Summer 9am-5pm; winter
10am-2pm, 5-7pm.

Luso
Spa
Open: May to mid-October

Viseu
Abel Lacerda Museum of Caramulo
Open: May to November 10am-
6pm (except Mondays).

Almeida Moreira House Museum
Largo Major Teles
Open: 10am-12.30pm, 2-5pm
(except Mondays and holidays).

Grão Vasco Museum
Largo da Se
Open: 10am-12.30pm, 2-5pm
(except Mondays and holidays).

Festivals

Buçaco
Senhora da Vitoria
27 September

Coimbra
Queima das Fitas
May

Rainha Santa Isabela
June

Vale de Maceira, near Oliveira do
 Hospital
Senhora das Preces
5 July

Vila de Moinhos, near Viseu
São João
24 June

Viseu
São Mateus
30 days of September

7 • Évora

The walled medieval city of **Évora**, although little known as a result of its geographical situation in the middle of the flat harsh landscape of the Alentejo, is the most beautiful city in Portugal, and was declared a site of World Patrimony by UNESCO in 1986. It is a delightful place whose maze of cobbled streets enclose architectural and artistic delights spanning almost two thousand years. It is, as one would expect from a town laid out in the Middle Ages, remarkably compact and can best be enjoyed as a walking tour.

The heart of the town and the best place from which to begin the tour is the Praça de Giraldo. On the square is to be found the town tourist office which will supply the visitor with a map.

The square has been the centre of the town since the Roman administration and it has witnessed many momentous events in the history of Portugal. It was here that the Inquisition held their inquiries and here too that that the last of the rebellious feudal nobles, the Duke of Bragança, was executed by João II in 1483. The square is named after Évora's legendary liberator from the Moors, Gerald Sempavor, or Gerald 'without fear'.

As Portugal's first king, Afonso Henriques, struggled to extend his domains in the middle of the twelfth century, Évora, which had been under Moorish occupation since the eighth century, was first conquered then lost again. The story goes that Gerald had fled Afonso's court for living a life of reckless self-indulgence and had decided to restore himself to the king's good graces by organising a small raiding party to capture castles from the Moslems wherever he could find them. In October 1186 in a daring scaling of the town's fortifications Gerald drew the town's defenders to its north-western edge, while on the far side of the city the main body of Gerald's men were able to enter the city unopposed. Having defeated the Moors Gerald handed the town over to Áfonso. So began Evora's golden

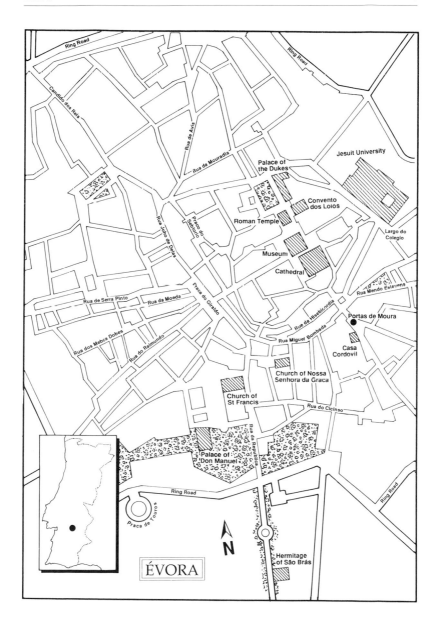

age when the first two dynasties of Portuguese kings had their home here and one of the country's first universities was established by the Cardinal King Henrique in 1551.

The Praça de Giraldo today is a pleasantly spacious and attrac-

A stone carving of Gerald Sempavor in Évora cathedral

tive square with the tables and parasols of nearby cafés laid out in the central area, made into something special by the arcades that lie along its north side. Dominating the square the Church of Saint Anthony and its fountain were both commisioned by the Cardinal Dom Henrique. The church, constructed on the site of an older Gothic building was designed by Manuel Pires in 1557 in the new style of the Renaissance. The baroque fountain in front of the church was built in a baroque style by Afonso Alvares in 1571. The fountain forms the meeting place in the early evening for young and old alike.

Just to the left of the fountain is the beginning of the Rua Serpa Pinto. Just a few yards down this road on the right after the picturesque old horse troughs is the entrance to a small local theatre. The company puts on shows throughout the summer and though they are usually in Portuguese, it is still worth a visit. The main reason for this is the nature of the auditorium which has a delicate tracery of vine trellisses for a roof. This creates a charming atmosphere on warm summer evenings. The productions are often of the sixteenth-century playwright Gil Vicente, the founding father of Portuguese theatre and a native son of Évora.

Returning to the Praça de Giraldo, however, the tour continues by following the Rua 5 de Outubro that leads off the square up the hill

The Roman Temple of Diana, Évora

towards the cathedral. Lying between the square and the town's two best known sights this narrow steeply rising street now plays host to a few tourist shops, specialising in the sale of the local speciality products, particularly cork but also very finely woven carpets from the nearby village of Arraiollos. With its wrought iron balconies and abscence of traffic it is a pleasant stroll. Facing the visitor at the top of the street is the cathedral of Évora and to the left and slightly around the corner are the striking remains of a Roman temple.

The most precious of the many precious buildings in Évora, the Roman temple is popularly known as the **Temple of Diana** and was built between the second and third centuries after Christ, in a settlement the Romans knew as *Liberalitas Julia*. Almost three sides of the temple remain intact and the ribbed pillars with their ornate Corinthian capitals are still marvellously well preserved. The fourth side was probably destroyed around the turn of the fifth century during the most determined of the Christian attacks upon paganism. The capitals and bases of the columns are built of marble from the Alentejan town of Estremoz, while the columns themselves are made of granite.

In the Middle Ages the temple was used as a fortress and in the last century as a slaughterhouse and perhaps these important social functions ensured that the marble and granite of the temple was not recycled for other uses by local people. Little is known of the use to which the Romans put the temple, the appelation 'Diana' was not used by the Romans themselves. There is no doubt though that it is the finest element in the architectural legacy left to Portugal by them. Its cool classical beauty can best be appreciated in the evening when it is lit up. Walking past the Museum of Évora the walker can now return to the main entrance and façade of the cathedral.

Not perhaps as purely beautiful as the temple but just as fascinating is **Évora Cathedral** It was built in a fortified style in the period of transition from the Romanesque to the Gothic. The final effect is not that of an integrated whole but the parts embody some of the finest aspects of the two styles. It was built on the site of the old mosque. The foundation stone was laid in 1186 and the cathedral was consecrated and dedicated to St Mary in 1204. Additions continued to be made until the choir was constructed in the sixteenth century and the original massive towers were topped with conical spires.

The external structure of the building with its twin towers in the main façade is Romanesque as are the general proportions of the building. In the inhospitable early Middle Ages churches were built as much for defence of the community as for worship and as late as the Napoleonic invasions the cathedral was used by local people as a place of refuge. The effect of the Romanesque style can be seen in the decoration and in particular in the deep only slightly arched main doorway, with its carved stone figures of the Apostles. Each of the figures carries the staff or book that would identify him to the faithful of the Middle Ages. The local sculptors who carved the figures in the first half of the fourteenth century have shown their faces as very similar to each other, embodying a common serenity of faith rather than a personal journey to salvation.

The interior, however, with its arched gallery and high arched roof is more evidently Gothic. The central nave, with broken barrel vaulting is 70m (230ft) in length and one of the longest in the country. It has two other naves of unequal height. The transept crossing before the altar has some fine features. A beautiful octagonal dome sits above the transept and the latter is lit at either end by rose windows. In a baroque chapel on the left of the nave is an unusual fifteenth-century polychrome statue of the Virgin, great with child. The statue is known locally as the 'Lady of the Mothers' and women still pray before it for fertilty.

Évora Cathedral and cloisters

Dominating the interior is the neo-Classical high altar designed by the German Renaissance artist Ludovice. The polychrome marble pillars of the altar are particularly beautiful. The figures are by the Paduan sculptor, Bellini and the painting of *Christ in Glory* is by Agostini Masucci.

The most delightful Rennaissance features of the cathedral, however, are to be found in the carved wooden stalls of the choir built above the cathedral doorway. These were completed by artists of the Flemish school, probably from Antwerp, in 1562. Each scene carved on the stalls depicts a scene from the Bible or from classical mythology. Some are deeply serious evoking the sufferings of the saints, such as Paul on the road to Tarsus. Others are witty and amusing, pointing out the vanity or foolishness of human beings. One, for example, shows a man being roasted on a spit by rabbits. All are beautifully executed with a cheerful blending of the religious and the secular that is typically Portuguese.

On the same staircase as the choir stalls is the **Cathedral Museum of Sacred Art**. This contains many examples of sacred vestments and vessels and some of these, such as an Italian baroque gold chalice from 1586, are very fine. The outstanding exhibit, without doubt, however, is the tiny ivory figure of the Virgin of Paradise. This thirteenth-century figure from the school of Paris opens up to reveal a triptych of exquisitely carved scenes from the life of the Virgin, including the Annunciation, the Nativity, her death and her Assumption into Heaven.

The Cathedral cloister is a Gothic work of elegant proportions with some intricate tracery in the window arches and a delightful low relief carving of the 'Fearless' Gerald. Statues of the Evangelists are to be seen in the four corners of the cloister.

On the same square as the Temple of Diana is the one of the finest *pousadas* in Portugal, now part of the **Palace of the Dukes of Cadaval**. It is still possible to visit the *pousada* even if you are not a guest by asking at the reception just to the right after the main door. Visitors arriving at meal times are, however, more likely to be refused access. The *pousada* occupies the old Monastery of Loios which was built in 1485 on the site of Évora castle, destroyed in a riot in 1385. The nobleman Dom Rodrigo Afonso de Melo founded the monastery, carrying on his own back to the site, so legend has it, the foundation stone. The building later fell into disrepair and the lower cloister with a remarkable Manueline arch by the famous Portuguese architect,

A painted ceiling in the Palace of the Dukes of Cadaval, Évora

Diogo de Arruda, whose work was deeply influenced by the Moors, lay buried and forgotten until it was excavated in the late 1940s. The vaulting, too, of the upper cloister, added in the sixteenth century, is very shallow, a feature of Moorish influenced architecture. Several of the rooms are kept open for visitors to view and contain attractive frescoed ceilings and walls and ornate antique furniture.

Next to the *pousada* is what was formerly the convent's church and is still the private chapel of the Duke of Cadaval and his family. For a small fee the **Church of St John the Evangelist** can be visited. Originally built in the fifteenth century the façade has been redesigned with the exception of the highly ornate doorway.

Of particular interest inside are extensive decorated tiles by, perhaps, the finest exponent of the art, the eighteenth-century craftsman Antonio de Oliveira Bernardes. The sequence of tiles that deco-

The tomb of Bishop Dom Afonso in the Musum of Évora

rate the nave illustrate the life of St Laurence Justinian. The church originally served as a mausoleum for the Melos family and before the altar can be seen several fine examples of early medieval figurative tombstones. The tombstone of Dom Francisco de Melo, the writer and tutor to the sons of King João III is a fine example, by contrast, of Renaissance art reckoned to have been designed by the Frenchman, Nicholas Chanterene.

Emerging from the church and the palace the visitor may wish to look round the small garden with colourful flower borders and benches on which to rest that lies to the right of the Temple of Diana; at its far end is a fine view over the Roman aqueduct and countryside that lies to the north of the city.

Directly facing the Temple of Diana is the **Museum of Évora** established in 1915 in what was formerly the archbishop's palace. It is a very fine musem with many treasures, exhibited in a cool, airy atmosphere that may come as a relief after exposure to the Alentejo heat. The building is baroque in style and was constructed in the last decade of the sixteenth century on the site of a primitive Gothic construction. The cloister just beyond the main entrance contains some fine Roman and medieval archaeological remains. The most precious is a low relief marble fragment of a vestal virgin found at the former Roman settlement of *Beja*. Among the late medieval exhibits the finest are probably a sixteenth-century Trinity in Anca stone and a fourteenth-century Annunciation in marble. Several interesting Manueline exhibits can be seen in a separate room in the ground floor. Named after the king who reigned from 1495 to 1521, Manuel I, also known as 'the Fortunate', the Manueline is Portugal's only indigenous architectural and artistic style and was prevalent from the end of the fifteenth century until around the end of the sixteenth century. It is an exuberant, highly decorative style that reflects the enormous wealth and variety of products that Portugal was gathering at this time from its overseas colonies. Many of the decorative motifs reflect that the source of these riches was due to the bravery of the country's mariners. Thus column or doorways will be twisted in rope-like coils. Globes and anchors are also featured as are leaves and flowers, pearls and acorns. The Manueline exhibits here include ornate window frames taken from the original town hall, destroyed in 1515, and frames taken from the original royal palace of Dom Manuel, a copy of which has been constructed in the public gardens to the south of the city.

The ground floor is completed with a Renaissance room exhibiting in particular the beautiful decorative frieze work of the French sculptor, Nicholas Chanterene. This can be particularly appreciated in the tomb of the Bishop Dom Afonso. The classical purity of the lines of the tomb is greatly enhanced by the masterly sculpture of the human figures and creatures from ancient mythology.

The museum's most impressive collection is, however, reserved for the second floor and consists of sixteenth- and seventeenth-century Flemish and Portuguese paintings. The similarity of styles arose from the close trading and cultural links between the countries during this period. The finest piece is perhaps the thirteen-panel *Life of the Virgin* commissioned by the Bishop Dom Afonso around the turn of the sixteenth century. Modern critics consider the work to have been completed in Évora by Flemish artists, and see in it the influence of established artists of the time. Up to 1717 the panels had formed the main cathedral altarpiece.

Outstanding among the other works is the nativity of Frei Carlos, the most important of the Flemish artists working in Portugal in the fifteenth century. A very beautiful tapestry from the nearby town of Arraiolos created during the reign of Dona Maria in the second half of the eighteenth century also hangs among the pictures of royalty. There are several portraits of the long suffering and, in Portugal, hugely popular, Catherine of Bragança, wife of the philandering king of England, Charles II.

Descending past the Palace of the Dukes of Cadaval onto the Rua de Menino Jesus one can appreciate the massiveness of the medieval walls of which the north tower, built into the walls of the palace, used to form a part. The medieval palace built around this tower was given by João of Avis to his faithful counsellor, Martim Afonso de Melo after the crucially important defeat of the Spanish at Aljubarrotta in 1390. The main façade of the bulding was remodelled in the seventeenth century.

Turning to the right on the Rua de Menino Jesus allows the visitor to walk through a section of the medieval town walls and through a small garden known as the Largo das Colegias. Parts of the wall that runs through the garden are considered to belong to the original first-century Roman wall which was reinforced in the seventh century by the Visigoths.

Above the wall at the far end of the garden can be seen the palace of the Dukes of Basto. Originally a Moorish palace it was here that the

The Cloister of Studies in the University Courtyard, Évora

medieval kings up to Dom Duarte lived when they were in Évora.It is a beautiful building, its towers and upper galleries being a meeting of Moorish, Manueline and Renaissance influences. In summer term time the Largo das Colegias garden is usually full of students relaxing and talking in the sun.

Across the main road at the bottom of the sloping garden is the complex of buildings that were formerly the Jesuit University of Évora, and therefore one of the oldest in the world and which now houses the modern state-run university.

The Jesuit **University** of the Holy Spirit was established by the Archbishop of Évora in 1551. Despite an illustrious record as a centre of learning the university was closed in 1759 when the effective dictator of Portugal at the time, the Marquis of Pombal, banned the Jesuits from the country. The university was re-established by parliamentary decree in December 1979.

The buildings are well worth visiting as they include the work of some of the finest of Portuguese architects of the sixteenth century, such as Afonso Alvares, Manuel Pires and Diogo de Torralva. Pires and Alvares worked in particular on the university church that lies on the corner of the buildings as one walks around to the main entrance. The façade is early baroque in style and the single nave is decorated with geometric panelling that accorded with the proportions laid down by examples in Rome of what a Jesuit church should look like.

Entering now the main courtyard of the university the visitor must surely immediately be impressed by the harmony and pleasing proportions of the what is called the Cloister of the Studies. The two-tiered arcade with their columns of marble create a sense of wealth and style. The pediment opposite the entrance sits above the doorway to the administrative centre, where decrees are bestowed, the Hall of Acts. The sculpted figures represent symbolically royal and ecclesiastical majesty and the inscriptions describe the values of the Jesuit Order. All around the courtyard are classrooms and these can be identified by examining the eighteenth-century tiles that adorn their outside walls; among the subjects represented are mathematics, philosophy and history.

Turning towards the cathedral and the centre of town on leaving the university there is a small pathway on the extreme right of the square that leads directly to the back of the cathedral. At the top of this narrow alley to the right just before the cathedral there is a

The Porta de Moura with the cathedral behind, Évora

remarkably attractive Gothic and Manueline sixteenth-century mansion belonging to the Counts of Portalegre. The effect of the balconies with their Moorish decoration is particularly picturesque.

Along the Rua de Cenáculo to the left of the cathedral is to be seen another fine mansion, the sixteenth-century home of the humanist scholar, Garcia de Resende. The first floor windows are beautifully decorated in the Manueline style. The meeting of Arabic and Manueline influences that can be seen in the marble and granite windows inspired the poet, Florbela Espanca, to write one of the most famous sonnets in Portuguese literature. Above the house of Garcia de Resende can be seen the majestic shape of one of the cathedral's massive conical-topped towers.

Descending from the Casa de Garcia de Resende away from the cathedral leads on to perhaps the most lovely fountain in Portugal, the fountain of the Porta de Moura. On either side of this, the former gateway to the medieval town, remain the imposing twin towers of the medieval walls. The picturesque square is dominated by the Renaissance statue which shows its Moorish influence in the unusual quadrangular pools of water that lie beneath it. The statue, the Fonte da Bola, consisting of a single column surmounted by a white marble sphere was built in 1556.

Facing the towers and adding to the picturesque square is the Casa Cordovil. This sixteenth-century mansion with its elegant belvedere represents a fine example of a hybrid of Manueline and Mudejar art. Horseshoe arches rest upon Arabic marble capitals and a conical cupola sits above it. The beauty of the square is further enhanced by the picturesque five-arched gallery of the sixteenth-century Casa Soure that also overlooks the fountain.

Retracing one's steps into the Porta de Moura and following either the Rua Miguel Bombarda or the Rua de Misericórdia leads to the small Largo de Alvaro Velho. Just beyond the Largo leading off to the left are the quaint steps or Travessa de Careca. Above the steps and cobbles are medieval arched buttreses and wrought iron lamps.

At the bottom of the steps is the classical baroque façade of the **Convent Church of Our Lady of Grace**, considered by some to be the first Renaissance building constructed in Portugal in the sixteenth century. The straight pillars and triangular pediments are in stark contrast to the Moorish influences that predominate in most of Evora's buildings. The church, which was originally granted by royal patronage to the Augustinian monks, was constructed in the 1530s. The male figures that sit on the roof represent, so local legend has it, the first four victims of the Portuguese Inquisition. The interior was largely destroyed in a structural collapse in 1884 and the treasures that had decorated the interior were redistributed to the nearby Church of St Francis and the Museum of Ancient Art. Included among those items removed to the museum were the tombs of the first Duke of Vimioso and his wife and that of Bishop Afonso. These tombs were all sculpted by the finest Renaisssance sculptor who worked in Portugal, Nicholas Chanterene.

To the left of the church lies what was once the main body of the monastery. This is now occupied by the Portuguese military and so is difficult to gain access to. However, if you approach with a specific request to see the cloister, which was designed in 1550, you may meet with some success.

Taking the narrow passage that leads out of the Largo de Graca opposite the church façade, turn immediately to the left and then just a little further on to the right to reach the **Royal Church of St Francis**. The church has recieved the denomination 'Royal' because so many royal weddings took place there during the later Middle Ages. The Manueline doorway is decorated with a pelican and an armillary sphere, symbols respectively of João II and Manuel I. The battlemented roofline and twisted conical towers are a more muted version of the full blown Manueline architectural style that is to be seen a little later in this walking tour in the Chapel of St Brás.

The interior of the church is of extremely pleasing proportions, designed in the form of a simple Latin cross. The nave is very high and there is usually a shaft of coloured light falling into the nave from the stained glass windows that flank the altar high above the ground. The vaulted roof with its bosses decorated with crucifixes and flowers is 24m (80ft) in height and the nave is over 36m (120ft) in length. The chancel contains two galleries, one to the left in the baroque style and the other to the right in the Renaissance style.

The Church of St Francis also contains one of the strangest chapels to be found in the whole of the Iberian Peninsula, the 'Casa Dos Ossos' or House of Bones. This is a small three-naved chapel built in the sixteenth century, the walls of which have been entirely covered with human skulls and bones. The bones were exhumed from the nearby Franciscan cemetery and the intention was that their presence would encourage purposeful meditation and prayer. The poet Ribeiro Chiado and the mystic, Brother Antonio das Chagadas were among those who prayed here. The inscription above the entrance bears the grimly humourous message, 'Our Bones here are waiting for yours'. Near to the entrance can be seen braids of hair hanging from the wall. These are left as offerings by young women about to be married in the hope of a happy future.

Directly opposite the church of St Francis on the Praça de Maio

The Royal Palace of St Francis (Palace of Dom Manuel), Évora

is the **Regional Handicraft Museum** which has fine examples of work in the traditional Alentejan materials of cork and wood, and fine carpets and tapestries.

Having walked almost an entire circle around the centre of Évora it is perhaps fortunate that the next sight of historical interest lies just to the south of the church of St Francis in the shade and quiet of a public garden. The gardens are cut through by a section of the town's fortifications that date from the seventeenth century. Dominating the gardens is the sixtenth-century palace, known popularly as the Palace of Dom Manuel, but whose correct title is the **Royal Palace of St Francis**. Originally a Franciscan monastery Afonso V was the first Portuguese monarch to extend the buildings. It was later to become a favourite residence of Manuel I, João III, Sebastiao I and the Castilian kings Philip II and III. The palace was the scene of the investiture of Vasco da Gama, the discoverer of a sea route to India in 1498 as the Duke of Vidigueira. It was also the place where the writer Gil Vicente penned some of his most famous verses in the sixteenth century. Unfortunately the Castilian kings changed much of the structure of the original building and only the Galeria das Damas or 'Gallery of the Ladies', was left largely intact. The gallery was built in the reign of Dom Manuel hence the popular name of the building. Much of the present building indeed actually dates from 1916 when a fire destroyed much of the original. The town council, however, went to great lengths to try to imitate exactly the proportions of the earlier building.

Like many of Evora's finest buildings it is composed of a number of architectural influences. The broad shallow vaulting of the arcades and the horseshoe arches of some of the windows are Moorish while the ancillary decoration of the windows and the conical summit to the tower are Manueline. The interior of the palace is not generally open but it is regularly used for cultural events through the summer, such as music recitals or dance groups and information on these can be obtained from the tourist office in the Praça do Giraldo.

Before returning to the centre of town two things remain that may detain the visitor beyond the southern city walls. In the large open space below the walls, an area that is generally used for parking, the city market is held here every Tuesday and Saturday morning. Much the best place to pick up a bargain, the market is full of noise and energy and a tremendous variety of livestock and wares including the regional handicrafts of weaving and pottery.

At the south end of the clearing that, apart from the market, is also used to accommodate the fair that regularly visits the town, is the fifteenth-century church of **São Brás** or St Blaise. This extraordinary church is certainly one of the best examples of an early Manueline work of art. In some ways it seems most closely to resemble that type of fairy tale castle with its pronounced battlements and round towers topped with dunce cap cones that Walt Disney has built in Florida and California. The church had its beginning in 1482 when João II ordered a wooden shelter to be built on the site to house the victims of the plague that was sweeping through the city. The church was used as a fortress by both the Castilians and the Portuguese during the various sieges of the city, and this resulted in much of the original sixteenth-century decoration being destroyed. The dome and belfry at the eastern end are Renaissance in style. The paintings in the panels of the altarpiece depict the Nativity and Resurrection of Christ and the Preaching and Martyrdom of St Brás.

Perhaps the final delight of the city that ought not to be missed is the sixteenth-century aqueduct that cuts across the city walls to the north of the town centre, the far side from the church of St Brás. Correctly entitled the Aqueduct of Agua de Prata (Silver Water) it was built between 1531 and 1542 and designed by the architect of the Tower of Belém in Lisbon, Francisco de Arruda. The water was originally conducted all the way to the starting point of our tour in the Praça do Geraldo.

Further Information

— Évora —

Tourist Information Office

Praça do Geraldo
☎ 066 22671

Places of Interest

Évora Museum
Largo da Se
Open: 10am-12.30pm, 2-3pm
(except Mondays)

Museu Artesenado Regional
Praça 1 Maio
Open: 10am-12.30pm, 2-3pm
(except Mondays)

Market
Tuesday and Saturday morning

Festivals

São João
Last ten days in June

Festival of Senhora das Candeis
2 February

Feira do Gado
Friday before Palm Sunday

Feira Nova
October

8 • The Alto Alentejo

The Alto Alentejo is a seemingly endless burnished plain of olive trees and cork oaks. It is not the most beautiful or varied of Portugal's landscapes yet it contains a number of exciting fortified towns such as Elvas and Marvão, and the unique 'marble' towns of Borba, and Estremoz, as well as the favourite palace of the last royal family of Portugal, at Vila Viçosa.

The Alentejo has been, despite its sweltering tranquility in the summer months, one of the most radical and revolutionary regions. A great stronghold of the Revolution of 1974 that ended the undemocratic rule of the dictator, Caetano, the succesor to the long-lived fascist dictator, Salazar, it remains a bastion of the Communist Party. Hatred of Salazar and support for the Revolution can still be seen in the fading graffitti on the walls of the small villages.

Unlike the conservative land of the Minho, with its numerous family smallholdings, the vast plantations, or *latifundias*, of the Alentejo have been the private property of successive occupiers for centuries. It was in this area so closely resembling the plains of Spain that the Moors put down their deepest roots and have had their greatest effect. Ruling the Alentejo for over five hundred years they divided the land into the vast estates that essentially remain to this day and forced the landless peasantry to work on them. When they were finally driven south and back to North Africa the new Christian nobility simply took over the established social system and with the religious orders fortified their strongholds of Elvas, Estremoz and Mourão, etc against their feudal rivals in the inland kingdoms of Aragon, Leon and Castile. When the religious orders were dissolved in the seventeenth century the large estates were still maintained and rich absentee landlords began to profit from the export of cork. Meanwhile the peasantry, still landless, many itinerant and working only seasonally, lived in abject poverty.

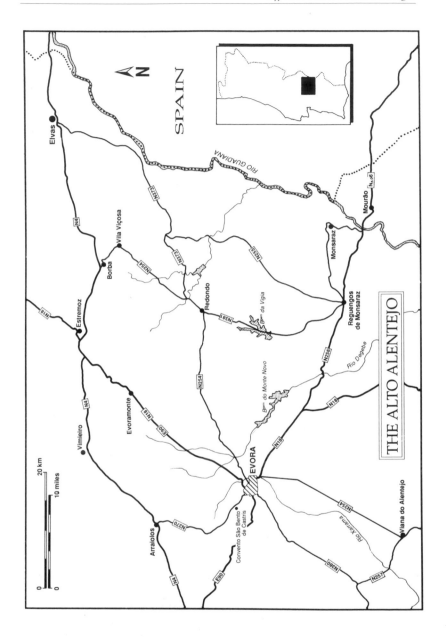

After the 1974 Revolution communists led the peasants in the establishment of co-operative production units. The Agrarian Reform Law subsequently passed by the new government made the individual holding of more than 50 hectares (123 acres) of irrigated land or 500 hectares (1,236 acres) of pasture land illegal. The co-operative production methods of the new estates benefitted the people greatly, and the units numbered at their peak, in the mid-1970s, over 900. However, the antipathy of successive social demo-cratic and right-wing governments to the units and the abiding lack of any investment or ownership of the units on the part of individual families has led to a gradual decrease in their numbers.

The main products of the area are, as they have been for centu-ries, cork, marble and wheat. As early as 1310 the farsighted King Dinis laid down laws for the careful cultivation of the cork oak. Today the Alentejo is the greatest cork producing region in the world, and the country as a whole contains over a third of the world's cork oaks. Bottle corks, floor and wall tiles and insulating materials form its major export uses, but when in the region it is worth looking out for the great variety of uses the local people have put it to, including doors, and decorations. Marble deposits around Borba and Vila Viçosa, as we shall see are very extensive. Most of the marble quarried is exported to Italy and Spain. A substantial proportion of Portugal's wheat is grown in the Alentejo.

Most of the roads and the transport of the Alto Alentejo ema-nates from the main town of Évora which has been described in an earlier chapter. Most places of interest can probably be reached from the town as a day trip until the tour moves north to the frontier town of Estremoz. At this point the visitor is advised to adopt a new base in the north of the region.

Three kilometres (2 miles) outside the walls of Évora on the N114-4 on the left-hand side is the monastery of São Bento de Castris. This is the oldest monastery in the south of Portugal. According to the chronicles of the Cistercian order of monks the site became a place of pilgrimage when an apparently supernatural light was seen there during the night of 21 March, the feast day of São Bento, in 1169. The sixteenth-century Manueline church is well worth seeing with its tiles depicting the life of St Bernard and its attractive vaulting. The highlight of the visit though is the sixteenth-century Luso Moorish cloister with its airy spacious arcades and paired horseshoe arches. There is a fine view over the surrounding countryside from the south side of the building.

Before continuing north to Arraiolos the visitor may consider it worthwhile to double back onto the ring road around Évora to take a brief detour to the south along the N380. Thirteen kilometres (8 miles) along this road is the episcopal palace and monastery of Bom Jesus of Valverde.

Founded in 1544 and granted to the Capuchin order of monks the building is now used as the offices of the rector of Évora University. It contains many vestiges of the original Manueline and Mudejar decoration but its highlight is the beautiful Renaissance church, designed by the Évora architect Manuel Pires around 1559, based on the strictures laid down by the Italian, Sebastiao Serlio. The chapel forms the shape of a Greek cross and the marble for the columns and floor came from Estremoz.

Twenty-two kilometres (14 miles) south of the turning to Valverde where the N380 meets the N2 is the small town of **Alcáçovas**, known throughout the region as the home of the production of cowbells. The bells are still made in the traditional way out of tin, copper and bronze, being hammered into shape and then fired in clay. The town has a small museum devoted to cowbells.

Returning to the N114-4 it is a journey of about 20km (14 miles) through the olive groves and cork oaks of the Alto Alentejo plain to the remarkable village of **Arraiolos**. This pretty village is similar to many in the region, built upon a hill, but is famous for two things, carpets and sausages, or *paios*.

The making of rugs and carpets here probably originated with the Moors who occupied Arraiolos for eight hundred years. It was, however, Portugal's early discovery of the sea routes to India and the East that led to a growing demand among the nobility of the sixteenth and seventeenth centuries to acquire the elaborately patterned carpets imported from Persia and India. In response to this demand a native industry, manufacturing carpets from linen and hemp and embroidering them with wool in the Persian manner, grew quickly in the area around Arraiolos. The original patterns have now been abandoned in favour of local designs. Carpets and wall hangings are available in the co-operative in the town, not cheap, but still considerably better value than elsewhere. The traditional white houses with blue frames of the region and the fourteenth-century castle make the village a pleasant place to walk in. The typical design of Alentejan houses, white with blue or yellow trimmings, incidentally, originated with the Moors. They considered that such colours around doors and windows would keep away evil spirits from the house.

Arraiolos is a good point from which to explore the fascinating towns of Évoramonte, Elvas, Estremoz and Borba. These frontier towns will be covered in some detail later in this chapter as a comfortable exploration of them necessitates moving to a new base other than Évora. Before doing so however it is worth considering a trip to the south-west of the city.

The N18 and subsequently the N256 to the frontier town of **Reguengos de Monsaraz** passes through fields of scattered cork trees and giant cactus and occasional fields of sunflowers and olive groves. Reguengos de Monsaraz is known for its wine, which is becoming widely available in supermarkets in Northern Europe, and its pottery. There is a wine co-operative in which to stock up. Though the town is not an apparently exciting one it plays host to many festivals and fairs throughout the year. The Feiras da Freguesia de Reguengos de Monsaraz takes place in January, May and August, the Feira de São Marcos do Campo in April, the Romaria de Santo Isidro at the end of May, the Festas de Santo Antonio in June, the Feira da Santa Maria da Lagoa and the Festa de Nosso Senhor Jesus dos Passos in September.

Accommodation in Reguengos de Monsaraz is limited to an *estalagem* and a manor house. Ask at the tourist office at Praça Dom Nuno Alvares Pereira for advice.

Just beyond Reguengos towards the frontier with Spain there is a dam and a very pleasant river beach on the River Alamo, next to an improvised camp site.

Beyond here there are two frontier towns that have ancient fortifications against the incursions of the Spanish, Mourão, and the more interesting of the two, Monsaraz.

From the approach road to **Monsaraz**, past the village of Xeres de Baixo, the town with its medieval castle encircling the town looks remarkably romantic. A steep climb onto the castle walls provides an amazing panoramic view over the surrounding countryside. The town is apparently also known in Portugal as the 'Ninho das Aguias', or Eagle's Nest, and it is easy to understand why. The streets within the castle walls are cobbled and forbidden to traffic and the sixteenth- and seventeenth-century houses, often emblazoned with coats of arms, are of traditional construction, built of slate with cork doors and with some very attractive ironwork grilles and balconies. The Museum of Sacred Art contains a fifteenth-century fresco on one of its walls and some eighteenth-century paintings and tapestries.

The castle walls, Monsaraz

The narrow side streets of Monsaraz

The parish church contains a fourteenth-century marble tomb of
Tomas Martins, with attractive carvings of a funeral procession. The
Misericord Hospital opposite the parish church has an interesting

and beautiful meeting hall on the first floor. There are rooms available on the main street of the town.

Monsaraz probably originated as a prehistoric hill settlement, or *castro*, and was later occupied in turn by the Romans, the Visigoths and the Moors. The town was liberated from the Moors in 1167 by the same Gerald Sem Pavor that liberated Évora. He handed the village over to the Knights Templar and subsequently the Order of Christ. The fortress was rebuilt by King Dinis in the thirteenth century and has now been converted into a small bull ring. The Portuguese bull fight is incidentally much less cruel than the Spanish variety and the bull is not killed. To see such a spectacle in such remote and unforgettable surroundings is a marvellous experience. It is worth checking in advance at the tourist office in Évora for the dates of bullfights in Monsaraz.

Just outside the town is a witness to a prehistoric community in this area, the Menhir of Outeiro, just off the Reguengos road. The 4.9m (16ft) high stone stands in the middle of a wheat field and decorative patterns can still clearly be seen on its sides. In the open country between Monsaraz and the River Guadiana is another prehistoric monument, the Monte do Xarez stones. They are comprised of a menhir 4m (13ft) high and a square of standing stones.

Seven kilometres ($4^1/_2$ miles) south of Monsaraz and on the far side of the River Guadiana is **Mourão**, another of the fortress towns that dominate this area. It is just 11km (7 miles) from the Spanish border. The original settlement here was at Vila Velha below the present town and near to the river. The prominent remains are the three towers of the original castle.

Returning to Évora via a small road to Reguengos through Telheiro and **Corval** the road passes the interesting church of São Pedro do Corval. It is to be found off to the left amid large almond groves. At first sight the church appears to be derelict but it is in fact still used and the women who live in the houses nearby will be only too pleased to bring the key. The church is of unusual construction with the main body being dominated by two side altars, and there being only a narrow gap to the main altar of St Peter. To the left is the enclosed chapel to Our Lady of the Rosary.

All over the chapel are hung votive offerings from people of the region and, according to our guides, from all over the country. Curious wax arms and legs, representing those parts of the body for which intercession was sought, sit or are hung from the altar along

View from the castle walls, Mourão

with the much more affecting photographs of young newly weds, hoping for a succesful marriage and the pictures of young recruits going to fight in the last Portuguese colonial war in Angola, placed there in the hope of a safe return. There is a fresco still partially visible above the main altar. This is a spot as off-the-beaten-track as it is possible to get in Portugal yet it reveals a great deal about the abiding attitudes and beliefs of the people.

A very similar sanctuary stands in fields near the town of **Viana de Alentejo** on the N254 directly south of Évora, the Sanctuary of Nossa Senhora de Aires. The white and yellow building with its twin towers and cupola was built in 1743, and it too is a place of pilgrimage and the depositing of votive offerings.

Moving now to the north of Évora and travelling along the N18 in the direction of Estremoz huge wheat fields scattered with the occasional cork oak line the route. The only point at which to pause along the way is the village of **Azuraja** with its prehistoric São Matias dolmen.

The medieval village of **Évoramonte** lies just a 1km ($^1/_2$ mile) above the modern village on the N18. It is signposted 'Castelo d'Évoramonte', and is a tiny fortified town, once occupied by the Moors and the Romans. Its walls, constructed between the fourteenth and seventeenth century, perch on the mountain high above the plain. It is a fascinating place, remote and, despite the fortifications, almost palpably peaceful.

The ancient castle, whose Gothic style is a fourteenth-century remodelling of an older structure, dominates the village. The massive keep was designed in Italian Rennaissance style in the sixteenth century, with four round towers and a simple decorative Manueline twisted stone rope. The vaulted chambers inside contain granite capitals that have been elaborately carved.

The village also contains several interesting churches. The parish or mother church, dedicated to Our Lady of Conception, is the finest. It was built towards the end of the first half of the sixteenth century, with a Gothic doorway, three naves and three transepts. The baroque altar is decorated with gold leaf. On the upper part of the main transept can be seen some fine sixteenth century frescoes in remarkably good condition. Represented on the left wall as one faces the altar are St Gregory, Mary Magdalene and John the Baptist, on the right St Anthony and St Barbara. They were probably painted around 1540 by the artist, Diogo Fernandes. Sixteenth-century raised surface Sevilian ceramic tiles are also worth seeing fronting the altar of Our Lady of the Rosary.

Every schoolboy and schoolgirl in Portugal knows Évoramonte best as the place where the convention was signed that brought the Portuguese Civil War to an end on 26 May 1834. A simple plaque in the wall of one of the houses on the Rua Direita indicates that here Miguel I's General accepted on his master's behalf abdication and exile as the price of defeat exacted by his brother, Pedro IV, Emperor of Brazil, after his defeat at the Battle of Asseceira. Miguel's niece, Maria, became Queen of Portugal.

Having visited the fortified eyries of Monsaraz and Évoramonte, the sight of a fine river beach 5km (3 miles) before Estremoz where it is crossed by the River Tera, may well be very welcome.

As well as being at the heart of one of the most important marble quarrying areas in the world, **Estremoz** has also been known since the sixteenth century as a centre for the production of pottery. The best place and time to buy it is at the market that is held in the main square, the Rossio, on Saturdays. Although unglazed the pottery of the region has always enjoyed a high reputation in the country. Royal patronage is remembered in the name of the *Pucaros dos Reis*, or 'King's Jugs'. The best known of the pots are the large globe shaped

The whitewashed houses of Évoramonte

water coolers, with two short spouts and one handle, known as *moringues*. The pots are often decorated with white marble chips, or are engraved. Perfect gifts for home are the brightly coloured figurines that are also produced here. Saints, peasants and animals are among the most favoured reproductions. The market is also believed, locally at least, to sell the finest cheeses, made from ewes' milk, in Portugal.

The Rossio itself is a fine place to rest and watch the traffic of people around the town. The houses and bars around the square have intricate, wrought iron balconies, and façades often decorated with tiles.

The lower part of the town also has two museums. The Rural Museum, number 62 on the Rossio, has an extensive collection of local handicrafts, produced in cork, wood and clay, among other materials. The Agricultural History Museum, at 87 Rua de Serpa Pinto contains other ethnographic exhibits.

The old upper town of Estremoz lies up a steep alley at the north end of the Rossio, beyond the Manueline pillory. The walk to the star-shaped inner fortifications of the old town is dominated by the thirteenth-century keep, topped by small pyramid shaped battlements. The view from the top of the tower of the Three Crowns, as it

The water jugs known as moringues *made in Estremoz*

is locally known, with the Serra de Ossa heights and the town of Évoramonte to the south is quite beautiful. The tower is 27m (88ft) high and built of white marble.

The upper town has been a point of strategic importance since before the thirteenth century when it was finally wrested from the Moors. King Sancho II and King Afonso III began the rebuilding of the castle, whose keep was completed by that inveterate builder of fortresses, King Dinis, at the beginning of the fourteenth century. The tower of the keep is known as the Tower of the Three Crowns because of the three kings who had a hand in building it: Sancho II, Afonso III and Dinis. Dom Dinis also built a palace from where he sought the hand of Princess Isabel of Aragon. The royal couple lived there for much of their lives and the queen, who was revered as a saint even in her own lifetime, died there in 1336.

Within the inner walls too is a chapel dedicated to her. The chapel is decorated with tiles showing scenes from the queen's life.

Her kindness and generosity to the poor were legendary and one scene depicted is the Miracle of the Roses. The queen, having loaded her skirts with gold from the king's coffers to distribute to the poor, was suddenly discovered by her husband. When called upon to open the pleats of her skirts, however, all that was revealed were rose petals.

In strictly historical terms however it was probably King Dinis' fortifications, rather than Isabel's good works, that have had the clearest effect on the status of the country. In the crucial battles to establish Portugal's independence from the Castilians, culminating in the Battle of Aljubarrota in 1385 Estremoz was the headquarters of Nun Alvares Pereira, the commander of the forces of the Portuguese contender for the throne, João of Avis. From here he led his army to defeat the Castilians at Atoleiros in 1384.

The old town also contains a *pousada*, that was formerly the armoury of King John V, and was built upon the ruins of the palace of Dom Dinis. Though luxurious and beautifully furnished it is, like many of the *pousadas*, less expensive than one might imagine for staying in a part of Portuguese history and it is, in any case, open for visitors. The restaurant, with its fine views is also recommended. Otherwise Estremoz has a good range of *pensions* and hotels, particularly around the Rossio in the lower part of town.

As an important regional town Estremoz has festivals almost throughout the year. The Festas de Santo Andre take place in November, the Festas da Cidade de Estremoz in September, a craftwork fair in July and an agricultural fair in May.

Estremoz is in the heart of one of the most important marble producing areas in the world. The Romans were the first to exploit the marble in the area and it became an important resource for them as Estremoz lay conveniently on the road between *Olisipo* (Lisbon) and *Emerita* (Merida in Spain). The first of the huge, deep quarries that are to be found between here and Borba lies just half a kilometre out of town on the right-hand side. The sheer white walls of marble descending as much as 60m (200ft) into the earth are a remarkable sight. Visitors are allowed to watch the marble being cut and winched up, and even to descend the iron steps down to the quarry bottom, though it is not recommended for the fainthearted.

One of the curious museums in which rural Portugal seems to specialise is located off the N4 on the road to Borba, in the tiny village of **Vila Lobos**. The Museu de Cristo has a collection of over 3,000

A herd of Alentejan bulls

Demonstrating traditional crafts in Évoramonte, Alto Alentejo

A quiet, sandy cove between Sines and Porto Covo, South-West Alentejo

The gilded and tiled interior of São Laurenço, Almansil, Eastern Algarve

Marble quarries just outside Estremoz

crucifixes, some over a thousand years old. Owned by the Lobo family, the collection,which is still being added to, was started over four decades ago and represents numerous artistic styles.

The archetypal marble town is undoubtedly **Borba**, just 11km (7 miles) west of Estremoz. Its environs are surrounded by marble quarries and even the humblest of houses in the town has marble door steps, window mantles and lintels. The cumulative effect is that of a remarkably clean quiet white town. There is a delightful garden on the road out of town towards Vila Viçosa which has a large eighteenth-century marble fountain and a café/bar made from a converted railway carriage. Some of the antique shops around the church of São Bartolemeu are said to contain some bargains.

Surprisingly, Borba is also the region which produces the fine Surbibor wines. The bottling plant is in the town centre and is open for visits. These *adegas* are also a good place to buy mature vintage wines at very reasonable prices. This wine producing area of the Alto Alentejo is apparently soon to be demarcated.

The area to the south of Borba is dominated by the huge palace of **Vila Viçosa**, just 6km (4 miles) away on the N255. This was the favoured residence of the last royal house of Portugal, the House of Bragança. As the N4 road enters Vila Viçosa, whose name means 'Shaded Town', the famous Manueline knotted gate of the palace can be seen on the right-hand side. This gate is part of the few remaining sections of the original sixteenth-century palace wall. Beyond the palace gate the road opens up to reveal the impressive proportions of the palace and the square before it. The statue at the centre is of the eigth Duke of Bragança, João IV, who acceded to the throne in 1640, at the end of the last period of Spanish rule.

The original palace dated, unsurprisingly, from the time of Dom Dinis, and construction began on the present massive structure in 1501, under the fourth Duke, Jaime I. The palace itself, as one might expect, contains many fine and valuable pieces of furniture, ceramics and painting. The most interesting of these are undoubtedly the vast seventeenth-century tapestries depicting the exploits of the Portuguese abroad.

Two of these hang in the well of the staircase to the first floor. One shows the fifteenth-century Battle of Ceuta in North Africa, victory at which started João I and Portugal upon a history of colonial exploration and exploitation. Another depicts the sixteenth-century Siege of Azamor by Jaime I. A surprising and intriguing revelation is that the wooden pannelled ceiling in the dining room is, in fact, an upturned caravel, the vessels in which the original explorers, such as Vasco da Gama, set sail.

Perhaps though the best way to enjoy the palace is to appreciate the character of the royal family that is revealed, particularly in the transverse wing which is largely given over to the apartments of the last but one king, Dom Carlos, his wife Marie-Amelia and their family. Carlos spent his last night here. Having been waved off the next morning he and his eldest son were assasinated when they arrived in Lisbon. The last king, Manuel II fled hastily with his mother into exile in 1910. He died in England in 1932. The present heir to the non-existent Portuguese throne practises ecological farming on his estate near Viseu.

The Braganças chose this as their residence because it was surrounded by 21,000 hectares (81 sq miles) of prime hunting land. The family indeed seems to have enjoyed a taste for the good life as is reflected in the choice of exhibits. The grossness of the huge antlers used as chandeliers in the dining room is reinforced by the idiosyncratic collection of royal beer mugs.

Whereas other royal families commisioned or collected works of art the Braganças chose to collect weapons, principally those useful in hunting, such as knifes, revolvers or rifles, but also weapons of war, such as cannons, swords and crossbows. The heads of game animals like stags and wild boars are proudly displayed around the palace. These were probably caught in the 'Tapada Real' or royal hunting ground, that lies behind the palace enclosed by 18km (11 miles) of walls.

The Bragança family character seems to dominate the place. This is particularly true of the private rooms with the family's beds still made up and dresses and suits hanging in wardrobes or lying on beds as if their owners might enter at any moment from a day's hard riding in the woods.

On his death in exile in England the last king, Manuel II, left all his property to the Portuguese nation and the palace archives contain a remarkable collection of fifteenth- and sixteenth-century books, including early editions of *The Lusiads* by Camões, the national poet.

Finally it is worth visiting the kitchens as no other place in the house with its vast coppers, long spits or gigantic mortar and pestle suggests so well the Hogarthian, indulgent lifestyle the royal family once seemed to have enjoyed. Before leaving try to visit the sixteenth-

A prehistoric dolmen near Elvas

century cloister with its boxwood hedges as it is delightfully cool. In the palace grounds there is also a coach museum containing examples from the eighteenth to the early twentieth century.

At the other end of the square are the ruins of Dom Dinis' original royal palace built at the end of the thirteenth century. The crenellated walls now house an archaeological museum, with exhibits from the Paleolithic, Neolithic and Roman periods. Two other buildings on the main square are worth visiting. The former Antigo Convento das Chagas, or Convent of the Wounds of Christ, contains within its Renaissance interior the tombs of the Duchesses of Bragança. The Augustine church, or Convento dos Agustinos, contains the white marble tombs of the Dukes of Bragança.

In August the largest animal fair in the Alentejo is held in Vila Viçosa in the Campo da Restauracão.

Further west from Vila Viçosa on the N4, having returned to the main road at Borba is the most impressive fortified town in the southern half of the Portuguese-Spanish border region, the walled town of **Elvas**. It is reached through sun-burnished fields which often enclose the hugely impressive black Alentejan bulls. The complex city walls are what gives the town its particular charm and grace. They are designed in the shape of a star and are made up of two distinct inner and outer walls. The original inner walls were built in the thirteenth century. The outer walls, moats and bastions were added in the seventeenth century according to the strictures of the French military architect, Vaubann. The extent of these defences reflects the historical animosity with Spain, and the proximity, just 17km (10 miles) away of the Spanish fortress of Badajoz. Unlike some of the other heavily fortified towns in Portugal, Elvas does, indeed have a history of proud defiance in the face of attack.

The number of dolmens and prehistoric remains to be found in the area of Elvas suggests that the town is of very ancient origin. Some historians believe that the first confrontation may have been between Celts, who had sailed up the Guadiana river from the Algarve settling on the hill tops in the Celtic fashion, and the Carthaginian General Maharbal. In 714 the Moors occupied the town and fortified it and were not removed until the liberator of Évora, Gerald the Fearless, attacked their fortress in 1166, and even then not conclusively. King Sancho II, who, most experts now agree, is pictured in the town's coat of arms bearing his standard, was the final Christian liberator in 1229.

During the War of Restoration against their Spanish rulers in 1644 Elvas was a crucial battleground. The Spaniards attacked with over 10,000 men but were repulsed by the stout defence of the townspeople. Besieged again by the Spanish in 1659 the castle walls still remained inviolate, despite an epidemic within them. In 1811, during the Peninsular War Elvas was the base for Wellington's successful assault on Napoleon's troops in Badajoz. Reinforced again and again during this glorious military career into one of the most formidable set of defensive walls in Europe, the scale of the walls is now such that lines of traffic can drive through the gates. The best way to appreciate their grandeur is to make a tour by foot of the 5km (3 miles) of walls.

This is the best way, too, to appreciate the remarkable Amoreira Aqueduct. Appearing at first sight as an extension of the fortifications, the aqueduct is a fine example of the confidence and exuberance of the Manueline period of the late fifteenth and early sixteenth century. The 7km ($4^1/_2$ mile) long structure was designed by Francisco de Arruda in 1498. It took 125 years to build with the first stream of water discharching in a fountain in the Largo de Misericordia in 1622. Paid for by a royal tax on the people of the town the aqueduct runs at ground level for $4^1/_2$km (3 miles), then 1,367m ($^3/_4$ mile)

The Amoreira Aqueduct, Elvas

underground and 1,238m ($^3/_4$ mile) on overhead arches.

The heart of the town lies around the old cathedral in the Praça de República, lying at the summit of the hill on which the town is built. The cobbled streets, with their whitewashed and iron-grilled sixteenth- and seventeenth-century houses, are a delight to walk around as the visitor approaches the main square. Bounded to the north by the old cathedral, the former town hall lies to the south and the tourist office is also in the square. A mosaic paving of geometrical shapes in sandstone, marble and basalt enhances its centre.

Elvas lost its episcopal status in 1882, and the cathedral is now more correctly known as the Church of the Assumption of Our Blessed Lady. Like the aqueduct it was built in the sixteenth century according to a design by the Manueline architect, Francisco de Arruda. Though it has been modified since, the rose window, the lateral doors, the stonework of the archways, and above all the conical tower all still pay witness to Portugal's only indigenous architectural style. The interior has three attractive naves and two fine paintings.

Behind the cathedral, reached via the road to the right of it, is a tiny but very attractive cobbled square, the 'Largo', or Square of Santa Clara, with a pillory at its centre. The four irons were used to

*The old cathedral at
Elvas*

chain up malefactors and date from the sixteenth century. The sixteenth-century pillory itself has some attractive Manueline decoration.

On the south side of the square is the Church of Our Lady of
Consolation. Unremarkable from the outside, its interior is composed of an almost perfectly symmetrical octagonal chapel. Built
between 1543 and 1557, according to the wishes of the military order
of the Knights Templar, almost every surface within was covered in
the seventeenth century with beautiful, multi-coloured ceramic tiles.
The church had also been part of a Dominican Convent, and the
panels that line the dome show the emblems of that order.

Beyond the square lies the original castle of Elvas, and to reach
it, one passes beneath an old Moorish gateway and loggia, flanked by
two towers. All of these buildings were part of the original tenth-
century defensive wall that surrounded the castle. The Moors occupied Elvas from the eighth century and were not finally removed
until 1229, almost a hundred years after the liberation of Lisbon.

Following the street beneath the arch the reason for the great
difficulty experienced by the Portuguese in dislodging the Moors

The sixteenth-century pillory in the Largo Santa Clara, Elvas

can be seen in the massive solidity of the castle and its two keeps. Though modified since, particularly in the fifteenth century, the fine views over the surrounding countryside give a good idea of the dominance the Moors could have exercised from its walls.

There is plenty of accommodation available, including the state-run *estalagem* of Sancho II, and to the south the *pousada* of Santa Luzia, that lies on the road to the fort of the same name. This fort, like the fort of Nossa Senhora da Graca, a kilometre to the north of Elvas was built in the Vaubann style. The Graca fort withstood a bombarding from Napoleon's troops with only slight damage, and within its walls contains a cistern with enough water to maintain a garrison for several months.

Elvas has two festivals, both in September. The Romaria ao Senhor Jesus da Boa Fe and the Feira de São Mateus take place at the beginning and the end of the month respectively. Elvas also has a good range of restaurants and some good sports facilities.

A final place to visit before leaving the Alentejo — rather a long way, 50km (30 miles) to the north-west of Elvas, but worth the trip — is to the stud and training centre for horses, the 'Coudelaria', at Alter do Chão. The town of **Alter do Chão** itself has a fourteenth-century castle and a sixteenth-century palace of the counts of Alter. Several *pensions* are to be found near the castle.

Three kilometres (2 miles) to the north of the town is the 'Coudelaria'. This is a world famous stud breeding the Royal Alter horses that were the Portuguese royal family's preferred breed ever since the stud was founded by a Portuguese king in 1748. The breed is descended from the Spanish Andalucian horse. For many years the breed was kept pure and was used by the Lisbon Riding School at Queluz. Unfortunately French mares were later introduced and the quality of the breed began to decline. Arabian stallions have since been used to try to re-upgrade the breed, with some success. The Alter Real is usually bay or dark brown in colour and has a short broad neck and large eyes. Close coupled, with a short neck and with a willing and obedient temperament, it is ideal for dressage and *haute ecole* training.

Over 130 people work on the 900 hectares (2,200 acres) of the farm, with over 300 horses and Andulusian donkeys in their charge. There are regular guided tours of the stables and yards of the stud throughout the day. The best time to visit though is in the morning when the horses are being exercised. The annual horse sale is the 25 April and is followed the next day by Alter da Chao's festival of Our Lady of Happiness.

Further Information

— The Alto Alentejo —

Tourist Information Offices

Alter do Chão
Largo de Pelourinho
☎ 045 62179

Elvas
Praça de República
☎ 068 62236

Estremoz
Largo da República
☎ 068 22538

Monsaraz
Rua Direita
☎ 066 55136

Vila Viçosa
Praça de República
☎ 068 42140.

Places of Interest

Alter do Chão (4km north)
'Coudelaria' Stud Farm
Open anytime before 5pm.

Elvas
Castle
Open: May-September 9am-12.30pm, 2-7pm.
Winter months closes at 5.30pm (except Thursdays).

Estremoz
Municipal Museum
Largo Dom Dinis
Open: 10am-12noon, 2-6pm.
Closed Mondays.

Rural Museum
Praça Rossio 62
Open: 10am-12noon, 2-6pm.
Closed Mondays.

Agricultural History Museum
Rua de Serpa Pinto
Open: 10am-12noon, 2-6pm.
Closed Mondays.

Vila Viçosa
Palace of the Braganças
Open 9am-1pm, 2-6pm Closed Mondays.

Markets

Elvas — Monday

Festivals

Alter do Chão
Annual Horse Sale
April 25

Senhora da Alegria
April 26.

Elvas
Senhor Jesus da Boa Fe
Early September

São Mateus
Late September.

Estremoz
Feira da Agricultura
May

Feira de Artesenato
July

Festas da Cidade de Estremoz
Early September.

Reguengos de Monsaraz
Festivals in January, April, May, June, August and September.

9 • South-West Alentejo

The coastline of the South-West Alentejo is arguably the most beautiful and unspoilt of the whole Iberian Peninsula. After the largely industrial, but still attractive, town of Sines there is an unbroken sweep of majestic headlands, picturesque coves and sandy beaches down to the old Arab town of Aljezur in the Algarve. There are no large centres of population and though some of the coastal villages have a small-scale tourist industry built around them, the majority of the fishing villages remain the tranquil, unhurried places they have always been. There are no major historical or artistic centres along the coast, though the native popular architecture of the traditional villages, such as Porto Covo, is simple and beautiful. But there is mile upon mile of extraordinary coastal scenery, precipitous cliffs and sandy dunes, with their accompanying wildlife. The ecology of the region is indeed so valued by the Portuguese themselves that the South-West Alentejo has been designated a protected area. Though strictly within the Algarve the area inland from the southern section of the protected zone contains the spectacular beauty of the Serra de Monchique and their delightful towns, Monchique and the elegant spa town of Caldas de Monchique.

Sines, in so far as it is known at all abroad, is known as the home of one of Portugal's largest oil refineries, and indeed it is one of the country's largest industrial centres. This should not deter the open-minded traveller, however, for as the birthplace of Vasco da Gama it retains much of its traditions and history as a fishing port, and plays host to an exciting music festival throughout the month of August with its climax on the fifteenth.

The town has regular train connections to Lisbon and to Portimão in the Algarve and the N120 road, which leads to Lisbon in the north and Lagos on the southern coast, is a good though not particularly quick road.

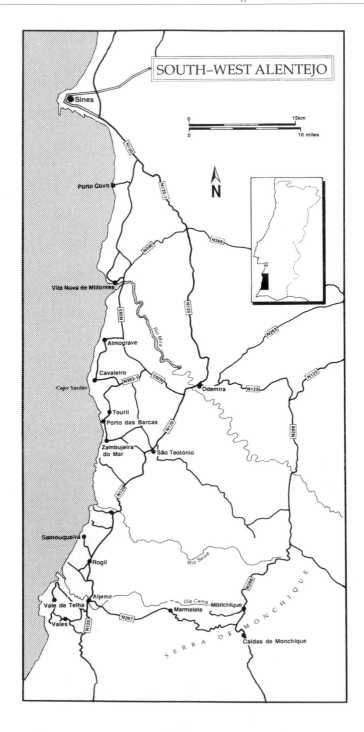

Sines harbour

Occupied by both the Romans and the Moors Sines was captured for Christendom in 1217 by the Knights of the Order of St John. Like other settlements along this coast it was also frequently the target of raids by pirates from Algeria and other parts of North Africa.

The old centre of the town is located around the medieval castle that was probably built for protection against pirates from North Africa and is now used by the communist-dominated local council as the atmospheric site for the summer's musical events. There are attractive terraced cafés in the shadow of the castle walls, popular with Portuguese tourists travelling on to the Algarve.

Inside the castle itself is a rather low key Natural History Museum, housed in what was formerly the governor's palace, where, according to tradition, Sines' most famous son, Vasco da Gama, was born. The castle walls afford a fine view of the natural harbour below. A statue of da Gama, the first man to discover a sea route to India in 1498, gazes out across the Atlantic.

To the right-hand side of the bay, north along the Avenida do Vasco da Gama, is Sines' still active fishing port. The men sit on the quays mending their nets. The brightly coloured fishing boats bob in the water. There is normally a catch brought in mid-afternoon and

The Manueline portal of Sines parish church

this is worth waiting a little to see as the hectic bargaining between fishermen and local market stall holders becomes quite animated.

Not surprisingly, there are fine sea food restaurants in Sines, serving rock lobsters, giant lobsters, spider crabs and dogwhelks as well as many types of fish. A good area to seek one out is directly above the fishing harbour around the Church of Nossa Senhora das Salvas. The views of the harbour from the restaurant terraces are very pleasing.

The brilliantly whitewashed church of Our Lady itself is worth pausing to admire. The church doorway is a most attractive Manueline portal, very unusual in being composed of a pink marbled stone. The Manueline is Portugal's only indigenous architectural and artistic style. It is named after King Manuel I who reigned from 1495 to 1521 during the country's great period of overseas expansion into Africa, Brazil and the Far East. The style which is mainly seen, as here, in decorative sculpture, uses motifs such as twisted coils like ropes, globes and anchors to reflect the importance of the newly discovered sea routes in Portugal's new conquests.

The rest of the façade of the church, with its cupolas, is sixteenth-century baroque, though it was remodelled in the seventeenth and eighteenth centuries. Local legend has it that the church was established when a Byzantine princess, Dona Vetaca, was saved after her ship had been wrecked along the coast.

Before leaving Sines it is worth mentioning that it contains a good range of accommodation and general facilities. There is a town beach nestling in the harbour with boats to hire, and at the left-hand end of the beach a nautical club can make available equipment for scuba diving. There is also a sports centre available to visitors opposite the tourist office on the Avenida General Humberto Delgado. For those interested in archaeology there is a museum collection derived from sites, particularly Roman, in the surrounding region, to be found near the town centre on the Rua Francisco Lopes.

Travelling south from Sines takes the traveller into the South-West Alentejo proper. The road to Porto Covo provides a good introduction to the economy of the area. As in many other parts of Portugal one can see new plantations of eucalyptus trees. The sandy soils of the region are not good, but nonetheless wheat is grown and there is pastureland for cattle. The cattle, like the roadside melon sellers, often shelter from the hot sun under simple wooden constructions, with roofs of eucalyptus branches.

The splendour of the Alentejan headlands can soon be appreciated by following the directions to the beach, or *praia*, of **São Torpes**. Stopping and walking at any point along this road before it reaches the beach will afford ample opportunity to appreciate the rugged beauty of the rocks.

Like Sines and many other towns along this coast São Torpes too has its shipwreck legend. The body of the Emperor Nero's chief steward, São Torpe, was said to have come ashore here and on the spot where he was found the first christian chapel in the country is claimed to have been built. The long stretch of sand that follows is a fine place to swim or relax.

Those who enjoy sports fishing should find their interest catered for here too. The Portuguese coast is indeed probably the richest in Europe in terms of the variety of fish that can be caught. This is principally because the two hundred or so varieties that appear in the countries fish markets are a mixture of the colourful Mediterranean varieties that migrate to this coast at varous times of the year and the cold water Atlantic varieties that are fished as far away as Norway and Iceland.

Common varieties caught are several different types of bass and bream, mackerel, mullet and groupers. The best place from which to fish is where there is a line of spray across the rocks, bearing in mind though that the tide rises between 2m and 3m (6-9ft). The best time to fish is when the skies are overcast and the tide is coming in. It should always of course be remembered by anyone fishing off the rocks that they can be slippery and treacherous.

Returning to the N120-1 and travelling south for 8km (5 miles) the turning to the exceptionally attractive Alentejan fishing village of **Porto Covo** appears on the right. Resisting the temptation to walk back along the coast to the, probably deserted, beaches of Morgavel, Olivierinha, and Burrinho the road leads into the main square of Porto Covo.

This is a beautifully simple jewel of popular architecture, dating back to the eighteenth century. The whitewashed houses are one storey with red terracotta tiled roofs and blue painted fringes to the door and window frames. The coloured fringes were introduced by the Moors who believed they kept evil spirits away. Should the neatness and simplicity of the village square, the Praça of the Marquis of Pombal, particularly appeal it is possible to rent rooms or an entire house in the village by inquiring at any of the local shops.

The Palace of Estoi, Eastern Algarve

Moncarapacho, Eastern Algarve

The main square in Porto Covo

There are quiet, craggy coves here and a tremendous view back to the port of Sines. The Fort of Ilha de Dentro on the shore was again built as protection against pirates and there is a fine view from its walls of the nearby island of Pessigueiro

Though the rugged and unexploited beauty of this coast is virtually unknown in Britain this is not the case with young people from Germany or with the Portuguese themselves. Thus Porto Covo, like many of the other villages on this coastline does have some shops selling beach wear and barbecue restaurants but the development is still small scale.

A short distance along the coast to the south is the beach and **Isla de Pessiguiero**. Local fishermen are usually around to take you to this sandy offshore island, and there is also a small seventeenth-century fort on the beach itself, which was partially destroyed in the great earthquake of 1775. Local legend has it that in 1660 a group of pirates murdered a hermit on this island and burnt his possessions including a statue of the Virgin. Some of the fishermen, however, found the image still intact amongst the ashes and built a chapel to Our Lady of the Burning to commemorate the miracle.

The beach also has one of the best bar restaurants to be found on this coast and it is a good spot from which to windsurf. The Isla de

*Bell tower at Vila
Nova de Milfontes*

Pessegueiro also contains the ruins of a Roman harbour and a chapel dating from the sixteenth century.

The main accommodation in this area is to be found 12km (7 miles) or so to the south of here at **Vila Nova de Milfontes**. The best of the camp sites is just outside the town. The Sitava site has tennis courts open to the general public, and opposite the site is a new nightclub. In the town there are *pensions*, and more expensive hotels, including rooms to let in the small castle that looks out over the sea at the resort's sea front.

Vila Nova de Milfontes is an old fishing port, becoming adapted for the tourist trade. Yet, set on the gently sloping sandy banks of the River Mira it still preserves much of its old charm. The old town is still huddled round the medieval castle, overlooking the sea. Built in 1603 it has a charming drawbridge. King João I made Vila Nova a sanctuary for those fleeing from justice on condition that they agreed to defend the castle against pirates from Algiers and Morocco. Unfortunately it is now privately owned and so cannot be visited, though it is possible to rent rooms inside. The whitewashed houses bordered with blue and yellow around the old town are again very attractive.

There are hotels here, though they can become quite crowded with Portuguese visitors from the North, as well as good restaurants. There are also sports facilities and canoe hire.

Perhaps the one specific sight worth visiting in Vila Nova is the church of Nossa Senora de Graca. It is interesting in the degree of contrast to the typical baroque churches of the north and centre of the country. The exterior is blindingly white with a bell tower and is simply fringed with blue, while the interior too is very plain and appealing. It is an example of the same kind of succesful popular architecture to be seen in the main square of Porto Covo.

The coast, south of Vila Nova, becomes a wild and beautiful series of cliffs, interspersed with coves and sandy beaches. As the road passes out of Vila Nova, however it is worth noting the dark green fields that can be seen in the flood plain of the River Mira. These, in such strong contrast to the dominant browns and yellows of the landscape, are rice fields. Much of Portugal's rice production, which is now in excess of 100,000 tons, comes from this area of the Alentejo.

The village of **Almograve**, 10km (6 miles) south of Vila Nova de Milfontes along the N390 is a fine place to enjoy the solitary, rugged beauty of this coastline. The beach here, the Praia Grande, is long and sandy and, unusually for Portugal, has a nudist section at its southern end.

Other than in the heat of the middle of the day the coast road to the south of the beach makes a fine area in which to walk and explore. A couple of kilometres (1 mile) below Almograve the cliffs rise to almost 40m (130ft) above the sea. The land here is slate and sandstone. As sandstone is a relatively soft rock, easily eroded, the headlands have been worn away into remarkable horizontal or vertical layered shapes of slate. The sea has gradually, too, worked its way into the land leaving small islands of towering slate high above the waterline. It is a delightful area for birdwatchers as the cliffs are home to several different species of gull and other sea birds. The village itself is very small but still has a couple of cafés and bars.

Travelling along the coast road to Cape Sardão, the route is lined

Cape Sardão

*The lighthouse at
Cape Sardão*

Alentejan chimneys in the village of Cavaleiro

with Scots pines and eucalyptus trees. In the fields beyond there are pumpkins, corn and chestnut-coloured long-horned cattle. Often seen feeding near the cattle, and only resident in this part of Portugal though occasionally found elsewhere in Europe, is the cattle egret, one of the heron family. Distinguishable from other herons by its stocky build, white plumage, and in the summer, at close range, its yellow legs and bill.

Just before Cape Sadão is the agricultural village of **Cavaleiro**. It is a pretty place with orchids and dog roses in the hedgerows. By the bridge to the cape itself there are fig trees and bamboo growing in the stream below.

At the cape there is a bright red lighthouse and some spectacular views over the cliffs. Wild garlic grows freely on the steep crags and common gulls and herring gulls swoop into their nests on the rock face. It is possible to fish off the rocks as the locals do and there is fine walking in either direction. It is a landscape far from our preconceptions of Portugal, and is certainly off-the-beaten-track.

Modern agricultural techniques and methods dominate the landscape from Cavaleiro to the villages of Touril and Porto das Barcas. A vast acreage is rendered fertile by the large grey pipeline that snakes its way across the land. Wells sunk deep into the earth can

An off-the-beaten-track village near Zambujeira do Mar

be seen at the roadside and large-scale mechanical sprayers irrigate the land. Most of the land thus cultivated is used for rice production.

The village of **Touril**, reached by following the N393 towards the coast, is an Alentejan village essentially unchanged from its traditional way of life. Firewood is still stacked outside the single-storey houses and the villagers can still be seen working in the fields with mules or donkeys. Hens and cockerels run across the cobbled street from their hen coops.

On the road between Touril and **Porto das Barcas** watch out for storks, standing perfectly still in the fields, sharing the pasture with the stately black Alentejan bulls. Storks can be found throughout this area of the Alentejo and they can easily be spotted by looking out for their unmistakeably large nests on old abandoned buildings, especially churches. The presence of these birds, so much a feature of the central Spanish plateau, is a reminder that it is this area of Portugal that most resembles its larger neighbour.

Zambujeira do Mar, just a few kilometres (2 miles) along the coast from Porto das Barcas is a very pleasant resort with an unpretentious, homely atmosphere, largely due to most of the visitors being Portuguese from the north of the country. The town is, again, built on the headland above a bay. In this case the promenade that sweeps down to the bay is lined with attractive pines. There are obviously a good range of restaurants and *pensions* here, a couple of nightclubs including one that promises traditional *fado* music and, at the nearby campsite, tennis facilities open to visitors. The highlight of the village is, without doubt, the beach that sits beneath an imposing cliff face.

From Zambujeira the coast road leads for the first time inland to **São Teotónio**. The way is lined with very tall eucalyptus trees, now being felled by the burgeoning timber industry. Beyond the trees are fields of sunflowers. São Teotónio, itself, is a pretty town, with trellised grapes growing between the houses in the backstreets and lots of exotic and colourful flowers growing in the main square before the parish church. The church of Santa Rita is itself worth visiting. It has an attractive clock tower and the altar inside, with its simple black and gold trimming, is very pleasing. There is a primitive painting above on the ceiling and the flooring is of cool marble.

Travelling from here to **Odemira**, the largest town of this area of the South-West Alentejo, the landscape changes quite dramatically. Away from the irrigated plains of the coast the bright orange of the

Alentejos relaxing in the shade in São Teotónia

stripped cork oaks, so typical of the rest of the Alentejo, appear for the first time. Portugal is, of course, the world's greatest producer of cork, and the bark is strippd every nine years. The road rises and twists around hairpin bends as it approaches Odemira. It thus affords fine views to the south to the foothills of the Sierra de Monchique.

Odemira is a rather sleepy but attractive town situated above the River Mira. It has an attractive centre in the Praça Sousa Prado, with ornamental pools, weeping willows and a small aviary. Though it must be said that the greylag geese and the sizeable carp look much more content in their respective pools than do the doves and golden pheasant in their cages.

There is a modern vegetable market on the hill above the town, worth visiting for such local specialities as the large bunches of herbs dried ready to sprinkle on salads. Odemira, too is a good place to seek local handicrafts, such as hand-woven baskets, rugs and clay pots.

Retracing the route back to São Teotonio, the road passes a large brickworks that uses the local red clay. There is also a large timber yard. The road beyond São Teotonio affords fine views of the Sierra de Monchique and a couple of picnic spots have been sited along the way. Three kilometres before Odeceixe at Baiona there is a large new

The pretty town of São Teotónia

campsite with a swimming pool open to visitors. Throughout this area, there are rooms available in private houses, normally advertised in bars or shops.

The best route to take to approach the excellent beach and charmingly situated village of **Praia de Odeceixe**, at which point one has officially entered the province of Algarve, is to follow the dirt road alongside the River Seixe that branches off to the right just before the bridge into the town. The course of the river estuary winds gently down to issue into the sea over gently sloping sands.

It is an idyllic place and if fairly well known by the locals there is still plenty of space to swim in the river or in the bay where, for once, the Atlantic does not pound the shore so fiercely that swimming is dangerous. There is good fishing in the river and surfing and windsurfing on the sea. The village of Praia de Odeceixe is perched decorously above the bay and can be reached by foot on a staircase cut into the rockface. The village is a maze of picturesque steep, cobbled streets. Nightlife consists of a discoteque 2km (1$^1/_4$ miles) south of the village, while accommodation is available in rooms in the town or in villas near to the beach.

The 16km (10 miles) from Odeceixe to Rogil are officially designated a scenic route and the views of the mountains of Monchique are indeed quite dramatic. Just before the village of Rogil for those particularly interested in natural history and walking there is a small road to the right leading to the village of **Samouquiera**. Parking at the end of the tarred road a path leads into a rare and valuable area of sand dunes. To the right a sand track borders the valley carved out by a small stream. This stream can be followed until it drops, forming a small waterfall, into the sea. From the rocky terrace, Cape Sardão can be made out to the north. Following the coastline to the south another beach, this time made up of tiny pieces of black schist, appears. A circular route is completed by following the course of another stream that crosses the path further south back inland.

Rogil itself, however, is disappointing consisting of no more than a few houses to either side of the through road. Just beyond Rogil though there is an excellent and inexpensive regional craft centre. It is also worth knowing that the red wine grown in the area round Rogil, and available in any of the local restaurants, is excellent.

There are clean and largely deserted beaches at Amoreira and Carreagem off the road to Aljezur. There is also a campsite with tennis courts and a swimming pool open to visitors.

At Odeceixe we crossed the boundary that divides the Alentejo and the Algarve. Divided physically, however, from the Algarve by the Sierra de Monchique, Aljezur, and indeed the mountain towns of Monchique and Caldas de Monchique, can all be included within this area. For conservation purposes the Portuguese government include the area around Aljezur in the South-West Alentejo.

The valley of the River Cerca in which **Aljezur** is set is very lush, green and fertile, after the umberous hues of the coast. The town as its name would suggest is an old Moorish settlement, dating from the tenth century. The original settlement lies to the west of the river while the new town lies to the east. Parts of the castle the Moors constructed still stands. It was captured from them by the master of the Order of St James, Dom Paio Peres, in 1246 and rebuilt. The castle was severely damaged in the earthquake of 1775. The view from the castle back towards the mountains is superb.

The Church of the Misericórdia, on the descent back into the town, is worth visiting as it contains some interesting paintings of Christ and at the centre of the altar, in a way that is particular to southern Portuguese churches is, not a crucifix, but a small statue of the Virgin. The church, originally built in the sixteenth century, was rebuilt in the eighteenth.

There are several *pensions* in the town and a couple of decent restaurants. The local delicacy is a sea food stew served with rice. Aljezur's craft workers specialise in wickerwork and baskets.

The coast to the west of Aljezur has two fine long stretches of sandy beach at Arrifana and at Monte Clérigo. Perhaps the most interesting development in the area, though, lies between the two at the **Vale de Telha**. This is a large area of several hundred acres given over to the development of holiday villas, holiday homes and leisure facilities. There is also a campsite here. Facilities available include horse riding, golf, fishing and shooting, and these are all open to non-residents. There is also a three-star hotel, a variety of shops and several swimming pools.

The road from Aljezur, through Marmalete, to meet the N266 to Monchique passes initially through a rather harsh, stony terrain of cork trees and olive groves. It is in this way very similar to Trás-os-Montes in the far north of the country. Some of the hills here, though, seem to have been deliberately cleared and terraced by the local timber industry in order to plant young, and relatively fast growing, eucalyptus trees.

The twisted and knotted ropes typical of the Manueline style around the doorway of the parish church, Monchique

Beyond **Marmalete**, as quiet a place as one could imagine, the hills are more densely wooded with their natural flora of pines. The road twists and turns as it rises, offering some fine views, occasionally even as far as the blue of the sea off the Algarve coast.

Monchique, sitting high in the mountains, is the main market town for all the farmers and smallholders in the surrounding area. The air is fresh and invigorating here and if hiking in the mountains all around is appealing, then Monchique has several *pensions* in which to be based. The town also has a couple of monuments that are well worth seeing. The Igreja Matriz, near the town centre has a beautiful doorway in the Manueline style. The interior of the church, too, is interesting with tiles on the walls and some attractive paintings. Once again the statue at the head of the church is of Our Lady, with Christ relegated to the side altar.

From the centre of town it is a pleasant walk past pretty one-storey houses their garden walls trailing bourgainvillea, up the hill to the ruins of the convent of Nossa Senhora Desterro. The convent is approached through a long avenue of tall cork oaks. The ruins are now home to one of the local resident's cows, but, nonetheless, the Renaissance façade of the building remains very impressive. The design of the shallow vaulting beneath the doorway, though it is unfortunately, rather covered with graffiti, is considered to have been influenced by the Moors. It is an atmospheric place with a fine view over the town.

Monchique has a couple of *pensions* and a several reasonable restaurants which provide an opportunity to sample local speciali-ties, such as eels in a tomato sauce with the distictive Algarvian bread. After the meal the locally produced brandy, *aguardente de medronho*, should be tried. This brandy is produced in the mountain villages of Ameixal, Alte, Salir and Querenca, and made from the berries of the wild arbutus bush. The berries are picked in October and November, with fermentation lasting for as long as forty days. The liquid is then distilled in a copper still.

There is an agricultural fair held every month in the town, the biggest of which is the one held during 26-28 October, when every-thing is on sale from livestock to local handicrafts. It makes an excellent base for hiking in the peace and beauty of the surrounding woods of cork, chestnut, eucalyptus, pines and oak.

From Monchique it is a drive of only a couple of kilometres to the the summit of Mount Foia, highest point in the Sierra de Monchique at 902m (2,960ft). A walk from Monchique to the summit affords an enjoyable opportunity to appreciate how the wooded landscape often includes ingenious terracing by local farmers. From the obelisk at its summit can be seen the bays of Lagos and Portimão, and the Sagres Peninsula. Apart from the tremendous view, however there is nothing much there apart from a radio mast, a souvenir shop and a restaurant.

From Monchique to the spa town of **Caldas de Monchique** is a delightful drive through some of the prettiest countryside in Portu-gal. The town itself is set at the head of a deep ravine. The best way to approach the town is by foot through the the stone gateway situated halfway down the slip road to the town from the main Monchique to Portimao road. This enables the visitor to walk down a stone pathway to the spa itself.

The spa at Caldas de Monchique

The medicinal effects of the spa were apparent as far back as Roman times and the waters are today considered to be particularly effective in the treatment of rheumatism and skin conditions. The natural spring is housed in glass and marble and a nurse offers the curative waters to anyone who wishes to try them. Below the spa is a hospital which makes extensive use of the natural springs, and the large building below that again is a bottling factory from which the waters of Monchique are distributed all over Portugal.

Caldas de Monchique was a fashionable resort for the wealthy Spaniards of the nineteenth century and it was they who constructed the mock Moorish casino, now a regional arts and handicrafts centre, that dominates the town square. In its cheerful vulgarity it is rather reminiscent of the English south coast resort of Brighton with its Pavilion. The extremely attractive square, set on a slightly raised platform of patterned stones, and shaded by the dense foliage of elm trees, is a delightful place to rest and to have a coffee from one of the nearby cafés. One of the restaurants on the square claims to have been founded in 1692.

To the right of the square, beyond the hotel with a swimming pool open to visitors for a small fee, is a small chapel. The classical columns of the exterior are unusual, but the figurative tiles of the interior, depicting scenes from the lives of St Anthony and St Christopher and a full-scale battle against the Moors, are fascinating.

Shaded from the heat of the sun by the steep sides of the ravine, there is an enjoyable walk alongside the stream away from the town to an old water mill. The walk begins, beyond the bottling factory with signposts to a picnic spot. At the water's edge are fig trees and cactus trees, $1^1/_2$-2m (5-6ft) high. The mill itself is about a kilometre along the path. It is an old flour mill and the machinery can still clearly be seen. The millstone is now a small picnic table nearby. The stream, diverted from its original path beneath the mill, continues to flow through and with the sunlight that streams onto the mill at the end of the ravine has created a tiny sub-tropical zone with palm trees and fronds growing abundantly. Very surprisingly, a family still lives among the trees next to the mill, their hen houses and stores being simple wooden constructions built around or propped against the trees. There is an old woman there who may greet you and invite you to taste the leathery pods from the carob tree that grows across the path to the house. It is a strangely idyllic place, though their lives are, obviously, very hard. It is certainly off-the-beaten-track and seems a thousand miles from the hotels, cafés and restaurants just a kilometre ($^1/_2$ mile) back up the ravine.

From Caldas de Monchique the N266 descends through beautiful wooded country to the beautiful climate and hotchpotch development of the Algarve.

Further Information

— South-West Alentejo —

Tourist InformationOffices

Aljezur
Largo do Mercado
☎ 082 98229

Sines
Av General Humberto Delgado
☎ 069 632952

Places of Interest

Sines
Sines Sports Centre
Avenida General Humberto

Aljezur
Vale de Telha
☎ 082 98179

Markets and Festivals

Porto Covo
Market 29 August.

Sines
Market fourth Sunday of every
month.

Fair 15 August and fourth Sunday
in October.

Monchique
Feira de Outubro 26-28 October.

10 • The Eastern Algarve

Cut off from the rest of the country in terms of geography by the mountains of Monchique, Caldeirão, Espinhaço de Cão, and Mesquita, and in historical terms by its long occupation by the Moors and associations with North Africa, the Algarve has an atmosphere and its people an attitude that is distinctly different from the rest of Portugal. All of the peoples who initially occupied the area, including the Turdetanos, the Phoenicians, and the Moors regarded it as a natural part of the same kingdom as North Africa.

The 5,000 sq km (2,000 sq miles) of the Algarve form a gentle declivity from the northern mountains down to the golden beaches, red cliffs and marshlands of the southern and western coast. It was from this that the region gained its name *Al-Gharb*, which in Arabic means the land that falls away to the west. The Moors included in this title the lands of North Africa, and it was the custom for succeeding kings of Portugal to style themselves also as kings of the Algarve. The area was attractive to these peoples as well as to the Greeks and to the Romans for much the same reasons as it is attractive to visitors today, the remarkable mildness of the climate which makes it feel like spring almost throughout the year, the great variety of flora and fauna, and a paricular clarity and freshness in the air that is unique to the area. Sadly, however, much of the traditional atmosphere and tranquility of the coastal resorts, particularly west of Faro has been destroyed by over hasty exploitation of the natural resources of sun, sea, and sand.

The Eastern Algarve from Vila Real to Olhão is a far less intensively developed stretch of coastline than that of the western coast. It is quite different from traditional images of the Algarve, the coastline being made up not of rocky, picturesque coves, but rather of long stretches of sandy beach, protected from the sea by long low-lying offshore islands. These islands themselves have long attractive

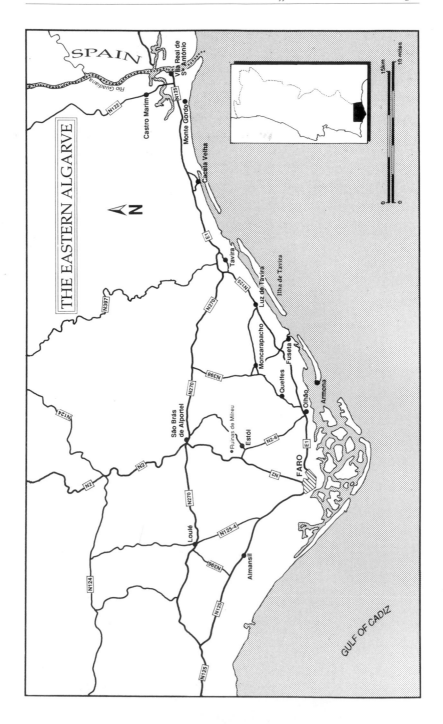

beaches as well as providing a unique environment for some of Portugal's most interesting wildlife. Inland from the coast too this region provides some fascinating historical and cultural sites in the Algarve, an area often thought of as a cultural wasteland.

Access to this area is very straightforward as there is a large and busy international airport, just 7km ($4^1/_2$ miles) from Faro with good connections to the town. Faro is also the meeting point of two major roads the N125 from the west and the N2 from the north. Faro, unfortunately, is one of the major resorts of the Algarve and very little of it could be said to be off-the-beaten-track. Nonetheless it is worth mentioning that the cathedral and bishop's palace stand in a very attractive square in the heart of the town, should the visitor have time to spare before a flight.

This tour of the Eastern Algarve begins with a small detour 16km (10 miles) to the west of Faro to the holiday village of **Almansil** along the N125. Unremarkable in itself, it is the best point from which to find the exceptional church of São Laurenço. The people of southern Portugal are much less religious than those of the North and the expulsion of the religious orders several centuries earlier in the south, combined with the great earthquake of 1755, has left very few churches of note in the south of the country. The church of São Lourenço is to be found just off the main route to Faro, the N125, about a kilometre before Almansil. The exterior of the church is a simple baroque façade. The interior, however is entirely covered, walls and ceiling, with tiles depicting the life of St Lawrence. The tiles were the work of Policarpo de Oliviera Bernardes, whose father, Antonio, founded an extremely influential school of ceramic design in Lisbon, and date from around 1730. The gilt altarpiece is very delicate and the domed ceiling above it is quite exquisite.

Part of the attractiveness of the church lies in the light, almost cheerful atmosphere that pervades it. The reason for this becomes clear with a closer examination of the tiles. The subject matter of many of the tiles is, in fact, essentially secular, depicting a bucolic idyll of plump cherubs, vines and cherries. Portuguese church architecture is in this quite different from the mystical, introspective atmosphere of Spanish tradition. The secular theme in the church is reinforced by the neo-Classical pillars and marble capitals in has relief on the side walls.

Just below the church of São Lourenço, on the right before the main road is the Cultural Centre of Almansil. Founded in 1980, this

Statue of a reclining woman by João Cutileiro at Almansil

is, in effect, a small art gallery, containing visiting exhibitions of
modern European art and a permanent collection of sculptures by
the modern Portuguese artist, João Cutileiro, whose most famous
sculpture of a reclining woman can be seen in the ornamental pool
before the Palace of Mateus in the remote northern region of Trás-os-
Montes. His small female figures are usually exhibited in the pleasant adjoining garden, along with the work of other Portuguese
sculptors. There is also a programme of musical performances, both
classical and jazz, thoughout the summer with artists coming from
all over Europe. Before leaving the centre the kitchen should be
visited to see the remarkably large-scale kitchen furniture, made by
craftsmen in the north of the country.

Almansil itself is an ugly modern tourist town, though if passing
through it is worth looking out for the ochre pottery painted in blues
and reds that is an traditional product of the town.

Six kilometres (4 miles) north of Almansil is the busy market
town of **Loulé**, birthplace of the present Social Democratic prime
minister of Portugal Cavaco da Silva. Reached by heading west out
of Almansil and then turning right on the N396, it is an attractive
town of whitewashed houses, old drinking fountains and castle
walls, best known in the region as a centre for craft workshops.

Loulé was originally a Roman settlement and within the castle walls, at the centre of the town, are some Roman remains in an archaeological museum. The castle has an impressive history, reckoned to have been first occupied by the Moors, it was captured by the Portuguese in 1249. Throughout its life it has recieved royal patronage. One of Portugal's earliest kings, Dom Pedro I, stayed for several days in the castle in 1359. The martyr king, Dom Sebastian stayed overnight in January, 1573, and Afonso V, after his conquest of the North African town of Alcacer, stayed here in November 1458. The castle walls are great fun to walk around and provide a good view over the town and an opportunity to examine the fret-cut, often filigree, chimneys that are unique to this region of the Algarve. The museum has an interesting collection of archaeological and ethnographic exhibits.

The tourist information office housed in the castle can offer detailed information on the good range of accommodation and on the variety of restaurants available in the city. Set off the coast accommodation can often be found in Loulé when it is at a premium elsewhere. Sports facilities, including a swimming pool, are available in the Municipal Gardens just at the northern edge of the town centre, off the Rua Assuncão. The greatest festivities in Loulé are during the blossoming of the almond trees in mid-February with a Battle of the Flowers and general merrymaking.

At the heart of the city is the market housed in a mock moorish building. It is a large market selling fish, fruit, meat, and leather goods. Some of the vegetables will probably be unfamiliar but the stallholders are lively and friendly and willing to point and mime their explanations for each vegetable's use. Specialities of this region are the soup *valdorejas*, tastily prepared chicken and delightful combinations of the locally grown figs and almonds.

In the streets surrounding the market place, particularly on the Rua 9 de Abril, are the small workshops of local craftsmen. The work of the Loulé craftsmen is considered to be particularly fine because many of them are believed to be descended from the Moslem artisans that remained in the town after the Christian re-conquest. They may be working in leather or in metals, but the local traditional crafts are those of doll making and the working of *esparto*, a type of grass, into mats, baskets and hats.

Loulé also contains several attractive churches. The parish church in the Largo Pr Da Silva, is an imposing Gothic construction

The busy market at Loulé

dating from the thirteenth century. The attractive tiles within date from 1720-30. The pulpit, too, is unusual in being made of wrought iron. The two side altars are dedicated to St Michael and St Brás. The latter chapel contains an interesting wooden sculpture of the eponymous saint from the early sixteenth century. Facing the church is the delightfully named Jardim dos Amuados or 'Garden of the Sulky Ones', and a stretch of the originally Moorish wall that defended the town against the Christians, rebuilt in the thirteenth century.

The Church of the Misericórdia on the Avenida Marcal Pacheco has a fine Manueline portal. In the churchyard there is a stone cross on which Christ has been sculpted on one side and Our Lady on the other. Behind the Misericordia on the Largo Tenente Cabecadas, dating from the twelfth and thirteenth centuries, is the now ruined Convent of Grace, though there still remains a valuable Gothic doorway. The former convent of the Holy Spirit, off the Largo Dom Pedro I, with its charming cloister has been converted into an art gallery for visiting exhibitions.

A kilometre ($^1/_2$ mile) to the west of Loulé on the N270, and affording a panoramic view of the surrounding area is the Church of Nossa Senhora de Piedade. The Renaissance church is no longer used for services but the local people still come to leave votive offerings at the altar as the statue of our Lady within is the *Mae Soberana* (literally Soveriegn Mother), or patron saint of Loulé. These are the curious wax limbs and locks of hair that can be seen. Though the main body of the church is quite dark the altar itself is lit by a skylight. The paintings on the sides of the church, and on the ceiling are interesting but quite faded.

The beehive-like construction behind the church is a new church that has yet to be completed. The platform before the church provides a fine view over the surrounding area. The great festival of Our Lady of Pity is on 15 April when her statue is taken down from the hill and placed in a church in the town to be venerated for fifteen days. The float bearing the statue is, apparently, carried back up the hill in procession at a trot which must be a remarkable sight given its steepness.

Moving on from Loulé along the N270 to the east, there is a tennis centre at the village of **Vilarinhos**, on the road to São Brás de Alportel, and an equestrian centre in the village of **Tor**. There is an excellent *pousada* at São Brás and an *estalagem* just before the village of Estoi.

São Brás de Alportel, for peace and tranquility in a beautiful rural setting within easy reach of the coast can hardly be matched. In the shadow of the Serra do Caldeirão, the village also provides easy access for walks in the mountains.

South of São Brás the landscape is quite harsh, the main produce from the area being from the cork oaks and arbutus bushes that are grown on mountainous areas. Where olive trees, carob and almond predominate, as is often the case in this area, the landscape is locally known as *barrocal*. The fields are also used as pasture for goats. The next place worth pausing at after turning south on the N2 is the village of Estói and the Roman ruins of Milreu.

Travelling first beyond Milreu to **Estói**, to the right off the main square stands the gateway to the grounds of a remarkable palace. It, and its gardens, are essentially baroque in design, although the decoration of the intricate staircase and the atmosphere of the gardens is decidedly late nineteenth century. It was built by the last Viscount of Estói in the eighteenth century and considerably added to between 1893 and 1909 by Jose Francisco da Silva.

Sadly, the palace has for some time been rather neglected and the interior is closed. The path from the gateway to the palace is lined with very tall palm trees, and on the right are the old stables. Signs

The stairway at the Palace of Estói

on the stable walls indicate that bulls were kept in the near side as one approaches and horses on the far side. At the base of the staircase to the palace itself there are orange and passion fruit groves which are now happily being tended by gardeners employed by the local council.

Beneath the bottom flight of stairs, and protected by iron railings is a statuary of life-size mythological figures, such as Diana and Venus. These are remarkable in themselves, but the quite beautiful mosaic animal figures on the walls of the statuary, such as the lion, for example, are, in fact original Roman mosaics transferred to the palace from the site of a Roman villa, a couple of kilometres away at Milreu.

The staircase as a whole is liberally decorated with very fine tiles, made at the turn of the century in Lisbon by such fine artists as Periera. These tiles, as at the church of São Laurenço at Almansil, depict scenes of a pastoral idyll, with cherubs, ducks, flamingos and full hipped female figures more Pre-Raphaelite than Classical, even when depicting Classical legends, such as that of Leda and the Swan. There are also, on either side of the staircase and, perhaps, as lovely as the Roman mosaics, two bas relief carvings in plaster or alabaster. One is becoming worn but the other is still in good condition and

Decorative painted tiles on the Palace of Estói

Mosaic of fish and shells at the Roman villa, Milreu

very fine. All along the balustrade at the top of the staircase and at the head of each flight of stairs are busts of political figures, such as Dom Carlos, the king of Portugal whose assasination in 1908 marked the beginning of the republic, and literary figures, such as Milton and the national poet of Portugal, the one-eyed Camoes. The whole place speaks of a confidence and optimism about the future which was soon to be irrevocably shattered by World War I in which Portugal suffered many casualties.

There is a fine view from the head of the stairs all the way to Olhão and the sea. It is to be hoped that before too long the council will have restored the interior of the palace so that its one-time sumptuous interior can be enjoyed. As a final example of the happy innocence that seems to pervade the place it is worth pausing to admire the ironwork of the bandstand, shaped as it is into lyres and musical staves. The Palace of Estói is certainly off-the-beaten-track, but it would be to its advantage if it did not remain quite so much so in the future.

Immediately after the small road bridge over the River Seco, before reaching the main Faro to São Brás road are situated the Roman ruins of **Milreu**. Built between the first and third centuries after Christ this was originally an important administrative centre

*An old irrigation
wheel in the fields
near Milreu*

for the surrounding agricultural area. It was subsequently, converted into a luxury villa for an important roman official. The design
of the building was that of a villa built around a central garden or
courtyard. All that remains of the original colonnade that surrounded the central open space now are half a column and the base
of another.

Much of the decoration that does remain is interesting, however,
in particular the mosaics of fishes, dolphins, and even prawns are
very lovely. The date of the villa has been established from the
presence on the site of busts of the Empress Agrappina, and the
Emperors Hadrian and Gallien, who reigned in the first, second, and
third centuries respectively. These, along with other items from the
site are kept in museums in Lagos and Faro. The site was discovered
in 1876 and is thought to be part of the Roman town of *Osssonaba*.

Milreu is an important archaeological site but it is not what is usually associated with the Algarve.

The roads from Estói to Moncarapacho and the coast, or the N2–6 from Estói to Olhão, wind their way through a landscape of disused waterwheels, orange groves, greenhouses of tomatoes, and trees heavy with pomegranates in the summer. The natural point from which to begin an exploration of this coast, avoiding Faro which is the effective heart of the mainstream Algarve tourist industry, is the town of Olhão.

The tourist industry has been developed to a limited extent in Olhão but the town still earns much of its living through its traditional industries of fishing and canning. The fish market on the dockside is, indeed, probably one of the finest in Portugal with fish, squid, swordfish, prawns and sardines constantly arriving through the day from the quayside. Each new catch brings with it a flurry of activity as the bar owners and restauranteurs gather round to appraise the quality of the catch. It is a noisy, smelly, lively place and interesting to watch the fish being expertly skinned and gutted.

Olhão is celebrated in Portugal for the beauty of its skyline, often being described as 'cubist' in style. The roofs of the town's buildings are typically flat and the staircases are often built onto the side of the houses. This style of building is very similar to that of towns in North Africa, though it is considered to have been adopted in Olhão through the relatively recent effect of trading links with North African cities rather than through any direct influence during the Moorish occupation.

The town shares with the nearby village of Fuseta the distinction of a style of chimney design that is unique in a province where great store is set by the aesthetic effect of chimneys. Unlike most others they are not designed in a complex lace-like pattern, but rather they have a relatively simple square one. Perhaps the best place from which to appreciate the effect, and the curious design of chimneys that is particular to the town is from the bell tower of the parish church, Nossa Senhora de Rosario on the central Avenida da República.

The church was founded in 1698, and before the church in the small square stands a small monument to the heroes of the 1808 rising against the French garrison of Napoleon's troops stationed there. After Napoleon's defeat a group of fishermen set out from the town in a small boat for Brazil to give the news to the exiled Portu-

A fisherman preparing his nets at Olhão

guese king, João VI. Navigating solely by the stars they brought the king the good news and the town of Olhão was shortly afterwads rewarded with the granting of a town charter.

At the rear of the parish church is the small chapel of Nossa Senhora dos Aflitos. This has been the place where traditionally the wives of sailors and fishermen have come to pray when there is a storm at sea.

The pleasant municipal gardens near to the fish market, the Joaquim Lopes park, provides the visitor with a first opportunity to appreciate the unique ecological environment that is formed by the Rio Formosa and its islands. The National Park of Rio Formosa runs along the Sota Vento coast from Ancão, to the west of Faro, to Manta Rota, 50km (31 miles) to the east of Olhão. The park, with an area of 15,000 hectares (60 sq miles), is composed of narrow shallow sandy streams and rivulets running between mudflats, and long peninsulas and islands of dunes.

The shallow streams and the mildness of the Algarvian winter makes the area a perfect wintering ground for many wading birds from Northern Europe. In the shallows protected by the islands of Culatra, Armona and Tavira are to be seen wigeons, shovelers, teal, little terns, pochards, bar-tailed godwits, curlews and grey plovers

The tiled interior of the church at Moncarapacho

among many other species. Entry to the port of Olhão lies between the first two of these islands. The rare species of flowers and plants that grow in the dunes are also of great interest to botanists. The area is also a great centre for the commercial culture of shellfish. Needless to say the proximity of the park to the country's premier tourist resorts places a great deal of pressure for the commercial exploitation of the islands. For the moment, however they serve the needs of many other species than humanity alone.

Ferries to reach the islands of Armona and Culatra leave from the jetties at the end of the municipal gardens. Of the two islands Armona is to be preferred though accommodation is probably easier to find on Culatra. On both islands, however, there are long stretches of deserted beach.

Inland from Olhão on the road to the small town of Moncarapacho is the unspoilt village of **Quelfes**. A small plaque on the wall of one of the buildings on the way into the town commemorates the fact that the famous Portuguese poet, Florbella Espança lived in the village. The parish church has retained some Romanesque and Gothic features, and some seventeenth-century decorative tiles. There is also a Roman bridge nearby.

The town of **Moncarapacho** appears initially to be an unpre-

An assortment of exhibits outside the museum at Moncarapacho

possesing place, but next to the town's small Chapel of Santo Cristo is one of the Algarve's most interesting and unexpected museums. Moncarapacho was in the past one of the region's centres of pilgrimage and had as many as ten churches. As the churches fell into disrepair the parish priest, who in 1991 was still living but in retirement at eighty-three years old, collected any objects of antiquity or artistic value that they contained. To the collection have been added gifts from other benefactors who heard of the priest's efforts. The private museum is now kept by a Swiss woman who speaks very good English. The small chapel, next to the museum, is in itself interesting. It was built in the seventeenth century, and the tiles on the interior walls were all hand made in the village.

The museum contains some fine examples of religious art, such as a Nativity scene, very finely carved in mother of pearl, and several religious figures in ivory, including a seventeenth-century ivory crucifix. There is also, incidentally, an ivory tusk weighing over 300lb. The Roman occupation of the area is remembered with several second-century wine jars or *amphora*, and some small coffins. Smaller scale, but still interesting reminders of the Arab occupation, too, can be seen in candle holders and jars.

The museum's finest exhibit, however, displayed in a glass case

A medieval watchtower near Luz de Tavira, a deserted part of the Algarve

in the centre of the upper floor, is an eighteenth-century Nativity scene, made in Naples, and preserved over the centuries in an airtight container such that its figures are in perfect condition. There are over thirty figures, the animals are made of wood and the human figures of china. The carving and the handsewing of the clothes are of the highest quality.

Many fine pieces of religious and secular art were stolen from Portugal during the Peninsular War, and an order granting permission to the French troops to loot, written by one of Napoleoon's Generals can be seen in one of the corner cabinets. Many of these stolen objects still reside in museums in France. All in all it is an interesting museum to find in such an unexpected corner of the Algarve.

Another unexpected place for a museum is at Monte Guerreira just outside the village of **Estiramentens** which lies about 8km (5 miles) to the north west of Moncarapacho. The house and museum of Jose Furtado de Mendonca contains collections of pottery, porcelain, silver, and glassware.

The holiday village of **Fuseta**, a few kilometres to the south of Moncarapacho, is rapidly expanding in a largely unplanned and unattractive way. There are two reasons to visit though, firstly, the

One of Portugal's finest Manueline doorways at Luz de Tavira

vines that can be seen in the roadside fields on approaching the town produce a fine local wine, and secondly, the busy restaurants in the town square which serve good, locally caught, sea food.

There is also a ferry from here to the long sandy spit of land, known as the island of **Armona**, where, with luck, one of the rarest and most unusual of dog breeds, the Algarvian Water Poodle can be found. These are large powerful dogs that bound across the sands and have traditionally been used by local fishermen to dive into the sea and drive shoals of fish towards the fisherman's nets. The breed have web-like membranes on their paws. The poodles have been known to dive as deep as 6m (20ft) and have been credited with saving many lives of sailors and fishermen. They were considered to have died out in the 1950s but there are now thought to be a thousand throughout Portugal.

Beyond Fuseta on the road to Tavira there are two places worth pausing at to take a closer look. **Luz de Tavira** is 5km (3 miles) from Tavira on the N125. It has a delightful sixteenth-century Renaissance parish church, with one of the loveliest Manueline portals above its side door of any in the country. Inside the three-naved interior is a

The bridge over the River Gilão at Tavira

Manueline font, some very rare Hispano-Arab decorative ceramic tiles and a painted vault. The town's traditional craft of basket weaving can also be seen by inquiring for the workshops of João Maria de Sousa or Joaquim Madeira.

The second is the medieval Torre de Ares. This old watch tower is to be found on the coast via a small road to the left, off the N125 just before a petrol station and just a few hundred metres before the town of Tavira itsef begins. Though not much of the tower is still standing the long blue lagoon that lies here between the island of Tavira and the coast is a beautifully deserted and tranquil part of the Algarve. There is no problem in escaping the crowds here. The island of Tavira, part of the Rio Formosa nature reserve, can be reached by foot at low tide. It is a perfect area for walking, fishing or windsurfing or just for sunbathing in peace with the crabs. The nearby village of **Santa Luzia** has, by reputation, the finest restaurants along this coast.

Tavira, the largest town on this coast between Faro and the border at Vila Real de Santo Antonio, is a happy, bustling town in which tourism takes its place as only one of several industries. The town has many churches and other historical sights that are well worth visiting.

Both Greeks and Romans are believed to have once been settlers in the area and its present name is a legacy of the considerable Moorish town of *Tabira* that once occupied the site. It was wrested from the Moors by the nobleman Dom Paio Peres Correia on 11 June 1242. Correia was responsible for liberating much of the Algarve, including the Moorish capital of Silves. Legend has it that the immediate reason for the Christian attack upon the town was in revenge for the murder of seven knights who were killed during a truce while they were hunting near the town.

The town's main church, Santa Maria of the Castle, sits on a hill overlooking the town and it is there appropriately enough that Correia's tomb and that of the seven treacherously murdered knights have been laid to rest in the chancel. Occupying the site of the former mosque, it was here that Henry the Navigator and João I's other sons were created knights after the reckless but successful Portuguese attack on the North African town of Ceuta in 1415.

Next to the church are the remaining walls of the medieval castle which provide a fine panorama of the city. The gardens surrounding it are attractive and the Gothic doorway to the church is beautifully carved with the kind of cheerful secular motifs that are to be seen elsewhere in the Algarve, such as leaves, grapes and starfish.

The town is built around the estuary of the River Gilão and there has been a bridge over the river at the point where the present bridge stands since Roman times, when it was part of the road that linked the Roman settlements of Faro and Mertola. On it there is a very attractive dedication in painted tiled to the soldiers who defended the bridge against the Moors on behalf of João 1 in 1383. The gardens, lined with palm trees, along the riverbank provide a very pleasant backdrop for some of the finest seafood restaurants in Portugal. The range of seafood available in Tavira is remarkable. Bream, red mullet, bass, sole, squid, clams, lobster, crawfish and crab are on the menu of just one restaurant. Riding, tennis and sailing boats for hire are all to be found here. Other than in high season accommodation is readily available and the best place for advice is in the helpful tourist office on the centrally located Praça de República.

Between the river and the castle lies the town's other main church, that of the Misericórdia, which is a fine example of Renaissance art. The doorway is flanked by the royal crown and the coat of arms of the city, with the image of Our Lady of Mercy at the centre.

Walking through the narrow streets of the old part of town is enjoyable in itself as the dorways are often decorated with coats of arms, and the peculiarly shaped four-sided roofs are topped with a great variety of prettily shaped chimneys.

At **Cabanas**, a village along the eastern coast reached along the N125, there is a ceramics workshop open to visitors and at **Conceicão** inland from Cabanas there are ceramics and earthenware workshops.

One of the most unusual spots in the Algarve is just a few kilometres further to the west just off the N125 at **Cacela Velha**. It is that great rarity: an unspoilt village on the Algarve coast. It is built around a small castle and fortified walls built in the seventeenth century on the site of a Roman fortress. Next to the fort is a sixteenth-century church with an attractive Renaissance doorway decorated with busts of St Peter and St Paul. The interior has three naves and curiously carved capitals. There is a very fine view back down the coast to Tavira, and there are steps down the steep headland to a small beach from which there is good swimming among the local fishermen's boats. The beaches on the island can be reached via a ferry run by an enterprising fisherman a little to the west of Cacela Velha at **Fabrica**. Fabrica also has a lively restaurant and bar. The area inland from here is also a favourite nesting area for the brightly coloured hoopoe bird.

Before the unashamedly commercial resort of Monte Gordo is reached is the vast wide expanse of white sand, known as the beach of Manta Rota. Though popular with locals it is such a large beach that a deserted stretch is to be found within a few minute's walk. The Portuguese seem to prefer to sunbathe relatively close together, though this is also based on safety considerations as the strength of the currents and the power of the breakers here can be quite intimidating.

The coast road from Manta Rota to the N125 to Tavira is flanked by fields of coarse straw, the main road itself is lined with cactus and olive trees, and vines growing on wooden frames. There is another fine beach at Alagôa. The land is also used for grazing for goats and even pasture for Fresian cows can be seen on the small road north to Casto Marim before Monte Gordo.

Castro Marim is as attractive a small town as the Eastern Algarve possesses. The hill on which the town is built is almost completely surrounded by the estuary of the River Guadiana. The Phoenicians from the Eastern Mediterranean were probably the founders of the

The fort of São Sebastião at Castro Marim

settlement and it was used as a crossroads in Roman times, when it was known as *Baesuris*. A stretch of the Roman road to Mértola can be seen near the town. It was also an important trading centre for the Arabs, and was granted a number of honours after the Christian reconquest. The most important of these was that it was made the first headquarters of the Order of Christ, an influential organisation of Christian knights, by King Dinis in 1319. It was for the defence of the knights that the complex formidable fortifications that still dominate the town were built. The order eventually moved their base to Tomar in 1334. The red sandstone walls of the medieval castle were badly damaged in the earthquake of 1775, and were heavily restored by Afonso III.

Within their walls are the remains of an even older castle, probably established by the Moors. Its square shape and round turrets are very similar to the castle at the old Moorish town of Aljezur in South-West Alentejo. There is an excellent view from the walls over the Lower Guadiana plain with its marshlands, reserved for wildlife, and salt pans in which salt is still extracted by traditional methods. Facing the castle over the estuary is the Spanish town of Ayamonte. The neatly laid out houses of Castro Marim below are very pretty with their brown tiled roofs and filigree chimneys.

The obelisk and main square of Vila Real de Santo Antónia

In the seventeenth century the fort of São Sebastião was built on the neighbouring hill. São Sebastião is an example of the furthest development of the design of the medieval castle by the seventeenth-century French military architect, Vauban. His complex designs became fasionable just as gunpowder was making the castle itself an anachronism. The medieval castle contains the ruins of the Misericórdia church with a Renaissance doorway as well as a small tourist centre and natural history library and a small museum explaining the history of the town, illustrated with archaeological and ethnographic exhibits.

The Castro Marim Marshland Nature Reserve covers 2,089 hectares (8 sq miles) in the districts of Castro Marim and Vila Real de Santo António. A great deal of information about the reserve can be gained from the castle tourist office. The nature reserve is a haven for migratory birds and provides an opportunity to watch and photograph white storks, oysterscatchers, marsh eagles, herons, snipe, avocet, kingfishers, dunlin, Kentish and ringed plovers, and the rare black winged stilt. Fishing in the river is also possible from here, the most plentiful varieties being grey mullet and barbel.

Five kilometres (3 miles) below Castro Marim on the west bank of the River Guadiana lies the border town of **Vila Real de Santo**

A basket weaver working in the countryside north of Castro Marim

António. It is an elegant, bustling town, with a long gardened promenade, usually packed with day visitors from Spain, who come over on the ferry from Ayamonte to take advantage of cheap Portuguese prices. With these people in mind the city authorities have made much of the town a pedestrian walkway.

At the heart of the town is a large, graceful square with a black and white mosaic surface that radiates out from a central obelisk in an elegant manner. The houses, too, are delightful whitewashed eighteenth-century buildings with balconies and balustrades. The fringe of the square is lined with orange and lime trees. The uniform architecture of the town is owed to the fact that the original town of Santo António de Areniha was washed away by the sea in a gradual process of erosion in the sixteenth and seventeenth centuries. The decision to reclaim the land was made by the prime minister and effective dictator of Portugal, the Marquis of Pombal, in 1774. Pombal applied the same principle that he had used in the Baixa quarter of Lisbon and laid out the streets in the form of a grid. The central area around the Square of the Marquess of Pombal was built in five months and was designed by the royal architect of the time, Reinaldo Manuel dos Santos.

There are fine hotels here along the Rua de República and the

Rua Teofilio Braga. There are sports facilities and regular river cruises up the River Guadiana to Foz de Odeleite. Bullfights can be seen throughout the summer at the Estadio de Lusitano.

The ferry to Ayamonte and Spain is fun, very cheap and runs every half hour, and cars can be taken across. Alternatively take the bridge that joins Portugal with Spain across the River Guadiana 6km (4 miles) north of Vila Real, which was opened in 1992. The culinary speciality of the town is fish salads, delightful for lunch, some of the fish at least brought from the fish farms at Castro Marim. Try also the dessert of caramel and eggs known as *Don Rodrigo.*

The road north from Vila Real to the Alentejo, the N 122, is in the process of being improved. Beyond Castro Marim there are basket weavers at the roadside weaving their wares from long strips of bamboo with no more advanced technology than a sharp knife. **Azinhal** and **Odeleite** are pleasant rural villages and the latter has an interesting parish church. The road begins to rise after these villages to the boundary between the Algarve and the Alentejo with the first stop the extraordinary eyrie that is the fortress town of Mertóla.

Further Information

— The Eastern Algarve —

Tourist Information Offices

Faro
Rua de Misericórdia 8-12
☎ 089 25404/24067

Faro Airport
Posto de Turismo
☎ 089 818582

Loulé
Edificio do Castelo
☎ 089 63900

Olhão
Largo da Lagoa
☎ 089 713936

Monte Gordo
Avenida Marginal
☎ 081 44495

Tavira
Praça de República
☎ 081 22511

Vila Real de Santo António
Avenida da República
☎ 081 43272

Places of Interest

Almansil
Vale de Lobo Sport and Leisure Centre
☎ 089 56842

Castro Marim
Castle and Museum
Open: 9:am-6pm (closed Sunday)

Faro
Rio Formosa Cruises
Quinta do Eucalipto, Montenegro
☎ 089 817301

Campsite
Reservations advisable in summer
☎ 082 24876

Churches in the Algarve are much less likely to be open than in the more religious North of Portugal. However be prepared to ask local residents for the key and they will usually prove of assistance.

Festivals

Festivals take place in the Algarve throughout the year though many are now either heavily commercialised or entirely commercial inventions. Some that still represent an ongoing tradition are as follows:

Loulé
Almond Blossom Festival
14-16 February

Romaria da Senhora da Piedade
17 April

Olhão
Shellfish Festival 11-13 August

Castro Marim
Festa da Senhora das Martires
14-15 August

Index

ACCOMMODATION AND EATING OUT

Portugal has a great range and variety of accommodation. *Pousadas* or State Inns, are often converted palaces, convents or castles. They may be luxurious or spartan but they are always memorable. They also usually have restaurants. Reservations and information on these can be obtained from ENATUR, Avenida Santa Joana a Princesa, 10A, 1700 Lisbon ☎ 01 88 12 21.

Hotels, *Estalagems* and *albergarias* are categorised by a star system which has been the basis for the Accommodation and Eating Out section of this book. *Residenciels* are 3-star and usually include breakfast in the price of the room. *Pensoes* are very reasonably priced, but it is always useful, and perfectly normal, to ask to see the room first.

Prices at almost all establishments vary between high and low season, and are usually clearly displayed at the reception desk. Single rooms are usually 60-75 per cent of the price of doubles. An extra bed in a double room will add 30 per cent to the bill, though rather less if it is for a child under eight years of age.

Similar to the *Pousadas*, and fairly common in the north, are the privately-owned stately homes and manor houses, known collectively as *Turismo de Habitaçao*. A publication available from the National Tourist Office, with whom bookings can be made, lists 120 such establishments. Most will accept reservations for less than three nights. Apartments and villas are also available in major tourist areas.

The best way to judge restaurants in Portugal is to try to assess the number of local people eating within. Breakfast in Portugal is normally continental. Lunches are served from 12.30pm to 2.30pm, though light snacks are usually available in bars and cafés at any time. Dinner is usually from 8pm. If uncertain of what to try ask for a regional speciality, or the 'dish of the day' the *Prato do Dia*.

Currency and Credit Cards

Portugal's currency is the 'escudo' (written with a $ sign where the decimal point usually is, eg 1½ escudos is 1$50) made up of 100 *centavos*. Major credit cards are accepted at most, but not all, hotels and restaurants. Foreign currency and cheques can be changed at most banks.

Telephone Services

When telephoning from Portugal it is best to use the metered phones available in Post Offices where you pay at the counter afterwards. It is just as simple to telephone from an hotel but you must expect to add a large connection charge. There are no cheap rate periods for either local or long distance calls.

For Directory Enquiries ☎ 12 in Portugal. ☎ 155 from Britain.

To telephone Portugal the international dialling code is: from the USA and Canada 011 351, from the UK 010 351 and from Australia 0011 351.

Tipping

Tipping of waiters, porters, taxi drivers etc is generally accepted and appreciated.

Tourist Information Offices

Britain

Portuguese National Tourist Office
22/25A Sackville Street
London
W1X 1DE
☎ 071 4941441

USA

Portuguese National Tourist Office
590 Fifth Avenue
New York
NY10036
☎ 212 354 4403

Canada

Portuguese National Tourist Office
500 Sherbrook West
Suite 930
Montreal
Quebec H3A 3C6
☎ 514 843 4623

Portuguese National Tourist Office
4120 Yonge Corporate Centre
Suite 414
Willowdale
Toronto
Ontario M2P 2B8
☎ 416 250 7575

Accommodation and Eating Out

✳✳✳ Expensive
✳✳ Moderate
✳ Inexpensive

Chapter 1 •
The Alto Minho

Accommodation

Arcos de Valdevez
Pensão Dom Antonio ✳
Rua Dr Germano de Amorim
☎ 058 52 10 10

Caminha
Pensão Galo de Ouro ✳
15 Rua de Corredoura
☎ 058 92 11 60

Melgaço
Pensão Boavista ✳✳
E.N. No 202-Peso
☎ 051 4 24 64

Monçao
Albergaria Atlântico ✳✳
15 Rua General Pimenta de Castro
☎ 051 65 23 55/6

Pensão Central ✳
Praça Deu-la-Deu
☎ 051 65 23 14

Ponte de Lima
Pensão Império do Minho ✳✳✳
Centro Ibérico
Avenida 5 de Outubro
☎ 058 74 15 10/1/2

Valença
Hotel Valença do Minho ✳✳✳
Av Miguel Dantas
☎ 051 82 42 11

Pensão Val Flores ✳✳
S. Gião-Edificio Val Flores
☎ 051 82 43 92

Pensão Rio Minho ✳
Largo da Estação
☎ 051 2 23 31

Viana do Castelo
Hotel Afonso III ✳✳✳✳
494 Av Afonso III
☎ 058 82 90 01/5

Pensão Vianamar ✳✳
215 Av Combateates de Grande Guerra
☎ 058 82 89 62

Hotel Viana Sol ✳✳✳
Largo Vasco da Gama
☎ 058 82 34 01

Eating Out

Arcos de Valdevez
Adega Regional ✳✳
Silvanes-Salvador
☎ 0580 6 61 22

Caminha
Barão ✳✳
Rua Barão de S. Roque
☎ 058 72 11 30

Napoleão ✳✳✳
Lugar de Coura-Seixas
☎ 058 92 21 15

Versalhes ✳✳
Largo Bento Coelho 114
☎ 058 92 15 42

Castro Labreiro
Estalagem de Castro Labreiro ✳
☎ 051 4 51 37

Monção
Danaide ✳
Largo S. João de Deus
☎ 051 65 22 88

Ponte de Lima
Encanada ✳
Praça Municipal
☎ 058 94 11 89

Valença
Monte de Faro ✳✳
Santuário Faro
☎ 051 2 24 11

Pousada de São Antonio ✱✱✱
☎ 051 22 22 52

Viana do Castelo
Alambique ✱
Rua Manuel Espregueira 86
☎ 058 2 38 94

3 Potas ✱✱
9 Beco dos Fornos
☎ 058 82 99 28

Vila Praia de Âncora
Verdes Lírios ✱✱✱
☎ 058 91 17 41

Chapter 2 •
The Costa Verde

Accommodation

Barcelos
Albergaria Condes de Barcelos ✱✱
Avenida Alcaides de Faria
☎ 053 81 10 61/2

Pensão Arantes ✱
35-1⁰ Av da Liberdade
☎ 053 81 13 26

Braga
Hotel Turismo de Braga ✱✱✱
Praceta João XXI
☎ 053 61 22 00

Hotel Carandá ✱✱✱
96 Av da Liberdade
☎ 053 61 45 00

Hotel João XXI ✱✱
Av João XXI 849
☎ 053 61 66 31

Esposende
Hotel Nélia ✱✱✱
Av Valentin Ribeiro
☎ 053 96 12 44

Pensão Acrópole ✱✱
Praça de São Sebastiâo
☎ 053 96 19 41/2

Gerês
Hotel des Termas ✱✱✱
Av Manuel Francisco da Costa
☎ 053 39 11 43

Pensão Central Jardin ✱✱
Av Manuel Francisco da Costa
☎ 053 39 11 32

Pensão Principe ✱
Rua de Cemiterio
☎ 053 39 11 21

Guimaraes
PensãoRestaurante Imperial ✱
111-119 Alameda Dr Sá Cameiro
☎ 053 41 51 63

Vila do Conde
Pensão Santa Marinha ✱
1330-1⁰ Via José Régio
☎ 052 927 15 20

Eating Out

Barcelos
Bagoeira ✱
53 Av Dr Sidónio Pais
☎ 053 81 12 36

Braga
A Ceia ✱
331 Largo Dr João Penha
☎ 053 2 39 32

Hotel Turismo ✱✱✱
Peta João XXI
☎ 053 61 22 00

Marisqueira de Braga ✱✱
157 Av Liberdade
☎ 053 7 42 42

Esposende
Chimmarão ✱✱✱
Lugar dos Alhos
Gândara
☎ 053 96 17 64

Fão
A Lareira ✱✱
5 Rua Bombeiros Voluntérios
☎ 053 98 15 88

Gerês
Noro Sol ✳
☎ 053 39 11 08

Pousada de S. Bento ✳✳✳
Ceniçada
☎ 053 64 73 17

Guimaraes
El Rei ✳✳
20 Praça de Santiago
☎ 053 41 90 96

D. Maria ✳✳✳
Hotel de Guimaraes
☎ 053 51 58 88

Jordão ✳✳
55 Av D. Afonso Henriques
☎ 053 51 64 98

Mesão Frio
Batista ✳
Cruz da Argola
☎ 054 41 62 16

Chapter 3 •
Porto

Accommodation

Porto
Hotel Ipanema Parque ✳✳✳
124 Rua de Serralves
4100 Porto
☎ 02 610 41 74

Hotel Tivoli Porto Atlântico ✳✳✳
148 Rua Afonso Lopes Vieira
4100 Porto
☎ 02 69 49 41/9

Grande Hotel de Batalha ✳✳✳
116 Praça da Batalha
4000 Porto
☎ 02 200 05 71

Hotel Inca ✳✳✳
52 Praça Coronel Pacheco
4000 Porto
☎ 02 38 41 51

Hotel Corcel ✳✳
135 Rua Camoes
4000 Porto
☎ 02 38 02 68/9

Hotel Malaposta ✳✳
80 Rua de Conceiçao
4000 Porto
☎ 02 201 43 52

Hotel São João ✳✳
120 Rua do Bonjardim
4000 Porto
☎ 02 200 16 62

Hotel Tuela ✳✳
200 Rua do Arq Marques da Silva
4100 Porto
☎ 02 600 47 47

Pensão Santo André ✳
990 Rua D. João IV
4000 Porto
☎ 02 231 58 69

Pensão Portuguesa ✳
11 Travessa Coronel Pacheca
4000 Porto
☎ 02 200 41 74

Pensão do Norte ✳
579 Rua Fernandes Tomás
4000 Porto
☎ 02 200 35 03

Hotel Paris ✳
27-29 Rua da Fabrica
4000 Porto
☎ 02 32 13 96

Eating Out

Porto
Abadia ✳
22 Rua Ateneu Comercial do Porto
☎ 02 200 87 57

Aleixo ✳
216 Rua Estacão
☎ 02 57 04 62

Capolira ✳
63 Esplanada do Castelo
Foz do Douro
☎ 02 68 15 89

Churrascão Gaúcho ✳✳✳
313 Avenida Boavista
☎ 02 60 9 17 38

Gunha ✳
41 Rue Guades Azeredo
☎ 02 31 41 31

Don Manoel ✳✳✳
384 Av Monterideu
☎ 02 61 7 23 04

Lagosteiro ✳✳✳
140 Rua C. de Burnay
☎ 02 56 66 78

Ó Macedo ✳✳✳
552 Rua Passeio Alegre
Foz do Douro
☎ 02 67 01 66

Portofino ✳✳
103 Rua de Padrão
Foz do Douro
☎ 02 617 73 39

Solar do Conga ✳
294 R do Bonjardin
☎ 02 200 69 34

Tripeiro ✳✳
195 Rua Passos Manuel
☎ 02 200 58 86

Varanda da Barra ✳✳
470-1⁰ Rua Paulo Gama
☎ 02 68 58 06

Chapter 4 •
The Douro Valley

Accommodation

Amarante
Hotel Amarento ✳✳✳
Edificio Amaranto
Murtas-Madalena
☎ 055 42 21 06/7

Hotel Navarras ✳✳✳
Rua Antonio Carneiro
☎ 055 42 40 36

Hotel Silva ✳
53 Rua Cândido dos Reis
São Gonçalo
☎ 055 43 31 10

Espinho
Hotel Praia Golfe ✳✳✳
Rua 6
☎ 02 72 06 30

Lamego
Albergaria do Cerrado ✳✳✳
Lugar do Cerrado
☎ 054 6 31 54/64

Hotel do Parque ✳✳
Parque Nossa Senhora dos Remédios
☎ 054 6 21 05/6

Pensão Império ✳✳
6 Travessa dos Loureiros
☎ 054 6 27 42

Pensão São Paulo ✳
22C Av 5 de Outubro
☎ 054 6 31 14/5

Pensão Solar do Espírita Santo ✳
Rua Alexandre Herculano
☎ 054 6 43 86

Mesão Frio
Hotel Panorama ✳✳
525 Av Conselheiro José Maria Alpoim
☎ 054 9 92 36

Peso da Régua
Pensão Dom Quixote ✳
Av Sacadura Cabral
☎ 054 2 41 51/2

Pensão Império ✳✳
8 Rua José Vasques Osório
☎ 054 2 23 99

Eating Out

Amarante
Amaranto ✳✳
Hotel Amaranto
☎ 055 42 20 06

Grelha ✳
Murtas-Madalena
☎ 055 42 37 72

Zé da Calcada ✳✳✳
Rua 31 de Janeiro
☎ 055 42 20 23

Lamego
Avenida ✳
Av Comb Grande Guerra
☎ 054 6 23 44

Nenufar ✴✴✴
43 Av D. Attredo de Sousa
☎ 054 6 44 44

S. Bernardo ✴
Largo Preguica
☎ 054 6 35 45

Tiviserro ✴
Serra-Meadas
☎ 054 6 33 80

Marco de Canaveses
Aldeia Turistica da Torre dos Nevões ✴✴
Tabuado
☎ 055 5 23 54

Mesão Frio
Hotel Panorama ✴✴✴
525 Av Conselheiro Jose Maria Alpuim
☎ 054 9 92 36

Peso da Régua
Gato Preto ✴
Av Voãs Franco
☎ 054 2 33 67

Rosmaninho ✴✴
☎ 054 2 23 20

Varanda da Régua ✴✴
Loureiro
☎ 054 2 47 49

Chapter 5 •
Trás-os-Montes

Accommodation

Bragança
Hotel Bragança ✴✴✴
Av Sá Carneiro
☎ 073 2 25 78/9

Pousada de São Bartolomeu ✴✴✴
Estrada do Turismo
☎ 073 2 24 93/4

Pensão Nordeste Shalon ✴✴
39 Av Abade de Baçal
☎ 073 246 67/8

Pensão São Roque ✴
Zona da Estacada
Lote 26-27
☎ 073 2 34 81

Chaves
Hotel Aquae Flaviãe ✴✴✴
Praça do Brasil
☎ 076 2 67 11

Hotel de Chaves ✴✴
25 Rua 25 de Abril
☎ 076 2 11 18

Pensão Bon Caminho ✴
Campo da Fonte
☎ 076 2 27 43

Macedo de Cavaleiros
Estalagem do Caçador ✴✴✴
Largo Manuel Pinto de Azevedo
☎ 078 42 13 54/56

Mirandela
Pensão Globo ✴✴
Rua Dr Trigo de Negreiros
☎ 078 2 21 11

Pensão O Viajante ✴
209 Rua da República
☎ 078 2 21 55

Vila Flor
Pensão Restaurante Campos ✴
Av Marechal Carmona
☎ 078 5 23 11

Vila Real
Hotel Tocaio ✴✴
45 Av Caivalho Araíyo
☎ 059 32 31 06/7

Eating Out

Bragança
Hotel Bragança ✴✴✴
Av A. Oliveira
☎ 073 2 25 79

Lá Em Casa ✴✴
R. Marques de Pombal
☎ 073 2 21 11

Pousada de S. Bartolomeu ✴✴✴
Estrada do Turismo
☎ 073 2 24 93

Chaves
Hotel Aquae Flaviae ✴✴✴
Praça do Brasil
☎ 076 2 29 41

Pote ✳
Estrada da Fronteira
☎ 076 2 12 26

Trajano ✳✳
Hotel Trajano
Tv Cãndido Reis
☎ 076 2 24 15

Macedo de Cavaleiros
Estalagem do Caçador ✳✳✳
Largo Manuel P. Azevedo
☎ 078 42 13 56

Mirandela
Paulino ✳
16 Rua República
☎ 078
078 2 20 54

Romeu
Maria Rita ✳
☎ 078 9 31 34

Vila Flor
Toni ✳✳
39 Av Marechal Carmona
☎ 078 5 23 15

Vila Real
Espadeiro ✳✳
Av Almeida Lucena
☎ 059 32 23 02

Nevada ✳
Miracongo Shopping Center
☎ 059 7 18 28

Chapter 6 •
Dão Lafoes

Accommodation

Arganil
Hotel de Arganil ✳✳
Av Forças Armadas
☎ 035 2 29 56

Buçaco
Hotel Palace do Buçaco ✳✳✳
☎ 031 93 01 01/2/3

Coimbra
Pensão Infante Dom Henrique ✳
43 Rua Dr Manuel Rodriques
☎ 039 2 21 42/3

Pensão Residência Almedina ✳✳
203 Av Fernãs de Magalhães
☎ 039 291 61/2

Hotel Tivoli Coimbra ✳✳✳
4 & 5 Rua Jão Machado
☎ 039 2 69 31

Coja
Pensão Piquenique do Paço ✳
Largo do Paço
☎ 035 9 21 56

Mangualde
Estalagem Cruz da Mata ✳✳
Lugar da Croz da Mata
☎ 032 61 19 45

Manteigas
Pensão Estrela ✳✳
5 Rua Dr Sobral
☎ 095 98 12 88

Nelas
Albergaria São Pedro ✳✳✳
Rua 4 - Baino das Toiças
☎ 032 94 0585

Viseu
Hotel Grão Vasco ✳✳✳
Rua Gaspa Barreiros
☎ 032 42 35 11/2/3

Pensão Virrato ✳
24 Largo Mousinho de Alberquerque
☎ 032 2 65 10

Pensão Rossio Parque ✳
55 Rua Soar de Cima
☎ 032 42 20 85

Eating Out

Caramulo
Pousada de S. Jerónimo ✳✳✳
☎ 032 86 12 91

Coimbra
Casa da Cerreja ✳✳
73 R. Calouste Gulberkian
☎ 039 3 23 05

D. Pedro ✳✳
58 Av Emidio Navarro
☎ 039 2 91 08

Espello de Água ✳✳✳
Parque de Manuel Braga
☎ 039 3 74 68

Piscinas ✳✳✳
Piscinas Municipois
Calhabé
☎ 039 71 70 13

Covilha
O Mário ✳
EN 18 crossroad Alcaria
☎ 075 7 41 62

Mangualde
Luciano ✳
Quinta do Salgueiro (Nelas Road)
☎ 032 62 36 32

Solar Beirão ✳✳
Hotel da Senhora do Castelo
☎ 032 61 16 08

Nelas
Quinta do Castelo ✳✳
☎ 032 96 46 42

Viseu
Cantinho ✳
Cabanões
☎ 032 46 11 77

Rodízio Real ✳✳
Bairro de Santa Eulália
Repeses
☎ 032 42 22 32

Alvorada ✳
24 Rua Gaspar Barreiros
☎ 032 2 58 43

Chapter 7 •
Évora

Accommodation

Evora
Pensão Diana ✳✳
2 Rua Diogo Cão
☎ 066 2 20 08

Pousada dos Lóios ✳✳✳
Largo do Conde de Vilar Flor
☎ 066 2 40 51/2

Estalagem Póquer ✳✳✳
Quinta de Vale Vagios
EN No 114
☎ 066 3 14 73

Pensão Os Manueis ✳
Rua do Raimundo
☎ 066 2 28 61

Pensão Policarpo ✳
16 Rua da Freira de Baixo
☎ 066 2 24 24

Pensão Riviera ✳✳✳
49 R. 5 de Outubro
☎ 066 2 33 04

Pensão O Ebonense ✳✳
1 Largo de Misericórdia
☎ 066 2 20 31

Eating Out

Évora
A. Torralva ✳✳
EN Évora-Arraiolos
☎ 066 3 25 31

Aqueduto ✳✳
13A Rua do Cano
☎ 066 2 63 73

Cozinha de Sto Humberto ✳✳
39 R. Moeda
☎ 066 2 42 51

Fialho ✳✳✳
Tv Mascarenhas
☎ 066 2 30 79

Guião ✳✳
81 Rua Republica
☎ 066 2 30 71

Mr Pickwick ✳
3 Alcárcora de Cima
☎ 066 2 69 99

Muralha ✳
21 Rua 5 de Outubro
☎ 066 2 22 84

O Antão ✳
5 R. Joãs de Dens
☎ 066 264 69

Pousada dos Lóios ✳✳✳
Largo do Conde de Vilar Flor
☎ 066 2 40 51

1/4 Pras Nore ✳
9A Pedro Simões
☎ 066 2 67 74

Chapter 8 •
Alto Alentejo

Accommodation

Elvas
Hotel Brasa ✳✳✳
Estrada de Badajoz
☎ 068 62 91 18

Estalagem Dom Sancho II ✳✳✳
20 Praça da República
☎ 068 62 26 84/6

Pensão Luso Espanhola ✳✳
Rua Rui de Melo
☎ 068 62 30 92/3

Estremoz
Hotel Alentejano ✳
50 Rossio do Marquês de Pombal
☎ 068 2 27 17

Pousada da Rainha Santa Isabel ✳✳✳
Largo D. Dinis
☎ 068 2 26 18

Pensão Residência Carralho ✳
27 Largo da República
☎ 068 2 27 12

Monsaraz
Estalagem de Monsaraz ✳
Largo de São Bartolomeu
☎ 066 5 51 12

Montemor-O-Noro
Pensão Sampaio ✳✳
12 Av Gago Coutinho
☎ 066 8 22 37

Eating Out

Arraiolos
Arca de Noé ✳
123 R. Sto Constestável
☎ 066 4 24 27

Marisqueira a Moagem ✳
2 R. de Fábrica
☎ 066 4 26 46

Borba
Beco ✳
☎ 068 9 41 61
Closed on Saturdays.

Elvas
A. Bolota ✳✳✳
Terrugem
☎ 068 65 61 52

Aqueduto ✳
Av de Badajoz
☎ 068 62 36 76

Chimarrão 4 ✳✳✳
Quinta da Espanhola
Piedade
☎ 068 62 99 56

El Cristo ✳✳
Parque da Piedade
☎ 068 62 35 12

Hotel Don Luis ✳✳
Av de Badajoz
☎ 068 62 27 56

Estremoz
Aguias d'Ouro ✳✳
Rossio Mq de Pombal
☎ 068 2 21 96

Pousada Rainha Santa Isabel ✳✳✳
Largo D. Dinis
☎ 068 2 26 18

Monsaraz
Estalagem de Monsaraz ✳✳
Lg São Bartolomeu
☎ 066 5 51 12

Chapter 9 •
South-West Alentejo

Accommodation

Aljustrel
Pensão Meia Encosta ✳
30 Rua Filipa de Vihena
☎ 084 6 24 97

Caldas de Monchique
Albergaria do Lageado ✳✳
Caldas de Monchique
☎ 082 9 26 16

Monchique
Estalagem Abrigo da Montanha ✳✳✳
Corte Pereiro
Estrada de Fóia
☎ 082 9 21 31

Pensão Bica Boa ✳✳
Rua de Sabóia
(Estrada de Lisboa)
☎ 082 9 22 71

Pensão Miradouro da Serra ✳✳
Rua Combatentes do Ultramar
☎ 082 9 21 63

Odemira
Pensão Paisagem ✳✳
Av das Escolas de São Teotónio
☎ 083 9 54 06

Pensão Paulo Campos ✳✳
São Salvador
Almograve
☎ 083 641 18

Sines
Hotel Apartamento Sinerama ✳✳✳
167 Rua Marquês de Pombal
☎ 069 63 38 45

Pensão Búzio ✳✳✳
14 Av 25 de Abril
☎ 069 63 21 14/5/6

Pensão Carvalho ✳
13 Rua Gago Coutinho
☎ 069 63 20 19

Pensão Veleiro ✳✳✳
19-A Rua Sacadura Cabral
☎ 069 63 47 51/2

Eating Out

Aljezur
Chefe Dimas ✳
Aldeia Velha
☎ 082 982 75

Fortaleza ✳
Praia da Arrifana
☎ 082 9 84 74

Caldas de Monchique
Albergaria Velha ✳✳
Caldas de Monchique Spa
☎ 082 9 25 92

Monchique
Mons Cicus ✳✳
Estrada de Fóia
☎ 082 9 26 50

Paraíso da Montanha ✳
Est de Fóia
☎ 082 9 21 50

Terezinha ✳
Estr. de Fóia
☎ 082 9 23 92

Porto Covo
Ilha ✳
Ilha do Pessegueiro
☎ 069 9 51 13

Vista do Mar ✳
Vale Vistoso
☎ 069 9 51 26

Sines
Atlântico Mar ✳✳✳
☎ 069 63 41 41

Esplanada Alentejana ✳
Praça da República
☎ 069 3 22 94

Mexilhão ✳✳✳
30 R. Sacadura Cabral
☎ 069 63 22 42

Varanda do Oceano ✳✳
1 Rua Rampa
☎ 069 62 23 03

Chapter 10 •
The Eastern Algarve

Accommodation

Almansil
Hotel Quinta do Lago ✳✳✳
Quinta do Lago ☎ 089 39 66 66

Faro
Hotel Faro ✳✳✳
2 Praca D. Francisco Gomes
☎ 089 80 32 76/8/9

Hotel Albacor ✳✳
23-25 Rua Brites de Almeida
☎ 089 80 35 93

Loulé
Hotel 'Louisé Jardim' ✳✳✳
Praça Manuel d'Arriaga
☎ 089 41 30 94/5

Pensão Ibérica ✳
157 Av Marçal Pacheco
☎ 089 41 41 00

Monte Gordo
Albergaria Monte Gordo ✳✳
Av Infante d. Henrique
☎ 081 4 21 24

Olhão
Hotel Ria Sol ✳✳
37 Rua General Humberto Delgado
☎ 089 70 52 67/8

Pensão Bela Vista ✳
65-67 Rua Teófilo Braga
☎ 089 70 25 38

Tavira
Hotel Apartamento Eurotel ✳✳✳
Quinta das Oliveiras
☎ 081 32 43 24

Pensão do Castelo ✳✳
4 Rua da Liberdade
☎ 081 2 39 42

Pensão Lagoa ✳
24 Rua Almirante Cândido dos Reis
☎ 081 2 22 82/52

Vila Real de Santo António
Hotel Apolo ✳✳✳
Av dos Bombeiros Portugueses
☎ 081 4 44 48/4/9

Eating Out

Almansil
Casa de Torre Ermitage ✳✳✳
Est de Vale do Lobo
☎ 089 39 43 29

Dio Giovanni ✳✳
Est Fonte Santa
☎ 089 39 72 05

Castro Marim
Manuel D'Água ✳
4 Estrada Mouro Vaz
☎ 081 4 38 80

Faro
Cidade Velha ✳✳✳
19 Largo da Sé
☎ 089 2 71 45

Loulé
A Casa Dos Arcos ✳✳
23 Rua sá de Miranda
☎ 089 41 67 13

Aux Bons Enfants ✳✳
Rua Eng Duarte Pacleco
☎ 089 6 20 96

Monte Gordo
Casino de Monte Gordo ✳✳✳
☎ 08151 22 44

Olhão
Aquarium ✳
R. Dr Voão Lúcio
☎ 089 71 35 39

Henrique ✳
B⁰ dos Pescadores
☎ 089 71 38 56

São Brás de Alportel
Pousada de São Bras ✳✳
☎ 089 84 23 05/6

Tavira
Ideal ✳
Cabanas de Tavira
☎ 081 2 02 32

Imperial ✳
R. Jose P. Padinha
☎ 081 2 23 06

Vila Real de Santo António
Caves do Guadiana ✳✳✳
90 Av República
☎ 081 4 44 98

Joaquim Gomes ✳
5 Rua 5 de Outubro
☎ 081 4 32 85

A Note To The Reader

The accommodation and eating out lists in this book are based upon the authors' own experiences and therefore may contain an element of subjective opinion. The contents of this book are believed correct at the time of publication but details given may change. We welcome any information to ensure accuracy in this guide book and to help keep it up-to-date.

Please write to The Editor, Moorland Publishing Co Ltd, Moor Farm Road, Airfield Estate, Ashbourne, Derbyshire, DE6 1HD, England.

American and Canadian readers please write to The Editor, The Globe Pequot Press, 6 Business Park Road, PO Box 833, Old Saybrook, Connecticut 06475, USA.

MPC

Discover a New World
with
Off The Beaten Track Travel Guides

Austria

Explore the quiet valleys of Bregenzerwald in the west to
Carinthia and Burgenland in the east. From picturesque
villages in the Tannheimertal to the castles north of
Klagenfurt, including Burg Hochosterwitz. This dramatic
castle with its many gates stands on a 450ft high limestone
cliff and was built to withstand the Turkish army by the
man who brought the original Spanish horses to Austria.

Britain

Yes, there are places off the beaten track in even the more
populated areas of Britain. Even in the heavily visited
national parks there are beautiful places you could easily
miss — areas well known to locals but not visitors. This book
guides you to such regions to make your visit memorable.

Greece

Brimming with suggested excursions that range from
climbing Mitikas, the highest peak of Mount Olympus, the
abode of Zeus, to Monemvassia, a fortified medieval town
with extensive ruins of a former castle. This book enables
you to mix a restful holiday in the sun with the fascinating
culture and countryside or rural Greece.

Italy

Beyond the artistic wealth of Rome or Florence and the hill
towns of Tuscany lie many fascinating areas of this ancient
country just waiting to be discovered. From medieval towns
such as Ceriana in the Armea valley to quiet and
spectacular areas of the Italian Lakes and the Dolomites
further to the east. At the southern end of the country, the
book explores Calabria, the 'toe' of Italy as well as Sicily,
opening up a whole 'new' area.

Germany

Visit the little market town of Windorf on the north bank of the Danube (with its nature reserve) or the picturesque upper Danube Valley, which even most German's never visit! Or go further north to the Taubertal. Downstream of famous Rothenburg with its medieval castle walls are red sandstone-built villages to explore with such gems as the carved altar in Creglingen church, the finest work by Tilman Riemenschneider — the Master Carver of the Middle Ages. This book includes five areas in the former East Germany.

Portugal

Most visitors to Portugal head to the Algarve and its famous beaches, but even the eastern Algarve is relatively quiet compared to the more popular western area. However, the book also covers the attractive areas of northern Portugal where only the more discerning independent travellers may be found enjoying the delights of this lovely country.

Scandinavia

Covers Norway, Denmark, Sweden and Finland. There is so much to see in these countries that it is all too easy to concentrate on the main tourist areas. That would mean missing so many memorable places that are well worth visiting. For instance, there are still about sixty Viking churches that survive in Norway. Alternatively many private castles and even palaces in Denmark open their gardens to visitors. Here is your guide to ensure that you enjoy the Scandinavian experience to the full.

Spain

From the unique landscape of the Ebrodelta in Catalonia to the majestic Picos d'Europa in the north, the reader is presented with numerous things to see and exciting things to do. With the mix of cultures and climates, there are many possibilities for an endearing holiday for the independent traveller.

Switzerland

Switzerland offers much more than the high mountains and deep valleys with which it is traditionally associated. This book covers lesser known areas of the high mountains — with suggested walks in some cases. It also covers Ticino, the Swiss Lakeland area near to the Italian Lakes and tours over the border into the latter. In the north, the book covers the lesser known areas between Zurich and the Rhine Falls, plus the Lake Constance area, with its lovely little towns like Rorschach, on the edge of the lake.

Forthcoming:

Northern France
Southern France

Touring the ancient fishing port of Guethary, hiking in the Pyrennees and visiting the old archway in Vaucoulers (through which Joan of Arc led her troops), are just a few of the many opportunities these two books present.

Scotland

Heather-clad mountains, baronian castles and magnificent coastal scenery, all combined with a rich historical heritage, combine to make this an ideal 'off the beaten track' destination.

Ireland

Ireland not only has a dramatic coastline, quiet fishing harbours and unspoilt rural villages, but also the natural friendliness of its easy-going people. *Off the Beaten Track Ireland* will lead you to a memorable holiday in a country where the pace of life is more relaxing and definitely not hectic.

TRAVEL GUIDE LIST

Airline/Ferry details ....
....
....
....
....

Telephone No. ....

Tickets arrived ☐

Travel insurance ordered ☐

Car hire details ....
....
....

Visas arrived ☐

Passport ☐

Currency ☐

Travellers cheques ☐

Eurocheques ☐

Accommodation address ....
....
....
....

Telephone No. ....

Booking confirmed ☐

Maps required ....
....
....

DAILY ITINERARY

Date ....

Places visited

....
....
....
....
....
....

Accommodation ....
....
....

Telephone No. ....

Booking confirmed ☐

Notes:

DAILY ITINERARY

Date ....

Places visited

....
....
....
....
....
....

Accommodation ....
....
....

Telephone No. ....

Booking confirmed ☐

Notes: